The
Singularity of
Shakespeare
and Other Essays

LIVERPOOL ENGLISH TEXTS AND STUDIES

GENERAL EDITOR: PHILIP EDWARDS

Titles in this Series

The Poems of William Habington
Edited by KENNETH ALLOTT

Rollo, Duke of Normandy or The Bloody Brother
Edited by JOHN D. JUMP

The Poems of Joseph Hall
Bishop of Exeter and Norwich
Edited by ARNOLD DAVENPORT

Poems by Nicholas Breton
Edited by JEAN ROBERTSON

John Keats: A Reassessment
Edited by KENNETH MUIR

The Poems of Henry Constable
Edited by JOAN GRUNDY

The Poems of John Marston
Edited by ARNOLD DAVENPORT

Life and Letters of Sir Thomas Wyatt
By KENNETH MUIR

Samuel Daniel: A Critical and Biographical Study
By JOAN REES

Collected Poems of Sir Thomas Wyatt
Edited by KENNETH MUIR and PATRICIA THOMSON

The Poetry of Sir Philip Sidney
By J. G. NICHOLS

Yeats and Anglo-Irish Literature
Critical Essays by PETER URE
Edited by C. J. RAWSON

Elizabethan and Jacobean Drama
Critical Essays by PETER URE
Edited by J. C. MAXWELL

Literature of the Romantic Period, 1750–1850
Edited by R. T. DAVIES and B. G. BEATTY

The Singularity of Shakespeare and Other Essays
By KENNETH MUIR

The Singularity of Shakespeare

and Other Essays

KENNETH MUIR

Emeritus Professor of English Literature
in the University of Liverpool

BARNES & NOBLE BOOKS · NEW YORK
(A division of Harper & Row Publishers, Inc.)

Published in the U.S.A. 1977 by
HARPER & ROW PUBLISHERS, INC.
BARNES & NOBLE IMPORT DIVISION

ISBN 0-06-495018-2

LIBRARY OF CONGRESS CATALOG
CARD NUMBER : 77-72251

First published 1977

Set in Monotype Fournier 12 pt. by
The Lancashire Typesetting Company Limited, Bolton
and printed and bound in Great Britain by
Hazell Watson & Viney Limited,
Aylesbury, Buckinghamshire

Preface

This collection of essays, written over the last thirty years, is selected from those concerned with drama. I have included three public lectures, delivered during the last few months: the Dill Lecture, the Byron Memorial Lecture, and the Annual Lecture to the Shakespeare Association of America. I am grateful to Queen's University, Belfast, the University of Nottingham, and my hosts in Washington, DC, for permission to print these. I am likewise indebted to publishers and editors for allowing me to reprint the other eleven essays: The British Academy, *The Cambridge Journal*, *The Modern Quarterly Miscellany*, Methuen and Co., D. W. Jefferson and Routledge and Kegan Paul, The Leeds Philosophical and Literary Society, Brian Morris and Ernest Benn Ltd., The English Association and John Murray, Elmer Blistein and the Brown University Press.

I have made a number of necessary alterations in these essays, but I have resisted the temptation to make my 1947 views conform to those I hold today.

Old spelling has been retained in 'The Uncomic Pun' (where it is necessary for the argument) and in the essay on *Edward III*, in accordance with the best edition.

KENNETH MUIR

Contents

Preface   v

1 Shakespeare and the Tragic Pattern   1

2 The Uncomic Pun   20

3 *Edward III*   38

4 *Timon of Athens* and the Cash-Nexus   56

5 The Conclusion of *The Winter's Tale*   76

6 This Side Idolatry   92

7 Some Freudian Interpretations of Shakespeare   110

8 The Singularity of Shakespeare   124

9 Robert Greene as Dramatist   138

10 The Comedies of Calderón   149

11 Congreve on the Modern Stage   159

12 The Plays of H. R. Lenormand   180

13 The Pursuit of Relevance   198

14 Poetry as a Criticism of Life   212

Index   233

I

Shakespeare and
the Tragic Pattern[1]

When my great predecessor at Liverpool, Andrew Cecil Bradley, wrote his book on *Shakespearean Tragedy*, he deliberately excluded not merely the early plays, *Titus Andronicus* and *Romeo and Juliet*, and the late play, *Timon of Athens*, because of its doubtful authenticity, but also the English and Roman historical tragedies. He suggested that Shakespeare himself would probably

have met some criticisms to which these plays are open by appealing to their historical character, and by denying that such works are to be judged by the standard of pure tragedy. In any case, most of the plays, perhaps all, do show, as a matter of fact, considerable deviations from that standard.

Without considering what Shakespeare might have said on the matter, we may raise several objections to Bradley's assumptions. In the first place, it is very doubtful whether we should segregate the English and Roman historical tragedies, and deny them the title of 'pure tragedy', whatever that may be. It was clearly a matter of convenience for the Folio editors to print the English Histories in chronological order, especially as some of them were neither comedy nor tragedy. But it can scarcely be doubted that *Richard II* and *Richard III* are closer to the other tragedies than they are to *Henry IV* and *Henry V*; and, indeed, the first quartos plainly entitled both plays as tragedies. I can find no evidence that Shakespeare regarded the Roman plays as different *in kind* from the other tragedies, or that he was at all hampered by the necessity of keeping close to the facts of history. Plutarch provided him with a source in which the facts of history had already undergone an artistic process of selection and arrangement; but, even so,

1. The British Academy Shakespeare Lecture for 1958. Some paragraphs were quoted in *Shakespeare's Tragic Sequence* (1972).

Shakespeare felt at liberty to omit, reinterpret, and rearrange his material, and to add corroborative detail both from another historical source—Appian—and from the plays of the Countess of Pembroke and Samuel Daniel.

The second objection we may raise to Bradley's remarks is that *Macbeth* and even *King Lear* were historical tragedies in the same sense as *Richard III* and *Richard II*. Both were based, at least in part, on Holinshed's *Chronicles*, and it would be a mistake to suppose that the Elizabethans made a clear distinction between the historical and the legendary. In any case, they went to history not primarily for factual truth but for appropriate morals. Professional historians would cheerfully distort the facts to drive home a useful lesson; and a professional playwright would have at least as great a licence. That Shakespeare substituted the murder of Duncan by Macbeth and his wife, from the story of Donwald in another part of the chronicles, for a conspiracy in which Banquo and other Scottish lords were involved, or that he changed Cordelia's suicide to a murder by Edmund, and placed the event before the death of the king, does not necessarily mean that Shakespeare felt freer to alter the facts of history than when he wrote *Antony and Cleopatra*. By these changes he did not merely make the plays more dramatic: he clarified the moral lessons of the two plays; for the dramatist, like the historian, was to some degree a moralist.

The third objection which may be levelled at Bradley's remarks is of greater significance. By his assumption that the four tragedies with which he deals are 'pure' tragedies while the others are not, he was in danger of exaggerating both the resemblances among the chosen four, and the difference between those four and the rest. What I am suggesting is that although Shakespeare's twelve tragedies, looked at as a whole, differ considerably from the Elizabethan tragedies of Kyd or Marlowe, and also from the Jacobean tragedies of Jonson and Webster, they are so different among themselves that it is misleading to regard them as belonging to a single category. There is no such thing as Shakespearian Tragedy: there are only Shakespearian tragedies.

Nearly all critics now refrain from the attempt to apply external rules to Shakespeare's plays. They have accepted the liberating principle, as proclaimed by Coleridge, of organic form, developing itself from within; but some critics are still tempted to seek for a formula which will fit at least the four tragic masterpieces, not fully realizing perhaps that Coleridge did not mean merely that every great author had to evolve a suitable form, but that each individual play will have a different form: that which is most suitable to the expression of the theme. This form will be influenced by several different factors, some of them, at one extreme, influencing all the writers of the period, and others, at the opposite extreme, being peculiar to a single poet. Elizabethan and Jacobean tragedy was clearly influenced by the physical structure of the playhouse, by the heterogeneous nature of the audience, and by the capabilities and peculiarities of the actors. It was likewise influenced, to take another obvious example, by the ideological mingling of Christian belief and classical education, with its excessive admiration for Cicero, and its undue regard for the plays of Seneca. In addition to such general influences, there were particular influences operating on the work of individual poets, influences of temperament, for example, which made Marlowe choose to write on Tamburlaine, Faustus, and Edward II, or which made Jonson write about Cicero and Chapman about Cato. There was, finally, the influence of the material itself on the form of the play, every dramatist being faced with the question of how best to embody the theme in dramatic form.

Towards the end of *Titus Andronicus* one of the few survivors comments in these terms:

> My heart is not compact of flint nor steel,
> Nor can I utter all our bitter grief,
> But floods of tears will drown my oratory
> And break my utt'rance, even in the time
> When it should move ye to attend me most,
> And force you to commiseration.

To arouse commiseration (as we know from Sidney) was thought by the Elizabethans to be one of the functions of tragedy; and it seems from these lines that Shakespeare hoped to achieve that end by means of effective oratory. The other feeling which tragedy should arouse (again according to Sidney) was admiration. The action of *Titus Andronicus* certainly arouses horror and admiration; but, under the influence of Seneca and Ovid, Shakespeare mitigates the horror by the cleverness of his conceited verse. It might almost be said that the oratory, instead of forcing our commiseration, acts as a shield between the horrors and our hearts.

For his next tragedies Shakespeare went to Marlowe for a model. The Machiavellian hero, Richard III, owes nearly everything to Marlowe's Machiavellians. The moral structure of the play was forced upon Shakespeare by the villainy of his hero, which in turn was determined by a century of tradition and propaganda. Richard is already committed to evil at the beginning of the play as the central character of *The Massacre at Paris* had been. Shakespeare shows him wading through slaughter to a throne and the inevitable nemesis which overtakes him. It is almost a morality play; and the moral is one that Sidney singled out as a suitable one for tragedy to teach: 'Make kings fear to be tyrants.' Richard is a bogey-man, and the only commiseration aroused in the play is for his victims: Clarence, the Princes in the Tower, Buckingham, the wretched queen. At a certain level the play is a masterpiece; but Richard is a stage-villain. His soliloquy on the morning of Bosworth Field comes too late to humanize an essentially melodramatic character, a character too wicked (Aristotle would have said) to be a satisfactory tragic hero, but not too wicked for a Senecan tragic hero.

The limitations of the play were largely imposed on Shakespeare by his subject. In his next tragedy, *Richard II*, he took *Edward II* as his model, technically a tyrant, but a weak rather than a wicked man. He learnt from Marlowe the trick of concentrating on his hero's weakness and vice before his downfall, and on his better qualities afterwards. This enabled him to stress the King's misgovernment, and so provide the usurper with some excuse, and afterwards to arouse the audience's sympathy for the King, and their horror at the sins of usurpation and rebellion. He selected incidents from his sources, and invented others, to arouse sympathy for his hero in misfortune; and for the first time he made use of iterative imagery. There are, of course, weaknesses in the play, and some scenes in it may belong to an earlier version; but I think that some critics have been unreasonably harsh in their judgement of it. Professor Charlton, for example, thinks that it 'presents a general social problem rather than a moral tragic dilemma', and he complains that it does not carry Shakespeare 'appreciably nearer to his tragic pattern'. Bradley likewise confessed that to him Richard is scarcely a tragic character, and that, if he is nevertheless a tragic figure, he is so only because his fall from prosperity to adversity is so great.

But to an Elizabethan—to one, that is, who had not had the opportunity of seeing the great Jacobean tragedies by Shakespeare and others—tragedy meant primarily the fall of those in high estate into misery. Shakespeare had not read *The Mirror for Magistrates* for nothing. Richard's lament for the fall of princes owes a good deal to that popular work:

> For God's sake let us sit upon the ground
> And tell sad stories of the death of kings;
> How some have been depos'd, some slain in war,
> Some haunted by the ghosts they have depos'd,
> Some poison'd by their wives, some sleeping kill'd,
> All murder'd . . .

And, although the play is not, as Professor Charlton thought, primarily political, it is a mirror for magistrates in its warnings both against misgovernment and against rebellion. In several ways, therefore, *Richard II* marked a considerable step forward. Shakespeare had aroused the proper commiseration for the hero, he had made the tragedy spring directly from the King's faults of character, he had given an *exemplum* of the changes and chances of this mortal life, he had drawn two exemplary political morals, and he had made the great discovery of the organic use of imagery. But, of course, if we compare Richard II with the tragic heroes of the later plays, it is obvious that there is something lacking. It is not merely that he plays a passive role—for Lear might be said to do that—but that he lacks the stature of a real tragic hero.

In *Romeo and Juliet* the lovers are destroyed by the family feud, and their death is the means of reconciling the families. This is the avowed theme of the play; and it is difficult to agree with those critics who imagine that Shakespeare was exhibiting the dangers of sexual passion. The imagery suggests that he regarded their love as a positive value contrasted with hatred, a lightning-flash in a dark night. It is true that the friar preaches long sermons to the lovers on the dangers of violent passion, but he is not sufficiently detached from the action to be regarded as a chorus. The lovers are star-crossed and death-marked, they are as unlucky as the protagonists of a novel by Thomas Hardy; and perhaps

Shakespeare tacitly admitted that he had been relying too much on accident, when he inserted the tragical mirth of Pyramus and Thisbe in his next play. But once again it is clear that Shakespeare knew perfectly well what he was doing. The accidents in the play illustrate the operation of the inauspicious stars.

Hamlet belongs to the same category of drama as *The Spanish Tragedy*: Shakespeare deals with a son avenging his father, instead of a father avenging his son. He borrowed other details, including a ghost, and a play within the play. But the revenge material is transformed so as to bring out the maximum of significance in the theme. Most revenge plays operate in a moral vacuum; Shakespeare revitalized the genre (we may suppose) by imagining a sensitive and civilized person, such as himself, in the role of the avenger. Hamlet is contrasted with the more conventional avenger, Laertes, who is bloody, bold, and resolute. He avenges his father, and acts in a way that many critics, including even Coleridge, suppose that Hamlet should have done. But he is put in the play precisely for the purpose of showing us what a Hamlet who unhesitatingly carried out his father's wishes would be. When Hamlet, in the duel scene, cries 'I'll be your foil, Laertes' the words are true in an ironical sense.

The function of Fortinbras is similar. Although Hamlet contrasts his own inactivity with the restless ambition of his rival, with some admixture of envy and shame, we are not really meant to admire wholeheartedly the

> delicate and tender prince,
> Whose spirit with divine ambition puffed,
> Makes mouths at the invisible event.

At first sight there might seem to be more reason for believing that Horatio was intended to show up Hamlet's weaknesses. The stoical friend, who is never passion's slave, is contrasted (we are assured) with the neurotic and hysterical prince. I am not, of course, arguing that Hamlet is a perfectly noble character; and I am quite prepared to admit that he has been sentimentalized; but some critics, Señor Madariaga and Professor L. C. Knights, for example, have gone to the other extreme. We are told that 'the desire to escape from the complexities of adult living is central' to his character; and that 'his attitudes of hatred, revulsion, self-complacence and self-reproach' are 'forms of escape from the difficult process of complex adjustment which normal living demands'. It is only fair to point out that an adulterous mother was not in Shakespeare's day, and cannot even now be regarded as, one of the demands of normal living, that there are few of us who have the misfortune to lose a kingdom to a usurping uncle, and that to learn that one's uncle has murdered one's father is still a comparatively rare experience. Shakespeare's admiration, then, for the Senecal man, Horatio, was genuine, but not unreserved. Although Horatio is a foil to Hamlet, Hamlet's weaknesses are the maladjustments of an extraordinary man, of one who suffers, as Lascelles Abercrombie put it, from 'the heroism of moral vacillation'.

T. S. Eliot came to regret his statement that *Hamlet* was an artistic failure; but it would, I think, be possible to show that every speech and every incident, even the advice to the Players, is strictly relevant to the themes of the play. The speech from the Dido play, for example, does not merely afford an opportunity for Hamlet to contrast the Player, who can weep genuine tears for an imaginary sorrow, with the John-a-Dreams he imagines himself to be; the murder of Priam, with Pyrrhus standing over his victim, is an exact parallel to the scene where Hamlet stands over the praying Claudius; Hamlet chooses this speech because Pyrrhus is the king-killer he would like to be himself; and Hecuba's grief is contrasted with the transitory grief of Gertrude.

One of the minor themes in the play is that of the inconstancy of Fortune. When Guildenstern declares that he lives in the middle of Fortune's favours, Hamlet remarks that she is a strumpet. The player, declaiming Aeneas' part, echoes the same sentiment:

> Out, out, thou strumpet, Fortune!

And anyone who had seen Hecuba after her downfall,

> With tongue in venom steep'd,
> 'Gainst Fortune's state would treason have pronounced.

The same themes were brought home to the audience in various ways. Hamlet complains of the drossy age which dotes on people like Osric, and in the graveyard he comments on the breaking down of class-distinctions; the tragedians of the city have been superseded in popularity by the child actors; and Hamlet tells Ophelia that the only hope of a great man's memory outliving his life half a year is that he should build churches. In *The Mousetrap* the Player King moralizes on the same theme:

> The great man down, you mark his favourite flies:
> The poor advanc'd makes friends of enemies.

The people who used to mock at Claudius now give a hundred ducats a-piece for his picture in little: and Rosencrantz compares the king's life to the wheel of fortune.

A counter-theme to that of fortune is that of providence, which is also stated in *The Mousetrap*:

> Our wills and fates do so contrary run,
> That our devices still are overthrown,
> Our thoughts are ours, their ends none of our own.

and taken up by Hamlet in the last act where he declares that

> There's a divinity that shapes our ends,
> Rough-hew them how we will;

or, defying augury, claims that there is a special providence in the fall of a sparrow. In such passages the theme of fortune is imbued with a religious significance. But elsewhere Shakespeare was displaying (in Sidney's words) 'the vncertaintie of this world, and vppon how weak foundations guilden roofes are builded'. It is known, indeed, that Shakespeare had read Sidney's *Defence of Poesy*, certainly before he wrote *Coriolanus*, and probably before he wrote *A Midsummer Night's Dream*. Whether by accident or design, there appear to be references in *Hamlet* to several points made by Sidney. Sidney quotes from Plutarch the story of a tyrant 'from whose eyes a *Tragedie* well made and represented, drew abundance of teares . . . so as he that was not ashamed to make matters for *Tragedies*, yet could not resist the sweet violence of a *Tragedie*'. So Hamlet tells us:

> I have heard
> That guilty creatures sitting at a play
> Have by the very cunning of the scene
> Been struck so to the soul, that presently
> They have proclaimed their malefactions.

Then Sidney, as we have seen, says that tragedy stirs 'the affects of *Admiration* and *Commiseration*'. So Horatio, at the end of the play, asks Fortinbras:

What is it you would see?
If aught of woe or wonder, cease your search.

There has been much discussion of the disease imagery in the play, Miss Spurgeon arguing that it reflects 'not only the outward condition which causes Hamlet's spiritual illness, but also his own state'; Professor Wilson Knight supposing that it serves to contrast the health and robust life of the Court with Hamlet's own sickness; and Professor Wolfgang Clemen suggesting that it proliferates from the Ghost's account of the effect of poison on his body. If one examines the individual images in their contexts, it becomes clear that their prime function was to reflect the rottenness of court and state—a rottenness caused by Claudius's crime—and only secondarily the paralysing effect of thought or conscience on action.[2]

Several of the images refer not to poison but to hidden disease and ulcers. Shakespeare may have been thinking of the function of 'high and excellent *Tragedie*, that openeth the greatest woundes, and sheweth forth the *Vlcers* that are couered with *Tissue*'. This would support the view that the disease imagery reflects the rottenness in the state of Denmark; and if Shakespeare had indeed been studying Sidney's *Defence of Poesy* it is not unreasonable to suppose that he had been considering afresh the nature and function of tragedy. I have tried to show that he was influenced by several different conceptions: the medieval idea of the man in high estate brought to his ruin by the workings of fate; the Senecan idea that calamity was inescapable and that man must endure; the idea that the essential function of tragedy was to warn people against pride, ambition, and other vices; the

2. I assume that in the lines:
>   Thus Conscience does make cowards of us all,
>   And thus the native hue of Resolution
>   Is sicklied o'er with the pale cast of thought
the word *Conscience* means not merely 'thinking too precisely on the event' but also the 'craven scruple' of which Hamlet speaks in the fourth soliloquy. Although right conduct can proceed only from a highly developed conscience, this highly developed conscience makes action of any kind more difficult. If we let god-like reason fust in us unused, we become less than human; and if we exercise reason and conscience to the full we become increasingly aware of the complexities of every moral situation in which we find ourselves. (Cf. D. G. James, *The Dream of Learning*, and Arthur Sewell, *Character and Society in Shakespeare*.)

Marlovian idea of man brought to his ruin by excess; and under-lying all the Christian idea that misery is often God's punishment for sin, the punishment falling on the innocent as well as on the guilty. I am not, of course, agreeing with those critics who suppose that Shakespeare wrote *Hamlet* to show that action was the chief end of human existence, or *Othello* as a warning to wives to look well to their linen, or *Antony and Cleopatra* to show that adultery is apt to interfere with one's career. But the fact that foolish morals have been drawn from Shakespeare's plays does not mean that the poet was not concerned, in a more fundamental sense, with moral issues. He knew, as well as Arnold, that all good poetry is a criticism of life, and he would probably have agreed with Sidney that the function of poetry was to teach delightfully.

But whether or not before writing *Hamlet* Shakespeare had been reconsidering the nature of tragedy does not affect my argument. In Hamlet, as in all the previous plays, he was mainly concerned with the dramatic problem—how to extract the maximum of significance from the revenge theme by the kind of duplication which I have described, by the complex character of the hero, illuminated from countless different angles, by playing with the difference between a scourge and a minister (as Professor Fredson Bowers has recently shown), and by introducing a coun-terpoint between fortune and providence.

There is no need for me to give an interpretation of the play. I do not believe that Shakespeare intended us to pluck out the heart of Hamlet's mystery, since the play is concerned partly with the mystery of human personality. But I think it could be shown that Hamlet is placed in a corrupt society and faced with a moral problem for which there is no ideal solution. He has to work out his own salvation in fear and trembling; he has to make a moral decision, in a complex situation where he cannot rely on cut-and-dried moral principles, or on the conventional code of the society in which he lives; and on his choice depend the fate of the people he loves and the fate of the kingdom to which he is the rightful heir. It has been said that he is like the man in Arnold's poem,

> Wandering between two worlds, one dead,
> The other powerless to be born.

And the place of his wandering was the blank page between the

Old and New Testaments. That is how Shakespeare revitalized the old revenge formula.

Othello is essentially a much simpler play, but in recent years it has provoked almost as much controversy as any play except *Hamlet*. On the one hand there is the orthodox view of the Noble Moor, not easily jealous, whose perfect marriage with Desdemona is destroyed by the devilish cunning of Iago. This is roughly the view of Coleridge, Pushkin, Dostoevsky, and Bradley, eloquently restated by Dame Helen Gardner in her 1955 lecture and by Professor John Dover Wilson in his recent edition. But the orthodox view has been questioned by numerous modern critics: by Professor Stoll who thinks that the Othello of the first act could not have behaved in real life as the jealous maniac of Act IV; by Mr. T. S. Eliot who accuses the Moor of *Bovarysme*; by Professor Bonnard who has written of the guilt of Desdemona and Othello; by Professor G. R. Elliott who thinks Othello is guilty of the deadly sin of pride; by Dr. F. R. Leavis who accuses him of 'a habit of self-approving self-dramatisation'; and by Professor Siegel and the late Mr. S. L. Bethell who reserve a place in hell for the unfortunate man. I doubt whether Shakespeare was as positive as his critics about the posthumous fate of his characters; or whether, after we have all been cured of the sickly habit of writing on the girlhood of Shakespeare's heroines, we should now fall into the doctrinaire one of writing about the fate reserved for his heroes in another world.

Some of this controversy could have been avoided if we had not followed Coleridge, Hazlitt, Swinburne, and Bradley in talking of the motiveless malignity of Iago. Nothing that the honest Ancient says should be believed, except what he tells us in soliloquy; but these critics seem to have believed much of what he says in conversation, and to have disbelieved everything he says in soliloquy. At the beginning of the play he tells Roderigo that he hates Othello because he has been passed over for the sake of Cassio. But very naturally he does not tell the fool Roderigo that he has another and deeper motive, one that is revealed in his first soliloquy:

> I hate the Moor;
> And it is thought abroad, that 'twixt my sheets
> He has done my office: I know not if't be true;
> But I, for mere suspicion in that kind,
> Will do as if for surety.

That he had indeed suspected his wife is confirmed by her complaint that some scandal-monger

> turn'd your wit the seamy side without,
> And made you to suspect me with the Moor.

The soliloquy is a means of informing us of Iago's thoughts during the preceding scenes. In the first scene of the second act we see him identifying himself with the supposedly amorous Cassio; and in the soliloquy at the end of the scene we learn why:

> Now I do love her too:
> Not out of absolute lust, (though, peradventure
> I stand accomptant for as great a sin),
> But partly led to diet my revenge,
> For that I do suspect the lusty Moor
> Hath leap'd into my seat: the thought whereof
> Doth, like a poisonous mineral, gnaw my inwards:
> And nothing can or shall content my soul,
> Till I am even'd with him, wife for wife;
> Or, failing so, yet that I put the Moor
> At least into a jealousy so strong
> That judgment cannot cure . . .
> I'll have our Michael Cassio on the hip:
> Abuse him to the Moor in the rank garb,—
> For I fear Cassio with my night-cap too.

These lines suggest that Iago's hatred of Othello and Cassio sprang initially from sexual jealousy, and that Cassio's promotion would not have rankled so much if he had not already hated the men for other reasons. The image of the poisonous mineral gnawing his inwards shows that his jealousy is not a pretence to justify his plot. It is, as Kittredge remarked, a raging torment. We learn one other thing from these lines, a thing we might have suspected from earlier passages in the play, that Iago (after his own perverted fashion) is in love with Desdemona. We should remember that in Shakespeare's source the Ancient's thwarted love is his primary motive. Iago is able to describe to Othello the torments of jealousy so vividly because he is drawing on his own experience. He knows the green-eyed monster and the dangerous conceits which burn like the mines of sulphur. His motives are not mysterious, but only too appallingly plain. He is a jealous man who is bent on infecting Othello with his own jealousy. The way in which he succeeds in dragging the Noble Moor down to his own level is emphasized, as Morozov and others have shown, by Othello's use of the same kind of imagery which had been used by Iago earlier in the play.

I am not suggesting that sexual jealousy was Iago's only motive. Near the end of the play, where he speaks of the advantages of having Roderigo kill Cassio, he reveals that his jealousy is a form of envy:

> If Cassio do remain,
> He hath a daily beauty in his life,
> That makes me ugly.

His evil passions are revealed as symptoms of his feelings of inferiority.

Just as in *Hamlet* we are given the contrasting portraits of two avengers, so in *Othello* we have a quadruple portrait of jealousy. Iago, Othello, Bianca, and Roderigo are all, in their different ways, jealous. But, as usual, Shakespeare did not start with a theme: he started with a tale; and what may have intrigued him in Cinthio's sordid little story was either his account of the way the villain's wickedness was unsuspected, or his remark, after his description of the murder of Desdemona, that the Moor loved her more than life. How did a man come to kill his beloved wife, how did a noble soldier come to commit an atrocious crime? Shakespeare deliberately exaggerated the disparity between the man and his crime so as to make the dramatic problem he set himself as difficult as possible. He solved it mainly by his subtle use of the colour question. The sense of 'otherness' which is a recurrent miracle in marriage can in a marriage of two different races be distorted and warped into alienation. The act of faith and commitment can be interpreted as a perversion, and the strangeness can appear as a mask hiding the real self. Nothing, moreover, in Othello's former life had served as a school for husbands, or as a protection against Iago. External evil combined with his own insufficiency to destroy him.

The same thing may be said of *King Lear*, since without the evil in Goneril, Regan, Edmund, and Cornwall, the foolishness of the King and Gloster would not have been fatal. But the play is much more complex in its organization. In place of the single, streamlined plot, there are two parallel plots in each of which the father is succoured by the child he has rejected. One father loses his reason and the other his sight, though Lear is wiser in his madness and Gloster sees more clearly in his blindness than they had before. Whereas in *Othello* the hero does not commit his fatal deed until the last scene of all, in *King Lear* the hero's fatal error is committed at the very beginning of the play, and Gloster's twenty years before—

> The dark and vicious place where thee he got
> Cost him his eyes;

and whereas in *Othello* we watch the moral disintegration of the hero, in *King Lear* both Lear and Gloster undergo a process of purification. For this reason, and because of the loyalty of Kent and the Fool, the integrity of Cordelia, the development of Albany and Edgar from their initial feebleness, and even the death-bed conversion of Edmund, *King Lear* is by no means so pessimistic as some critics have believed; and even in *Othello*, though we see a noble mind overthrown and Desdemona murdered, we see also the courage of Emilia in the face of death, Desdemona's attempt to shield her husband, and his final recognition that she was the pearl of great price which he had wantonly thrown away.

All the great tragedies exemplify Keats's famous maxim:

> The excellence of every art is its intensity, capable of making all disagreeables evaporate, from their being in close relationship with Beauty and Truth.

There are many disagreeables in *Othello* and *King Lear*, but they are evaporated. The plays strike at the roots of human complacency, acting on our unconscious minds and revealing our hidden selves. 'An aged man', as Goethe said, 'is always a King Lear'; and the play reveals, with terrifying and parabolic clarity, the ambivalent attitude of parents to children, and of children to parents. Lear in the storm, and Gloster bound to the chair, are symbols of nightmares which are perhaps universal; and every human relationship is threatened by the alienation that befalls the apparently perfect marriage of Othello and Desdemona.

In spite of the universality of the tragedies, they became so by Shakespeare's resolute refusal to generalize. In each case, as I have tried to show, he began by considering how best to present on the stage a story that had kindled his imagination, how to squeeze from it its essential meaning. One of the main reasons why it is worth while to study his source-material is that we can derive hints from it of the way his shaping spirit of imagination was operating. In some cases we can deduce without much difficulty the reason for his changes—why, for example, he omitted Iago's child, and why he did not allow Desdemona to be battered to death with a sandbag. In other cases the changes are more complicated: the grafting of the story of the Paphlagonian King on the Lear story, the invention of Lear's madness, the disguise of Edgar as Poor Tom with details taken from Harsnett, Gloster's attempted suicide, and the substitution of Cordelia's murder for the suicide of the sources are all pointers to the way Shakespeare was organizing his material for thematic purposes. Some of his inventions—the trial of Goneril and Regan and the meeting of Lear and Gloster at Dover—since they are strictly irrelevant to the plot, show even more clearly what Shakespeare was doing. Although he was still trying to arouse commiseration and admiration, still disclosing the ulcers that are covered with tissue, still showing 'vppon how weak foundations guilden roofes are builded', and still teaching the uncertainty of this world, Shakespeare had by this time left Elizabethan theory far behind. He was not merely revealing ulcers, he was stripping man of everything, and showing unaccommodated man as he really is. There are still traces of Seneca in remarks scattered through the play and in the continual stress on endurance and patience; but in spite of the pagan setting the Senecanism has been impregnated with Christian feeling. Bradley rightly stressed the secular nature of Elizabethan drama; yet although compared with medieval drama it is manifestly secular, it was after all written for the most part by Christians for Christians. Tragedy is necessarily concerned with man (as Newman says) 'implicated in some terrible original calamity'; and from the very nature of man Shakespeare rediscovers what he may not, as a poet, assume.

In *Macbeth* Shakespeare abandoned the double plot he had used in *King Lear*, and produced the shortest and most condensed of his tragedies. Only two episodes have been regarded by some critics as not strictly necessary: the Porter scene, and the scene in England. Both, of course, are essential: the Porter scene well illustrates Shakespeare's creative use of anachronism, as a means of linking the play with contemporary events and as a means of universalizing the murder; and the scene in England is necessary partly to show the way Macbeth's crimes have created an atmosphere of terror and suspicion, partly to establish the qualities of order and kingship violated by Macbeth, and partly to show the gathering of the forces of liberation.

Macbeth is closer to *Richard III* than to any other tragedy; but in spite of superficial resemblances the tone is quite different. Richard is entirely a villain, committed to evil from the start; Macbeth becomes a villain, but we watch his temptation and fall from within, and he never entirely alienates our sympathies. He remains a man like ourselves, not a bogey-man. Nevertheless the movement of the play reverses that of *King Lear*. Macbeth's descent into damnation is continuous and unalleviated, and he dies like a trapped beast. When in the last act he expresses the utter futility of life, we are not to take it as a reflection of Shakespeare's own pessimism, nor even to suppose (as Lascelles Abercrombie did) that Macbeth exhibits his grandeur as a tragic hero by savouring to the full the meaninglessness of life, and, by so doing, transcending it. In fact the meaninglessness is transcended, not for Macbeth, but for us—we realize, that is, that life is not

> a tale
> Told by an idiot, full of sound and fury
> Signifying nothing—

because we know that Macbeth has destroyed the significance of life by his own acts. The moral retribution which has overtaken him reinforces for the audience the conviction that life is full of meaning, that a moral order exists however much the individual may violate it.

It is significant that *Macbeth* has more direct echoes of Seneca than any other of Shakespeare's tragedies. It is an indication, perhaps, that even after writing *Othello* and *King Lear* he was still looking over his shoulder at the ghosts of Sidney and Holofernes. Perhaps, indeed, the fact that the play was written for King James made Shakespeare take the precaution of refreshing his memory of Seneca, and of adopting a more classical structure.

I want finally to say a word about the Roman plays for which the historical material had already been digested by a great writer. The three plays are as different from each other as they are from the other great tragedies. All three deal with significant moments in the history of Rome; and Shakespeare made a great effort of historical imagination to paint convincingly the varying backgrounds as well as the characters of the chief actors. He was not primarily concerned with the political issues involved. It is not Autocracy versus Oligarchy but the self-deceptions of the idealist, Brutus, which is the real theme of *Julius Caesar*; and in *Coriolanus*, though the political struggle is brilliantly conveyed, Shakespeare concentrates on the relationship between mother and son.

Each theme requires and receives a totally different treatment. It is noteworthy, for example, that the two portraits of Antony, though both are derived mainly from Appian and Plutarch, are deliberately varied to suit the plays in which they appear. We see nothing in *Julius Caesar* which would make us suspect that Antony was a great warrior and a great lover, an inspirer of love and loyalty in his followers. In *Antony and Cleopatra* the stature of Antony is increased by references to his ancestor, Hercules, by comparisons with Mars and Bacchus, and even by the grudging admissions of his enemies.

Morley was the first critic to suggest that the theme of *Antony and Cleopatra* was, unlike Dryden's play, 'All for Lust, or the World ill-lost'; but Bradley is surely right when he says that when we judge the tragic heroes we have slipped from the tragic position. Other critics, of whom Professor Danby is the most notable, have argued that Shakespeare is deliberately objective, and does not, even at the end, expect us to choose between passion and power, between the cold-blooded Octavius and the man who proclaims that the nobleness of life is to love. I think that this view ignores the development in Cleopatra's character and the way she becomes imbued with Antony's spirit after his death. It is clear from Plutarch that she lies about the amount of her treasure, not because she is thinking of coming to terms with Caesar, but to make him think she is not going to commit suicide; and if she kills herself partly to avoid being taken to Rome in Caesar's triumph, and only partly for love of Antony, mixed motives are as legitimate in drama as they are unavoidable in real life. When Cleopatra says 'Husband I come', and 'I am fire and air', we must believe her. Her suicide is her triumph. Indeed, the triumphant note at the close of the play was one of the reasons why Bradley felt that the play was not properly tragic. It is a different kind of tragedy from *King Lear* and *Macbeth*, perfect in its kind; and if there is one thing that emerges from a study of Shakespeare's twelve tragedies it is that after each masterpiece he wished, in Keats's phrase, to devote himself to other sensations.

The nature of *Coriolanus* was partly determined by the tradition within which Shakespeare was writing. The fable of the Belly and the Members of the Body which is one key to the interpretation of the play was known to Shakespeare in a number of different versions, and the Coriolanus story itself was told in five books written or translated just before Shakespeare wrote his play. Dudley Digges used the story to show that war is better than luxurious idleness, and that it can be used to cure internal dissensions. Bodin's long criticism of democracy uses the banishment of Coriolanus as an example. Forset's *Comparative Discourse* is an elaborate comparison, starting from Menenius's fable, between the human body and the body politic. He stresses the fact that the faults of great men are most dangerous and shows that amputation is sometimes necessary, a point made by Sicinius about Coriolanus. Goslicius blames the Tribunes for the troubles in Rome, but refers to Coriolanus's invasion as wicked and unnatural; and William Fulbecke again alludes to the banishment of Coriolanus as an example of the evils of democracy.

Shakespeare, in spite of the suggestion that he was exhibiting the terror of a landowner at the Warwickshire insurrection, was much more critical of the patricians, and more sympathetic to the plebians than any of the writers I have mentioned. He depicts Coriolanus as inordinately proud, and as something of a schoolboy. When his son tears a butterfly to pieces we are meant to suppose that the child is father of the man. The kind of play to which *Coriolanus* belongs is the tragical satire. The hero's renunciation of vengeance is often regarded as the triumph of love in his heart, as in a sense it may be; but Shakespeare depicts him as refusing the plea of the exquisite Virgilia and surrendering to his mother, the old Roman matron whose 'virtue' is as destructive as the lust of Cleopatra or as the murderous ambition of Lady Macbeth.

I have touched all too briefly on nearly all Shakespeare's tragedies so as to show that each play is unique and *sui generis*. The generalizations which have been made about Shakespearian tragedy—even those in Bradley's brilliant introductory chapter—do not seem to me to be very helpful, since the differences between one play and another are more significant than the resemblances. The sense of waste, for example, is apparent in all the tragedies, but the kind of waste differs greatly from play to play. We may discern a tragic flaw—a dram of eale—in all the tragic heroes, but there is such a difference between the flaw in Romeo and that in Richard III, or between that in Hamlet and that in Macbeth, that it becomes a difference in kind. Or, again, Professor G. R. Elliott's statement that all the tragic heroes fall through pride can be justified only on theological grounds. We must, as Mr. J. C. Maxwell says, 'grant artistic autonomy to the individual work'.

All the alterations which have been made in adapting Shakespeare to suit the tastes of later ages, and all the generalizations which have been imposed on his work, have been caused by timidity. The adaptors and the critics have shrunk from the appalling clarity of Shakespeare's vision. They have wanted to pretend that evil does not have certain inevitable consequences, so they have married Edgar to Cordelia, and restored Lear to his throne; or they have pretended that Othello was not really jealous, or that Iago is merely an abstraction; or they have denied Shakespeare's negative capability and turned him into a stoic or an Hegelian whose thesis and antithesis lead to a comfortable synthesis. But Shakespeare always refused to impose an ideological pattern on his material: the only pattern that emerges is an artistic one. As a poet he was primarily concerned with imposing order on chaos, with extracting the maximum of significance from the situation with which he was dealing. He might, if the material allowed, show that crime does not pay, or reveal that pride is destructive and self-love suicidal. But such morals are not imposed on his material: they emerge as the simple facts of life. He holds, as it were, a mirror up to nature.

2

The Uncomic Pun[1]

In his essay on *The Dramatic Poetry of the Last Age* Dryden
complained that even so correct an author as Jonson

was not free from the lowest and most grovelling kind of wit, which we
call clenches, of which *Every Man in his Humour* is infinitely full; and,
which is worse, the wittiest persons in the drama speak them.

Shakespeare was likewise guilty of 'the jingle of a more poor
paronomasia'. What to the Elizabethans had been natural and
satisfying had come to seem tasteless and unnatural. A hundred
years after Dryden the gulf between the taste of Shakespeare and
that of his critics was wider than ever. Dr. Johnson complained
in his great Preface:

A quibble is to *Shakespeare*, what luminous vapours are to the traveller;
he follows it at all adventures; it is sure to lead him out of his way, and
sure to engulf him in the mire. It has some malignant power over his
mind, and its fascinations are irresistible. Whatever be the dignity or
profundity of his disquisition, whether he be enlarging knowledge or
exalting affection, whether he be amusing attention with incidents, or
enchaining it in suspense, let but a quibble spring up before him, and he
leaves his work unfinished. A quibble is the golden apple for which he
will always turn aside from his career, or stoop from his elevation.
A quibble, poor and barren as it is, gave him such delight, that he was
content to purchase it, by the sacrifice of reason, propriety and truth.
A quibble was to him the fatal *Cleopatra* for which he lost the world,
and was content to lose it.

Some attempt to revive the pun was made in the circles of
Charles Lamb and Leigh Hunt, but their puns were always used
for comic purposes; and in the humorous verse of Thomas Hood
the pun was turned out mechanically as an end in itself. The
popularity of this sort of quibble made it difficult to defend

1. Published in *The Cambridge Journal* (1950).

Shakespeare's very different use of it, though Coleridge in his lectures made a half-hearted attempt. In answer to Richard's question to Gaunt, Can sick men play so nicely with their names? Coleridge replies:

Yes! on a death-bed there is a feeling which may make all things appear but as puns and equivocations. And a passion there is that carries off its own excess by plays on words as naturally and, therefore, as appropriately to drama, as by gesticulations, looks, or tones. This belongs to human nature as such, independently of associations and habits from any particular rank of life or mode of employment . . . No doubt, something of Shakespeare's punning must be attributed to his age, in which direct and formal combats of wit were a favourite pastime of the courtly and accomplished. It was an age more favourable, upon the whole, to vigour of intellect than the present, in which a dread of being thought pedantic dispirits and flattens the energies of original minds. But independently of this, I have no hesitation in saying that a pun, if it be congruous with the feeling of the scene, is not only allowable in the dramatic dialogue, but oftentimes one of the most effectual intensives of passion.

Elsewhere Coleridge argues that if punning is the lowest, it is at all events the most harmless, kind of wit, because it never excites envy; and he suggests that

this form of speech is generally produced by a mixture of anger and contempt, and punning is a natural mode of expressing them.

At the present day, with one or two exceptions to which I shall refer, it is still usual to deplore the bad taste of the age in which Shakespeare lived, which could enjoy such a low form of humour; or at least to excuse Shakespeare on the grounds that he is less guilty of quibbling than his contemporaries. But as a matter of fact Shakespeare is fonder of the quibble than Jonson, Marlowe, or Webster, and perhaps than any of his contemporaries; and we can scarcely excuse him by pretending that he fell into bad company.

Yet it is quite needless to be apologetic about Shakespeare's puns. The comic ones justify themselves as amusing examples of contemporary wit, heightened no doubt for dramatic purposes; and however much we have been taught at school that such wit is unworthy to evoke our laughter, it continues to do so. But tragedies, no less than comedies, contain numerous puns; and

they are used at moments which make it impossible to suppose
that Shakespeare intended a laugh. In editing *Macbeth* I have been
struck by the prevalence of puns, many of which have been left
unnoted, if not unnoticed, by previous commentators; and I
propose in this article to examine a number of the puns and quibbles
in this play and try to classify them so as to determine their
dramatic function.

The first thing one notices, as I have suggested, is that few of
the puns are used for comic purposes. Only in the one semi-comic
scene of the play, the Porter scene, are the puns intended to arouse
laughter. We may instance the following piece of dialogue, which
contains a large number of quibbles:

PORTER: . . . Therefore much Drinke may be said to be an Equivocator
with Lecherie: it makes him, but it marres him; it sets him on, and it
takes him off; it perswades him, and disheartens him; makes him
stand too, and not stand too: in conclusion, equivocates him in a
sleepe, and giving him the Lye, leaves him.
MACDUFF: I beleeve, Drinke gave thee the Lye last Night.
PORTER: That it did, Sir, i' the very Throat on me: but I requited him
for his Lye, and (I thinke) being too strong for him, though he
tooke up my Legges sometimes, yet I made a Shift to cast him.

Here there are quibbles on *lie*, which can mean 'falsehood', or
'sexual intercourse', or be a term in wrestling, and on *cast*, which
can mean 'throw' (in wrestling again), 'vomit', or 'urinate'. The
purpose of these puns was clearly to arouse laughter by equivo-
catory references to obscene subjects, although, indeed, the
Porter's mention of Equivocation recalls the equivocator 'who
could not equivocate to heaven' and the 'equivocation of the
fiend that lies like truth'.

But if we turn to a quibble in the preceding scene, it is obvious
that there, just after the murder of Duncan, laughter was the last
thing that Shakespeare intended. Lady Macbeth announces that
she will try to incriminate the grooms by daubing them with
Duncan's blood in these words:

> If he doe bleed,
> Ile guild the Faces of the Groomes withall,
> For it must seeme their Guilt.

It is difficult for us to put ourselves in the place of Shakespeare's
original audience. Clearly such a quibble was not meant to be

funny. It was intended rather to suggest the overwrought condition of Lady Macbeth's nerves and her contempt for her
husband's lack of self-control. It has the effect, moreover, of
reinforcing the logical sequence with a phonic sequence. To an
audience, though not to a reader, the similarity of *gild* and *guilt*
seems to clinch the sentence. It should also be noted that the image
of gilding looks forward to Macbeth's description of Duncan's
corpse:

> His Silver skinne, lac'd with his Golden Blood.

Another quibble of the same simple kind occurs in the scene in
England, where Rosse brings the news of the murder of Macduff s
family:

> Your Castle is surpriz'd: your Wife, and Babes
> Savagely slaughter'd: To relate the manner
> Were on the Quarry of these murther'd Deere
> To adde the death of you.

where *deer* is part of the metaphor of the chase, but also a quibbling reference to Macduff's dear ones. Here again laughter is the
last thing that Shakespeare wanted.

Most of the other puns are more subtle, and less apparent, than
these. There are a large number of concealed quibbles, of which
Shakespeare himself was probably unconscious; as, for example,
when Macbeth addresses Night before the murder of Banquo:

> Come, seeling Night,
> Skarfe up the tender Eye of pittifull Day,
> And with thy bloodie and invisible Hand
> Cancell and teare to pieces that great Bond,
> Which keepes me pale.

Here the word *seeling*—a term in falconry referring to the way
hawks were tamed by stitching up their eyelids with a thread tied
behind the head—suggested the word *bond* by way of *sealing*; and
bond suggested *pale*, Macbeth's white face resembling parchment,
and as a bond is also a fetter it may also have suggested *pale* in the
sense of fenced-in land.

Similarly, in the preceding scene Macbeth tells the murderers:

> Now, if you have a station in the file,
> Not i' th'worst ranke of Manhood, say't . . .

where *file* in the old sense of catalogue suggested *rank*, by way of *file* in the military sense. There is another example in the last act of the play when Macbeth remarks:

> this push
> Will cheere me ever, or dis-seate me now . . .

where *cheer* suggested *dis-seat* through the intermediate *chair*, the pronunciation of the two words being similar. Or again, in the scene of the discovery of the murder of Duncan Macbeth declares:

> The Wine of Life is drawne, and the meere Lees
> Is left this Vault, to brag of.

where *wine* and *lees* both suggest the vault, which may be either a wine-cellar, a tomb, or the vaulted arch of the sky.

Sometimes the use of overt or concealed puns causes an ambiguity, which enables the passage to be interpreted in two different ways; and it is not always possible to be sure whether Shakespeare was conscious of both meanings, or of one only, and if of one only which of the two. In the scene in which Macduff visits Malcolm in England, the latter is suspicious of his visitor because he thinks that he may be seeking to betray him to Macbeth. He tells him:

> A good and vertuous Nature may recoyle
> In an Imperiall charge.

This is generally taken to mean: 'give way under pressure from a monarch'. The image may be either that of retiring before the charge or onslaught of a superior force, or that of a gun which recoils when the charge is too great. *Charge* can thus mean 'duty', 'onslaught', or 'gunpowder'. The probability is that the word was suggested to Shakespeare by the double meaning of 'recoil'. We weaken the effectiveness of the passage by ignoring the subsidiary meanings.

A similar example is to be found in *Romeo and Juliet* (III. vi) in a passage which was the cause of a heated controversy in *The Times Literary Supplement* in 1943. When Juliet arrives at the Friar's cell to be married, he announces her approach in these lines:

> Here comes the Lady. Oh so light a foot
> Will nere weare out the everlasting flint.

> A Lover may bestride the Gossamer,
> That ydles in the wanton Summer ayre,
> And yet not fall, so light is vanitie.

One critic complained that the second of these lines was vacuous, since no foot, however heavy, will wear out the everlasting flint. He therefore urged that *nere* is 'near' rather than 'ne'er', and that *wear out* means 'outwear' or 'outlast', as in *King Lear* (v. iii. 17–18):

> We'll wear out
> In a wall'd prison, packs and sects of great ones.

But it was pointed out that it was a commonplace of Latin and Elizabethan poetry that 'even the lightest attrition in the end wears out even the hardest material' and that 'the Friar's point is that Juliet's step is so light as to defy a recognized law of nature'. Another critic argued that the image was suggested by an earlier one, a few lines before:

> These violent delights have violent endes,
> And in their triumph die; like fire and powder,
> Which as they kisse consume.

This, I think, is probable, though I part company with this critic when he goes on to suggest that Shakespeare was referring to the new musket which was provided with a flintlock, the flint of which was everlasting in comparison with the earlier iron pyrites; and that the 'light foot' of Juliet was an allusion to the lightly armed infantry, who would stand no chance against the deadly fire of the new musket. The lines are, in fact, a continuation of the Friar's warning to Romeo against violent delights:

> Therefore Love moderately, long Love doth so,
> Too swift arrives as tardie as too slow.

Then he sees Juliet flying to meet her lover and hardly seeming to touch the ground. She has her head in the clouds, and does not come down to solid rock or the flint of the pathway. The word 'light' is itself a kind of quibble: it means not only that Juliet weighs less than a hundredweight, but also that she is light as vanity, i.e. frivolous, out of touch with reality. This is surely the main meaning of the lines, though *light* was suggested by *delight* and the image of gunpowder, and *flint* was suggested either by the same gunpowder image or by the word *light*.

A more complicated example is to be found in the second act of *Macbeth*, just after the murder of Duncan, where the hero speaks of sleep:

> *Macbeth* does murther Sleepe, the innocent Sleepe,
> Sleepe that knits up the ravel'd Sleeve of Care,
> The death of each dayes Life, sore Labors Bath,
> Balme of hurt Mindes, great Natures second Course,
> Chiefe nourisher in Life's Feast.

In the First Folio the word 'sleave' is spelt 'sleeve'; and a few commentators have assumed that the clause means 'knits up the frayed sleeve'. But nearly all editors have spelt the word 'sleave', which is defined as 'a slender filament of silk obtained by separating a thicker thread'. But it seems also to mean 'coarse silk', for Florio translates *sfilazza* as 'any kinde of ravelled stuffe, or sleave silke'. Macbeth's phrase would then mean 'knits up the tangled silk'. Both meanings are quite possible, and Shakespeare may have intended either, or both. Another phrase in this passage is also ambiguous. 'Great Nature's second course' probably means the second race or career after the death of each day's life; but, by a quibble, it suggested to Shakespeare the second course, in the sense of the joint or roast: pudding being in those days the first course. The succeeding phrase, 'Chief nourisher in Life's feast', may also have been suggested by another meaning of *ravelled*. Ravelled bread was made from flour and bran; and wholemeal bread, the staff of life, could be regarded as the chief nourisher— indeed a *whole meal* in itself.[2]

2. The passage owed something, perhaps, to a passage in Golding's *Metamorphoses* (xi. 723 ff.):

> Sweete sleepe, the peace of minde with whome crookt
>   care is aye at ods:
> Which cherishest men's weary limbes appalld with
>   toyling sore,
> And makest them as fresh to worke, and lustie as before.

As Seneca's *Hercules Furens* is echoed elsewhere in *Macbeth*, the phrase 'balm of hurt minds' may reflect the situation where the Chorus invokes sleep to cure the madness of Hercules. Jasper Heywood translates thus:

> And thou O tamer best
> O sleepe of toyles, the quietnesse of mynde,
> Of all the lyfe of man the better part.

Another example, for which I am partly indebted to S. L. Bethell, is to be found in Macbeth's soliloquy (I. vii):

> If it were done, when 'tis done, then 'twer well
> It were done quickly: If th'Assassination
> Could trammell up the Consequence, and catch
> With his surcease, Successe: that but this blow
> Might be the be-all, and the end-all—heere,
> But heere, upon this Banke and Shoal of time,
> Wee'ld iumpe the life to come.

These seven lines contain a large number of ambiguities. 'Trammel up' can mean 'entangle, as in a net', 'fasten the legs of horses together, so that they cannot stray', or possibly 'hang up'— derived from a *trammel*, an iron device for suspending pots over a fire. 'Surcease' may be a legal term derived from the Old French *sursis*, meaning the stay of proceedings; in which case the pronoun *his* refers to *consequence*. But Shakespeare elsewhere uses the word as a euphemism for *die*:

> If they surcease to be that should survive

and it may here mean *death*, the pronoun referring to Duncan. 'Success' may be used in its ordinary modern sense, or it may mean *consequence* or *succession* to the throne. Editors have cheerfully plumped for a single meaning of each of these three words, and have dismissed all the other meanings out of hand. But Shakespeare and his audience presumably had more than one meaning at the backs of their minds. A more significant phrase is 'bank and shoal of time'. 'Shoal' is Theobald's brilliant emendation for the

---

There is a similar passage in the first chorus of Seneca's *Agamemnon*, which is also echoed elsewhere in *Macbeth:*

> Sleepe that doth overcome and break the bonds of griefe.

There is also a parallel, pointed out by Malone, with the opening of Sidney's most famous sonnet:

> Come Sleepe, O Sleepe, the certaine knot of peace,
> The baiting place of wit, the balme of woe.

With *knot, baiting, balm* and *woe* may be compared *knits, feast, balm* and *care*. Shakespeare seems also to have read the pirated edition (1591) of *Astrophel and Stella* which has *bathing* for *baiting*, a more obvious parallel to Macbeth's *bath*. Shakespeare's lines were probably created by an unconscious coalescence of the phrases of Ovid, Seneca, and Sidney.

'Schoole' of the Folio. This is now generally accepted, especially
as 'schoole' is a possible seventeenth-century spelling of 'shoal'.
Theobald explained:

> This Shallow, this narrow Ford, of humane Life,
> opposed to the great Abyss of Eternity.

One or two critics, however, have argued for the original
reading, taking 'bank' to mean 'bench'. Elwin paraphrased:

If here only, upon this bench of instruction, in this school of eternity,
I could do this without bringing these, my pupil days, under suffering,
I would hazard its effect on the endless life to come.

Bethell, who is one of the few modern critics to defend 'school',
assumes that 'bank' is the judicial bench (OF *banc*), not the school
bench. The word was certainly current in this sense in Shakespeare's time. Bethell argued[3] that

Time is thus seen as the period of judgment, testing, or 'crisis', and as a
school.

If we reject this interpretation, as I think we must, it should not be
because, as some have complained, it is less poetic—for it would
not be very different from Keats's great parable of the world as a
school and as a vale of soul-making—but because, in spite of
Bethell's denial, Shakespeare often couples words together like
'bank and shoal', and because the preposition 'upon' fits 'bank',
but not 'school'. The true explanation is that we have here another
example of an unconscious pun. Shakespeare intended 'shoal'; but
the alternative meaning of 'bank' would lead naturally to 'judgement' a few lines later and 'schoole' would suggest 'teach',
'instructions', and 'taught'.

> But in these Cases
> We still have iudgement heere, that we but teach
> Bloody Instructions, which being taught, returne
> To plague th'Inventer.

In the same soliloquy the phrase 'Angels, Trumpet-tongu'd' is
closely followed by the image of

> Pitty, like a naked New-borne-Babe,
> Striding the blast,

3. *The Winter's Tale* (1947), pp. 126–7.

in which the blast of the storm was suggested by the blast of the
trumpet. When Macbeth describes the discovery of the murder
the phrase 'Breach in Nature' is linked by a pun with the word
used to describe the daggers of the supposed murderers, 'Un-
mannerly breech'd with gore'. In the scene in England Malcolm
declares:

> I should forge
> Quarrels uniust against the Good and Loyall,
> Destroying them for wealth.

The surface meaning of these lines is plain enough; but as a
quarrel was also a square-headed arrow for a cross-bow and
Holinshed speaks of

> crossebowes set readie bent with sharpe quarrels in them,

Shakespeare probably used the verb *forge* with this secondary
meaning of *quarrel* at the back of his mind.

The same thing may have happened in the scene before the
murder of Banquo—

> Light thickens,
> And the Crow makes Wing to th' Rookie Wood.

The primary meaning of *Rookie* is simply 'black and filled with
rooks'; but many editors, since the carrion crow is not gregarious,
have regarded the line as tautological and in need of emendation.
They have therefore proposed a variety of words, including
'roky' (= misty), 'rouky' (= perching), 'reeky' (= steamy), and
there is apparently a variant of this in Scots and Northern
dialects: 'rooky' (= misty), 'rouky' (= chattering), and 'rucky'
(= multitudinous). If we combined these last two suggestions,
we should get a portmanteau equivalent for the Meredithian
phrase, 'multitudinous chatterings'. But we need not take too
seriously these attempts to relieve the poet of the responsibility of
writing one of his most magical lines, though it is possible that one
of these dialectical words was hovering at the back of his consciousness when he used the word 'rooky' to mean something
more straightforward.

In the same scene Lady Macbeth makes an ambiguous remark
about Banquo and Fleance:

> But in them, Natures Coppie's not eterne.

This is usually taken as a reference to copyhold, meaning that the tenure of their lives by Banquo and Fleance under nature would cease with their deaths: in other words, that they would not live for ever. Certainly there is another legal metaphor twelve lines later; but elsewhere Shakespeare invariably means by *copy* a thing to be copied or the result of imitation, and the phrase has been paraphrased 'the particular cast from Nature's mould'.

There are several examples of quibbling in the scene in England. Macduff, on hearing of Malcolm's suspicions of him, exclaims:

> Bleed, bleed poore Country,
> Great Tyrrany, lay thou thy basis sure,
> For goodnesse dare not check thee: wear thou thy wrongs,
> The Title is affear'd.

The last word is invariably emended to 'affeer'd', which means 'confirmed'; and the primary meaning of the passage is that the title of Macbeth to the country he rules is confirmed by the cowardice of the good. But 'The Title is affear'd' may also bear the meaning 'The rightful king is afraid'. Shakespeare was probably conscious of this pun as he must have been of the one a few lines later:

> my Desire
> All continent Impediments would ore-beare
> That did oppose my will.

Here *continent* can mean either 'restraining' or 'chaste', and *will* means both 'lust' and 'determination'.

It is sometimes impossible to be sure which meaning Shake-speare intended. In the lines:

> ere to black *Heccats* summons
> The shard-borne Beetle, with his drowsie hums,
> Hath rung Nights yawning Peale, there shall be done
> A deed of dreadfull note

the epithet *shard-borne* may mean either 'dung-bred' or 'borne on scaly wings': the *Oxford Dictionary* supports the former inter-pretation and most editors the latter. When Donalbain asks his brother:

> What should be spoken here, where our Fate
> Hid in an augure hole, may rush and seize us?

Shakespeare may have been thinking of the passage in Scot's *Discovery of Witchcraft* which refers to the way that witches can go in and out of auger-holes; or he may have meant merely that Donalbain thinks that his fate lurks in a hole made by a dagger. When Macbeth first conceives the murder of Duncan he declares:

> My Thought, whose Murther yet is but fantasticall,
> Shakes so my single state of Man,
> That Function is smother'd in surmise.

It is usually supposed that in the phrase 'my single state of man' Shakespeare was referring to the microcosm, the little kingdom of man, as in Brutus' well-known lines:

> the state of a man,
> Like to a little Kingdome, suffers then
> The nature of an Insurrection.

But Steevens pointed out that 'double' and 'single' used to signify 'strong' and 'weak'; and 'single state' may mean no more than 'weak condition'.

One last example of ambiguity will suffice. In Act v, scene ii, Menteith speaks of the English army led by Malcolm, Siward, and Macduff:

> Revenges burne in them: for their deere causes
> Would to the bleeding, and the grim Alarme
> Excite the mortified man.

The word *burn*, with its association with fever, suggested *dear causes*; for this phrase could mean 'sore diseases' as well as 'grievous wrongs' or 'grounds of action'. The sickness metaphor is continued in *bleeding* and *mortified* and in the later speech:

> He cannot buckle his distemper'd cause
> Within the belt of Rule.

Bleeding was, of course, a remedy for fever; but it may have been suggested by the superstition, mentioned by Holinshed in this part of the *Chronicles*, that the corpse of a murdered man bled afresh in the presence of the murderer. 'Excite the mortified man' may mean 'raise up the dead' or 'stir up the numbed': *excite* being derived from *excitare*, to call forth, or quicken. The whole passage, therefore, means either that the justice of their cause would rouse even the dead to take an interest in the battle, or else that it would excite the sluggish to fight.

A few examples may be given of puns from another tragedy I
have edited, *King Lear*. In the scene in which Cordelia and Lear
are reconciled, we have these lines:

> Was this a face
> To be oppos'd against the warring winds?
> To stand against the deepe dread-bolted thunder?
> In the most terrible and nimble stroke
> Of quick crosse lightning? to watch—poor *Perdu*—
> With this thin helme?

A perdu was a sentry in a dangerous advanced post, and this is
undoubtedly Cordelia's primary meaning. But the effectiveness of
the word depends partly on an undertone of meaning suggested
by its derivation: Lear is a poor lost one. When Gloucester
decides to make Edmund his heir for revealing Edgar's supposed
treachery, he calls him 'loyal and natural boy'. 'Natural' here is the
opposite of unnatural; but as it also means illegitimate, and (in
some contexts) legitimate, it reminds us of Edmund's bastardy.
In a later scene Gloucester prays to the gods that the 'superfluous
and lust-dieted man' that slaves their ordinance may feel their
power quickly. The word 'slaves' means enslaves, but the poet
was also thinking of a word pronounced the same which means
'rends asunder'. The lust-dieted man tears up the ordinance, as well
as treating it as his slave. Regan tells Gloucester that she and
Cornwall have come to visit him,

> Thus out of season, thredding darke-eyed night.

She means that she has traversed the darkness, but by a quibble
the image suggests the threading of the eye of a needle.

In III. vii Gloucester upbraids Regan for her treatment of her
father:

> The Sea, with such a storme as his bare head
> In Hell-blacke night indur'd, would have buoy'd vp,
> And quench'd the Stelled fires.

'Stelled' means fixed, as in Sonnet 24, where Shakespeare says that
his eye 'hath stelled Thy beauty's form in table of my heart'. The
stelled fires are the fixed stars, as opposed to the wandering stars,
or planets. But it is difficult to doubt that the poet was conscious
of the Latin word *stella*. Even in Lear's death-scene there appears
to be a quibble:

> He hates him
> That would vpon the rack of this tough world
> Stretch him out longer . . .

i.e. stretch him for a longer time, or elongate him further on the rack.

As a last example from *King Lear* we may take Kent's words about Oswald:

> My Lord, if you will giue me leaue, I will tread this vnboulted villaine into morter, and daube the wall of a Iakes with him.

'Unbolted' is taken by editors to mean unsifted, coarse. Unbolted mortar is made of unsifted lime, the lumps of which have to be broken up by treading on them with wooden shoes. But coarse is a strange epithet to apply to Oswald, who has previously been described as a glass-gazing, finical barber-monger, that is, as effeminate. If one considered the words without reference to the mortar, one might take them to mean 'released villain', one who is unrestrained in his villainy, a jailbird. But it is significant that Shakespeare uses the word *unbolt* in *Timon of Athens*, a play written soon after *King Lear*, in the sentence 'I will unbolt to you', meaning 'I will reveal to you'. It is quite possible, therefore, that unbolted villain means revealed or apparent villain. The word has to mean unsifted, as part of the mortar image; but there is no reason why the other senses should not also be understood. (Indeed, as a bolt could mean a phallus, unbolted may well mean effeminate too.)

Other plays are equally full of quibbles. According to William Empson, the character of Iago is 'a critique on an unconscious pun', that is, on the possible meanings of honest.[4] And the climax of Shakespeare's most profound comedy, *Measure for Measure*, is Angelo's wonderful quibble of repentance. When he kneels before the Duke, who had until a moment before been disguised as a friar, Angelo cries:

> Oh, my dread Lord,
> I should be guiltier than my guiltinesse,
> To thinke I can be vndiscerneable,
> When I perceiue your grace, like powre diuine,
> Hath look'd vpon my passes.

4. *The Structure of Complex Words* (1951), p. 230.

The Duke is not merely his grace in a secular sense; for a moment he becomes a symbol of the one from whom no secrets are hid. How easily Shakespeare is able to hint at such a meaning without incongruity and without blasphemy! And he could do this only because the quibble was at his disposal.

The examples that have been given, selected out of a much larger number in these two plays, may suggest certain conclusions with regard to Shakespeare's use of the quibble. Previous critics have, of course, discussed the matter. As long ago as 1794 Walter Whiter pointed out that in Shakespeare's plays

> certain terms containing an equivocal meaning, or sounds suggesting such a meaning, will often serve to introduce other words and expressions of a similar nature: This similarity is formed by having in some cases a coincidence in sense, or an affinity from sound; though the signification, in which they are really applied, has never any reference and often no similitude to that, which caused their association.

Yet neither Whiter, nor Kellett in the present century, really examined the dramatic effect of the hidden puns they brought to light. The most valuable work on the subject is Empson's *Seven Types of Ambiguity*. He analyses the different kinds of ambiguity with great subtlety, though he is not directly concerned with the dramatic effect of puns.[5] Cleanth Brooks, in his book *The Well Wrought Urn*, has admirable chapters on 'The Language of Paradox' and 'The Heresy of Paraphrase', but he is concerned more with ambiguities than with actual puns and he seems to regard the paradox as the chief criterion of poetry.

There are four main functions of the serious pun in dramatic poetry. First, puns—and especially hidden puns—provide as we have seen an illogical reinforcement of the logical sequence of thought, so that the poetic statement strikes us almost as a remembrance: as Keats said that poetry should do. Secondly, such puns often link together unrelated imagery and act as solvents for mixed metaphors. Thirdly, they make the listener aware of a complex of ideas which enrich the total statement, even though they do not come into full consciousness. Fourthly, they seem to shoot out roots in all directions, so that the poetry is firmly based on reality: a reality which is nothing less, if nothing more, than the sum total of experience.

5. See note at end of this essay.

It is no accident that the best period of English drama, from 1590 to 1625 coincided with the poetry of the metaphysical school. Donne used the serious pun in much the same way as the dramatists, and to him and his fellows it served as a means in conjunction with the imagery of enriching the complexity of a poem. No one now imagines that his 'Hymn to God the Father' is insincere or frivolous because in each stanza it repeats the pun:

> When thou hast done, thou hast not done.

It will be remembered, too, that the pun was used by divines as well as by poets. Lancelot Andrewes obtained some of his most splendid effects by means of the quibble, as in the well-known passage from one of the Nativity sermons:

The *Word was made flesh.* I add yet further: what *flesh?* The flesh of an *Infant.* What, *Verbum Infans,* the *Word* an *Infant?* The *Word,* and not be able to speak a word? How evill agreeth this?

The detailed dissection of the text, which is a characteristic of many sermons of the period, displays the same kind of interest in words as the poets did in their quibbles. Another passage by Lancelot Andrewes will illustrate this point—

First, by *Solvite* (that is) *dissolving* is meant *death. Cupio dissolvi,* ye know what that is: And *tempus dissolutionis meae instat,* the *time of my dissolution* (that is, *my death*) *is at hand.* For, *death,* is a very *dissolution:* a *loosing* the cement, the soule, and bodie are held together with. Which two, as a *frame* or fabrique are compaginate at first; and after, as the *timber* from the *lime,* or the *lime* from the *stone,* so are they taken in sunder againe. But *death,* is not, this way only, a *loosing*; but a further than this. For upon the *loosing* the *soule* from the *body,* and the life from both, there followes an universall *loosing,* of all the bonds and knots here: of the *Father* from the *Son*; and otherwhile, of the *Son* from the *Father* first: Of *Man* from *Wife,* of *friend* from *friend,* of *Prince* from *People*: So great a *Solvite* is *death*; makes all, that is fast, *loose*: makes all knots flie in sunder.[6]

A third example may be given, in which Donne plays on the two meanings of heaven, as a place and as a state:

For all the way to Heaven is Heaven; and as those Angels, which came from Heaven hither, bring Heaven with them, and are in Heaven here,

6. Andrewes, *XCVI Sermons* (1641), p. 485.

So that soule that goes to Heaven, meets Heaven here; and as those Angels doe not devest Heaven by coming, so these soules invest Heaven, in their going.[7]

There are two things wrong with the verse tragedies of the age of Dryden. The poets did not take their subjects seriously; they merely played with them, even when the stage was littered with corpses: and they virtually adopted for poetry as well as prose the fatal canons of the Royal Society, which exhibited an essentially static attitude to language. Dryden is said to have written his plays first in prose, and then translated them into verse. Whether this is true or not, his remarks about the style of Shakespeare and Chapman show that the tradition of dramatic poetry had been fatally interrupted during the Commonwealth period. The Restoration dramatists were admirably lucid, but their use of language was, in the last resort, unimaginative. The banishing of the pun except for comic purposes was the symbol of a radical defect: it was a turning away from the genius of the language. If we consider the tragedies of Young and Thomson, the unactable closet dramas of the Romantic poets, and the still more abortive plays of the great Victorians the lack of a living tradition of dramatic verse is even more apparent. Not till the 1930s did we get anything resembling good dramatic verse.

Great drama went out with the serious pun because by its use Shakespeare and other Jacobean dramatists were able to bring into their plays a much wider range of experience. The texture of nearly all the poetic dramas of the eighteenth and nineteenth centuries was intolerably thin; and it is significant that with the renaissance of poetic drama in the last twenty years, disappointing though it has been, we have had the return of the quibble and of the conceit. I am thinking particularly of Eliot's plays and, on a different level, Christopher Fry's *The Lady's not for Burning* which delighted audiences with its verbal acrobatics.

It is not so much the pun itself that should be defended with uncompromising vigour, but the attitude to language which the use of the quibble demands. Language is called upon to perform two main functions—to convey thoughts, and to express feelings or states of mind. For the former function an unemotive, precise language is required. If we want to talk about the theory of

7. Donne, Sermon LXVI, ed. Q, 1921, p. 55.

relativity or nuclear fission, we should be as unambiguous and as straightforward as possible in our use of language: though certain modern scientific writers seem to lose themselves in metaphors and analogies. But if we are expressing complicated human feelings, the more scientifically precise we are, the greater the distortion. Where the human mind is in question we must take into consideration that the language has a life of its own, that every word has a different pedigree and a different emotive history, and that its relationships and derivations necessarily suggest to the speaker and to the listener the kind of association which is, in its most obvious form, the pun. In Henry Moore's sculpture it is always possible to perceive how his actual medium has influenced the finished work of art. He has collaborated, as it were, with the grain and texture of the wood or the markings on the stone so that his reclining figures look almost as if they were works of nature rather than works of man—figures that were inherent in the tree or stone. In much the same way the artist in words must collaborate with the genius of the language. If he tries to write without due regard to his medium, his work will be thin, artificial, and sterile. We can master language only by submitting to it.[8]

8. M. M. Mahood's *Shakespeare's Wordplay* (1957) is the best treatment of the subject of this essay. Part of her first chapter appeared in *Essays in Criticism* in 1951.

3

Edward III[1]

English history provided the plots of many Elizabethan plays. But
readers of Mr. Irving Ribner's recent survey of the subject are
likely to feel that, apart from Marlowe's *Edward II* at the beginning of the period and Ford's belated masterpiece, *Perkin
Warbeck*, a generation later, there are no English history plays
written by Shakespeare's contemporaries which are worth reading
for their own sake. They were, for the most part, written by hack
writers to satisfy a public demand—a demand aroused perhaps
both by the sense of national pride which resulted from the defeat
of the Spanish Armada and by the tireless efforts of Tudor propa-
gandists. The historical matter, moreover, was easily available in
Stow, Holinshed, Hall, Froissart, and other chroniclers, and this
must have been a consideration to poorly paid writers, pressed
for time and anxious to satisfy the public's voracious demands for
new plays.

   Edward III, whoever wrote it, is a much more impressive play
than Peele's *Edward I* or *The Famous Victories of Henry V* or *The
Troublesome Raigne of King John*—even when allowances have
been made for the bad texts of those plays. It was planned as a
whole; or at least the authors (if there were two) worked in
collaboration, using the same sources, and taking care to link the
Countess scenes with the rest of the play. The King in Act II looks
forward to his French campaign:

> Away, loose silkes of wavering vanity!
> Shall the large limmit of fair Britannye
> By me be overthrowne? and shall I not
> Master this little mansion of my selfe?
> Give me an Armor of eternall steele;
> I go to conquer kings.

1. From *Shakespeare as Collaborator* (1960).

In the next act the King of France refers to Edward's pursuit of the Countess:

> For whats this Edward, but a belly god,
> A tender and lasciuious wantonnes,
> That th'other day was almost dead for loue?

Not only are the two sections of the play linked together in this way, but even the war scenes are competently written. It seems probable, however, that the play was written by Shakespeare in collaboration, for some scenes one would be unwilling to ascribe to him at any period of his career—not because they are bad, but because their badness is unlike Shakespeare's. The very first scene may be taken as an example. It was probably imitated from *The Famous Victories*, and for this reason resembles the first scene in *Henry V*; but the badness of the latter seems to be due to Shakespeare's attempt to turn into verse an intractable passage of Holinshed about the Salic law, while the badness of the *Edward III* passage is absolute. As in *Henry V* and *The Famous Victories*, the exposition in *Edward III* is followed immediately by the arrival of the French ambassador. Warwick's lines:

> Byd him leaue off the Lyon's case he weares;
> Lest, meeting with the Lyon in the field,
> He chaunce to teare him peece-meale for his pride.

were probably suggested either by *The Troublesome Raigne* or by *King John* itself. The blank verse of this scene is monotonous, and nearly all end-stopped, only a line here and there being at all memorable. One line,

> See, how occasion laughes me in the face!

is reminiscent of one in *Hamlet*:

> Occasion smiles upon a second leave.

One image happens to fit in with the group of masking images which (as I have shown) is characteristic of the Shakespearian parts of the play; but this is probably accidental.

The Countess of Salisbury is introduced in the second scene; and though the Shakespearian portion is generally thought to begin at l. 95, the earlier part is much better written than the first scene. There are a number of fine lines, as for example the one describing the bagpipes which

> Bray foorth their Conquest, and our ouerthrow,
> Euen in the barraine, bleake, and fruitlesse aire.

There is a more sustained passage in which King David boasts:

> And neuer shall our bonny riders rest;
> Nor rusting canker haue the time to eate
> Their light-borne snaffles, nor their nimble spurres;
> Nor lay aside their Iacks of Gymould mayle;
> Nor hang their staues of grayned Scottish ash
> In peacefull wise vpon their citie wals;
> Nor from their buttoned tawny leatherne belts
> Dismisse their byting whinyards, – till your King
> Cry out: *Enough, spare England now for pittie!*

The early part of the scene, before King Edward's entrance, is lively and amusing. The dividing of the spoil by the Scots before they have captured Roxborough Castle is nicely contrasted with their precipitate flight on the approach of the English forces; and the Countess's fliting of the cowardly braggarts is spirited and effective. But although it would be difficult to tell from the verse alone that this was not by the same author as the later part of the scene, it might be argued that the undaunted woman therein depicted does not quite harmonize with Warwick's description of her a few lines later as one

> whose beauty tyrant feare,
> As a May blossome with pernitious winds,
> Hath sullied, withered, ouercast, and donne.

The rest of the scene, appropriately enough, is written in a more lyrical style, the last forty lines being in rhymed couplets, and some of the imagery recalling that of the *Sonnets*, *Romeo and Juliet*, and *Love's Labour's Lost*.

> Now, in the Sunne alone it doth not lye,
> With light to take light from a mortall eye;
> For here two day stars that mine eies would see,
> More then the Sunne steales myne owne light from mee ...

> Let not thy presence, like the Aprill sunne,
> Flatter our earth and sodenly be done ...

> For where the golden Ore doth buried lie,
> The ground, vndeckt with natures tapestrie,
> Seemes barrayne, sere, vnfertill, fructless, dry;

> And where the vpper turfe of earth doth boast
> His pide perfumes and party-colloured cost,
> Delue there, and find this issue and their pride
> To spring from ordure and corruptions side.
> But to make vp my all too long compare,
> These ragged walles no testimonie are,
> What is within; but, like a cloake, doth hide
> From weathers Waste the vnder garnisht pride.

These last lines, spoken by the Countess, are not particularly in character: but they are intended to show that she is intelligent as well as beautiful, and thus go some way to justify the King's infatuation:

> As wise, as faire; what fond fit can be heard,
> When wisedome keepes the gate as beuties gard?

The whole of the second act is devoted to the King's unsuccessful attempt on the Countess's chastity. It resembles in some ways the scene in *3 Henry VI* in which Edward IV's advances to Lady Grey are repelled so that he is constrained to offer marriage, but it is altogether more serious and mature in its treatment of the theme. The conversation between Edward IV and Lady Grey, observed from a distance by Clarence and Gloucester, is carried on for the most part in single-line speeches:

K. EDW. No, by my troth, I did not mean such love.
L. GREY. Why, then you mean not as I thought you did.
K. EDW. To tell thee plain, I aim to lie with thee.
L. GREY. To tell you plain, I had rather lie in prison.
K. EDW. Why, then thou shalt not have thy husband's lands.
L. GREY. Why, then mine honesty shall be my dower.

This stychomythia is expertly managed, but the effect is inevitably artificial. The verse offers room neither for development of character nor of argument, nor for the use of imagery. The situation is reduced to its lowest terms—Virtuous Woman rejects Lustful Monarch, who is converted to the idea of matrimony. The second act of *Edward III* is much longer and more complex; the author has plenty of room to develop situation and character; the King's temptation is not as blunt and crude as Edward IV's had been, the guilty love being tempered by poetry; and both the King and the Countess are furnished with long and eloquent speeches. The King, moreover, makes use of Lodowick and the Countess's father, Warwick, to weaken her resistance.

Algernon Charles Swinburne, who analysed the scene in some detail, but not without prejudice, convinced himself that Shakespeare had no hand in it. Some of his arguments are difficult to take seriously. He appears to have been outraged by the character of Lodowick, whom he described as poet and pimp. The indignation comes a little oddly from Swinburne, who was fresh from the composition of *Poems and Ballads* and who was even then meditating his great poem on adulterous love, *Tristram in Lyonesse*. Nor is the moral character of the poets depicted in Shakespeare's acknowledged plays so lofty that we can assume that Lodowick's portrayal is beneath him. The time-serving poet in *Timon of Athens*[2] and the lynched poet in *Julius Caesar* are neither idealized; and Sir Thurio is advised by Proteus to

> lay lime to tangle her desires
> By wailful sonnets, whose composed rhymes
> Shall be full-fraught with serviceable vows.

Lodowick is not a professional poet; he is a lord, the King's friend and confidant. He is full of admiration for the Countess's beauty before he is asked to compose a poem to express the King's love. This is made clear by the soliloquy in which he compares the King's blushes to hers:

> His cheekes put on their scarlet ornaments;
> But no more like her oryentall red,
> Then Bricke to Corrall or liue things to dead.

It should also be noted that although Lodowick doubtless guesses to whom his poem is to be sent, the King does not tell him; and that the lines he composes serve only to remind the King of the Countess's chastity:

> More faire and chast then is the queen of shades,
> More bould in constancie then Iudith was.

If Lodowick were a pimp he would be a singularly ineffective one, and a disgrace to his profession. It is surely more reasonable to suppose that he is an honest man who does his best to deter the

2. But I have argued (*Essays in Criticism*, iii, pp. 120–1) that the poet in *Timon of Athens* was not as bad as he is usually painted.

King from his adulterous passion, and that he does not deserve the hard things said of him by Swinburne.

The temptation of the Countess may be divided into four sections. In the first, after a soliloquy by the King, he asks Lodowick to write a poem in praise of his unnamed mistress, but he decides finally that only a lover can write of love (II. i. 25–183). In the second section the King makes his first proposal to the Countess, who assumes, or pretends to assume, that he is testing her virtue (184–276). In the third section the King tricks Warwick into pleading for him, and the Countess, to her father's joy, repels his advocacy (277–459). In the fourth section the King, on seeing his son, momentarily repents; but he again presses his suit on the entrance of the Countess. She shames him into repentance by threatening to stab herself, but not before he has offered to murder the Queen and the Countess's husband (II. ii. 1–211).

The four sections exhibit a rising tension from the King's opening soliloquy, through the Countess's first repulse of his suit, and the tragic dilemma of her father, to the final impassioned argument culminating in the threat of violence. The only dramatic objection to this act is that the remaining three acts of the play are something of an anti-climax, not merely because they are generally inferior in style, but because the qualities they possess are epic rather than dramatic.

Tucker Brooke, who regarded the unknown author of *Edward III* as 'one of the truest poets of his generation', nevertheless complained of the 'rather cloying sweetness' and 'quibbling mawkishness' of the Countess scenes. The date of the play is not known, but it is likely to have been written after 1593—because of its allusion to *Lucrece*—and it must certainly have been written before December 1595, when it was entered in the Stationers' Register. If one reads Elizabethan plays—even *Romeo and Juliet* and *Richard II*—written during these years one can find many passages which could as justly be dismissed as 'cloying sweetness' and 'quibbling mawkishness'. But the sweetness is not cloying to all readers; the quibble was an admired grace of style used by Shakespeare throughout his life and not deserving the contempt with which it was treated by critics from Dryden to Bradley; and the mawkishness is a matter of opinion.

The dialogue between the King and Lodowick is interesting for a number of reasons. One, the misjudged character of Lodowick,

I have already mentioned. A second is the fact that the King is given better poetry to speak when he is instructing Lodowick on the theme of the poem he wants him to write than the poem itself. Thirdly, the lines provide an interesting account of how an Elizabethan poet set to work, and it may possibly reflect the author's own habits of composition.

The King states, though not in so many words, that the function of poetry—of the poet when inspired by a 'golden muse' —is to express emotion and to arouse a similar emotion in a reader. Then he complains of the inadequacy of language to express the praises of his mistress, a theme touched on in the *Sonnets* and in *Love's Labour's Lost*:

> Better then bewtifull thou must begin,
> Deuise for faire a fairer word then faire,
> And euery ornament that thou wouldest praise,
> Fly it a pitch aboue the soare of praise.

The King then makes a kind of inventory of his mistress's qualities—her rank, her voice, her hair, her eyes—in a way which corresponds to the favourite method of Elizabethan sonneteers. But the inventory is complicated by the King's own objections to his comparisons. He compares the Countess's voice to that of the nightingale, and then recalls the danger of referring to the story of Philomel:

> The nightingale singes of adulterate wrong,
> And that, compared, is too satyrical.

Or, in comparing her hair to various things:

> Her hair, far softer then the silke wormes twist,
> Like to a flattering glas, doth make more faire
> The yelow Amber—

he realizes that the comparison can be used more appropriately elsewhere:

> *like a flattering glas*
> Comes in too soone; for, writing of her eies,
> Ile say that like a glas they catch the sunne,
> And thence the hot reflection doth rebounde
> Against my brest, and burnes my hart within.

When the Countess appears the King tricks her into swearing to do all she can to remedy his discontent, and then demands her love in fulfilment of her vow. She fails at first to understand him, and this inevitably leads to the quibbling of which Tucker Brooke complained; but when she does understand she rebukes him with a dignity which never violates the respect due to her sovereign.

> But that your lippes were sacred (O) my Lord,
> You would prophane the holie name of loue.

She accuses him of wishing to commit high treason against the king of heaven,

> To stamp his Image in forbidden mettel,
> Forgetting your alleageance and your othe,

and she concludes that he must be testing her virtue on behalf of her husband. The first round goes to her. The author preserves a nice balance of sympathies. Although we are made to approve wholeheartedly of the Countess's virtue, which is never allowed to seem priggish, we are never in danger of thinking that King Edward is a villain. He is intermittently aware of the sinfulness of his conduct, recognizing her words as 'sweet chaplaines to her bewtie' and wishing he

> were a honie-gathering bee,
> To beare the combe of virtue from this flower,
> And not a poison-sucking enuious spider,
> To turn the iuce I take to deadlie venom!

His adulterous love, inspired as it is by the Countess's virtues as well as by her physical attractions, is not as uncompromisingly evil as the overpowering lust of Angelo, who is attracted likewise by the virtues of Isabella.

The next stage in the pursuit of the Countess is the employment of her father as unwilling pandar. The method employed by the King to achieve this end is a repetition of his opening gambit with the Countess. He tricks Warwick into swearing that he will buy the King's ease even with the loss of his own honour, and then asks him to persuade his daughter to commit adultery. The dialogue at this point is closely knit and closely argued, the King pressing his points home with deliberate ambiguities, and by seizing on Warwick's admissions. After he has sworn, for example, the King asks:

> What office were it, to suggest a man
> To breake a lawfull and religious vowe?

Warwick replies:

> An office for the deuill, not for man.

And the King immediately pounces:

> That deuilles office must thou do for me.

If Warwick were given time to think, he would realize that his own vow was not lawful and religious, and that he could not properly be bound by it. But his daughter appears while he is still staggering under the King's request. The way in which he is torn between his feelings of loyalty to the King and his sense of right and honour is neatly indicated both in the soliloquy and in the scene which follows. Alternate lines in the soliloquy counteract the lines which precede them:

> Ile say, she must forget her husband Salisbury,
> If she remember to embrace the king;
> Ile say, an othe may easily be broken,
> But not so easily pardoned, being broken;
> Ile say, it is true charitie to loue,
> But not true loue to be so charitable;
> Ile say, his greatnes may beare out the shame,
> But not his kingdome may beare out the sinne;
> Ile say, it is my duety to perswade,
> But not her honestie to giue consent.

So he prefixes his solicitation of his daughter with a warning which will put her on her guard:

> I am not Warwike, as thou thinkst I am,
> But an atturnie from the Court of hell,
> That thus haue housd my spirite in his forme,
> To do a message to thee from the king.

His argument that she should consent to the King's proposal is continually checked by references to honour, shame, and 'the bitter potion of reproch'; and he concludes his speech by admitting that he has

> Apparaled sin in vertuous sentences.

When the Countess scornfully repudiates his arguments, declaring that she will die rather than consent to the King's 'gracelesse lust', Warwick strengthens her resolution by retracting what he has said and giving her a series of sentences on the other side of the question. This speech, which includes a line from one of Shakespeare's *Sonnets*, is the best poetry in the play:

> The freshest summers day doth soonest taint
> The lothed carrion that it seemes to kiss: . . .
> That sinne doth ten times agreuate it selfe
> That is committed in a holie place:
> An euill deed, done by authorite,
> Is sin and subbornation: Decke an Ape
> In tissue, and the beautie of the robe
> Adds but the greater scorne vnto the beast.
> A spatious field of reasons could I vrge
> Betweene his glorie, daughter, and thy shame:
> That poyson shows worst in a golden cup;
> Darke night seemes darker by the lightning flash;
> Lillies that fester smel far worse then weeds;
> And euery glory that inclynes to sin,
> The shame is treble by the opposite.

In the following scene, the conflict in the King's mind is well suggested by his slip of the tongue when he tells Derby in reference to the Emperor's letters:

> Ile looke vpon the Countesse minde anone—

and by his almost hysterical annoyance when he hears the sound of a drum. He threatens to use the parchment as his writing-paper, and to hang the drummer in the braces of his drum unless he learns to play the lute. When Prince Edward enters, the resemblance of the boy to his mother corrects the King's 'straid desire' and makes him decide to sail for France; but the announcement that the Countess 'with a smiling cheere' desires access to him makes him suppose that she is about to surrender:

> That verie smile of hers
> Hath ransomed captiue Fraunce.

The Countess smiles because she has made up her mind what to do. She turns the tables on the King by doing with him what he had previously done with her and with her father. She exacts a

vow from him that he will remove the hindrances between his
love and hers. Not realizing the implications of the vow, the King
duly swears; and the Countess demands the death of her husband
and of the Queen. She hopes by this to shame the King to repentance; but instead he agrees to their deaths, swearing that he will
outdo Leander by swimming through a Hellespont of blood, and
blaming the Countess's beauty for his intended crimes. To which
the Countess replies:

> O periurde beautie, more corrupted Iudge!
> When to the great Starre-chamber ore our heads
> The vniuersall Sessions cals to count
> This packing euill, we both shall tremble for it.

Finally, she produces two daggers and threatens to commit suicide
unless he swears to abandon his unholy suit. The King again
swears, and this time his repentance is permanent. Awakening
from his 'idle dreame', he sets out immediately for his French
campaign. As he has now mastered his passions, he can proceed
to the lesser victories of war.

The rest of the play is concerned with the sea-battle off the
coast of Flanders and the land-battles of Crécy and Poitiers. The
sea-battle is described by a French sailor in two long messenger
speeches, inspired partly, we may suspect, by the defeat of the
Spanish Armada, though it is the English fleet which is described
as

> Figuring the horned Circle of the Moone.

Although the speeches are not without some vivid touches, the
blank verse is stiff, unvaried, and mostly end-stopped, and the
imagery is conventional. The ensigns are described as

> Like to a meddow full of sundry flowers,
> Adornes the naked bosome of the earth.

The flagships are compared to fiery dragons. The sea pouring
through leaks is described in stilted phrase:

> As did her gushing moysture breake into
> The crannied cleftures of the through shot planks.

And the effect of the cannon-balls is described in a somewhat
inappropriate simile:

> Heere flew a head, disseuered from the tronke,
> There mangled armes and legs were tost aloft,
> As when a wherle winde takes the Summer dust
> And scatters it in middle of the aire.

The author is striving hard for epic grandeur, but achieves it only at moments. The best touch is provided by the arrival of the white-faced messenger to announce the defeat, and King John asks:

> Say, mirror of pale death,
> To whome belongs the honor of this day?

The remainder of the third act is taken up with the long speeches of invective exchanged between the French and English kings, the ceremonial arming of Prince Edward, and the battle of Crécy, in which the English forces are victorious, largely through the personal valour of the Prince. The writing of these scenes is competent, but undistinguished. In the fourth act we are introduced somewhat belatedly to the Earl of Salisbury, who has reinstated Lord Mountford as Duke of Brittany. He makes no reference in this or later scenes to his Countess, the heroine of the second act: and this is a slight indication that the scenes in which he appears were not by the same author. The Salisbury scenes are concerned largely with a little drama of military honour, as the Countess scenes had been concerned with marital honour. Salisbury releases Villiers without a ransom on condition he procures him a safe-conduct to Calais. Villiers swears that if he fails to obtain the passport from Charles, Duke of Normandy, he will return to Salisbury as his prisoner. When he arrives at the French camp Charles refuses the passport, and Villiers tells him he must return to prison. Charles thinks his scruples are absurd, and there ensues the following passage of dialogue:

> VIL. Ah, but it is mine othe, my gratious Lord,
> Which I in conscience may not violate,
> Or else a kingdome should not draw me hence.
> CH. Thine othe? why, that doth bind thee to abide:
> Hast thou not sworne obedience to thy Prince?
> VIL. In all things that vprightly he commands:
> But either to perswade or threaten me,
> Not to performe the couenant of my word,
> Is lawlesse, and I need not to obey.

CH. Why, is it lawfull for a man to kill,
     And not to breake a promise with his foe?
VIL. To kill, my Lord, when warre is once proclaymd,
     So that our quarrel be for wrongs receaude,
     No doubt is lawfully permitted vs:
     But in an othe we must be well aduisd,
     How we do sweare, and, when we once haue sworne,
     Not to infringe it, though we die therefore:
     Therefore, my Lord, as willing I returne,
     As if I were to flie to paradise.

The way in which one's obedience to a prince is limited by the over-riding moral law links up with the problem confronting Warwick and the Countess in the second act; and just as King Edward is converted by the Countess, Charles is converted by the virtue of Villiers. Armed with safe-conduct so procured, Salisbury is captured by the French forces; and King John forthwith orders him to be hanged on the nearest tree. Charles, infected with Villiers's sense of honour, protests hotly:

     I hope your highnes will not so disgrace me,
     And dash the vertue of my seale at armes:
     He hath my neuer broken name to shew,
     Carectred with this princely hande of mine;
     And rather let me leaue to be a prince
     Than break the stable verdict of a prince:
     I doo beseech you, let him passe in quiet.

King John tells him that he can overrule any promise made by one of his subjects; and Charles exclaims bitterly:

     What, am I not a soldier in my word?
     Then, armes, adieu, and let them fight that list!
     Shall I not giue my girdle from my wast,
     But with a gardion I shall be controld,
     To saie I may not giue my things awaie?
     Vpon my soule, had Edward, prince of Wales,
     Ingagde his word, writ downe his noble hand
     For all your knights to passe his fathers land,
     The roiall king, to grace his warlike sonne,
     Would not alone safe conduct giue to them,
     But with all bountie feasted them and theirs.

Just as Charles had been converted by Villiers, so King John is shamed into allowing Salisbury to go free.

The Crécy scenes have been praised by Tucker Brooke for their verve and exhilaration, and they are certainly exciting. The arming of the Prince, the King's refusal to send aid, the despair of his friends who think him doomed, and his triumphant entrance form an obviously effective sequence of incidents; but the actual poetry is disappointing. The imagery is perfunctory at times, and at other times laboured, as when the Prince compares his fight to a voyage:

> And now, behold, after my winters' toyle,
> My payneful voyage on the boystrous sea
> Of warres deuouring gulphes and steely rocks,
> I bring my fraught vnto the wished port,
> My Summers hope, my trauels sweet reward.

Some of the verse, moreover, is extremely feeble:

> Let Edward be deliuered by our hands,
> And still, in danger, hele expect the like:
> But if himselfe himselfe redeeme from thence,
> He will haue vanquisht cheerefull death and feare,
> And euer after dread their force no more
> Then if they were but babes or Captiue slaues.

The Poitiers scenes, on the other hand, reach and maintain a much higher poetic and dramatic level. They resemble in many ways the Agincourt scenes in *Henry V*. In both the English forces, heavily outnumbered, are in an apparently hopeless situation. In both the French are gorgeously arrayed and over-confident, though in *Edward III* they are depicted more sympathetically. There is real splendour in Audley's description of the French army, and the successive heralds who demand surrender, bring a horse so that the Black Prince may escape, and finally offer a prayer-book so that he may prepare his mind for death, not merely characterize the French, but enable the Prince to exhibit a notable courage in the face of death. Henry V never loses hope, but the Black Prince accepts what he regards as the certainty of defeat and death.

> Audley, the armes of death embrace vs round,
> And comfort haue we none, saue that to die
> We pay sower earnest for a sweeter life.

These lines occur at the beginning of one of the best scenes in the play. The description of the French army whose

> new-replenisht pendants cuff the aire
> And beat the windes, that for their gaudinesse
> Struggles to kisse them:

which rises to a climax in the lines:

> And on the Hill behind stands certaine death
> In pay and seruice with Chattillion—

and the image used by the Prince when he asks Audley for consolation in the face of death:

> Thy selfe art bruis'd and bit with many broiles,
> And stratagems forepast with yron pens
> Are texted in thine honorable face;
> Thou art a married man in this distresse,
> But danger wooes me as a blushing maide:
> Teach me an answere to this perilous time.

are excellent; but other lines in the same scene are so feeble, that one is driven to suspect corruption in the text. Just before the lines just quoted, for example, the Prince is made to say:

> Now, Audley, sound those siluer winges of thine,
> And let those milke-white messengers of time
> Shew thy times learning in this dangerous time.

This confused passage in which Audley's white hair is apparently compared to the white plumage of an angel, and his voice to the beating of an angel's wings, is unlikely to have been written by the same poet in that form. The repetition of *time* at the end of a line suggests that the confusion may be due to the compositor.

Audley's speech of consolation, it has been said, reads like a rough draft for the Duke's advice to Claudio, as the Prince's reply resembles Claudio's. Audley says:

> For, from the instant we begin to liue,
> We do pursue and hunt the time to die: ...
> If, then, we hunt for death, why do we feare it?
> If we feare it, why do we follow it?

The Prince exclaims:

> Ah, what an idiot hast thou made of lyfe,
> To seeke the thing it feares! and how disgrast
> The imperiall victorie of murdring death, . . .
> I will not giue a pennie for a lyfe,
> Nor halfe a halfpennie to shun grim death,
> Since for to liue is but to seeke to die,
> And dying but beginning of new lyfe.
> Let come the houre when he that rules it will!
> To liue or die I hold indifferent.

The two other scenes relating to Audley also contain some superb passages, and the poorer parts there are due to the lapses of the author rather than to those of the compositor. Audley is mortally wounded, and he is asked how he fares. He replies:

> Euen as a man may do
> That dines at such a bloudie feast as this.

He asks his squires to carry him to the Prince,

> That in the crimson brauerie of my bloud
> I may become him with saluting him.

The Prince, on seeing him, says:

> Speake, thou that wooest death with thy careless smile,
> As if thou wert enamored of thyne end:
> What hungry sword hath so bereaud thy face,
> And lopt a true friend from my louing soule?

The first two lines are magnificent, the others a sad anticlimax; and when the Prince continues with absurd bombast it is difficult to understand how so good a poet could be guilty of such lines:

> If thou wilt drinke the blood of captyue kings,
> Or that it were restoritiue, command
> A Health of kings blood, and Ile drinke to thee.

A moment later the poet recovers himself, giving Audley the splendid, if over-rhetorical, lines:

> If I could hold dym death but at a bay,
> Till I did see my liege thy royall father,
> My soule should yeeld this Castle of my flesh,
> To darkenes, consummation, dust, and Wormes.

It would appear that the author of these scenes was a young poet, 'able to bombast out a blank verse as the best' of the University Wits, as Greene said of Shakespeare, but liable to strange lapses; one whose sense of situation was superior to his power of characterization.

In the last act the incident of the burghers of Calais is dealt with in a very perfunctory way. It is followed by the arrival of Copland with King David of Scotland, Copland's attiude to his prisoner resembling that of Hotspur in *1 Henry IV*. The rest of the scene is taken up with a long speech of Salisbury describing what he thinks is the defeat of the Black Prince at Poitiers, followed by the arrival of the victorious Prince with his French prisoners. As the audience already know the result of the battle, the effect of the contrast is somewhat spoilt; but it serves to remind us of the way in which victory had been snatched from the jaws of certain defeat.

Edward III as a whole is not an entirely satisfying play. The first two acts, in spite of the links to which we have called attention, are not sufficiently related to the remaining three. Critics have shown that the King, by conquering himself, makes himself worthy to conquer France; and the Salisbury–Villiers scenes provide us with an *exemplum* of military honour to set beside the *exemplum* of marital honour in the Countess scenes. Both of them, moreover, define the limitations of a subject's obedience. But there is, nevertheless, a switch of interest. Of the three main characters in the first two acts only King Edward appears in the second half of the play, and there his role is subordinated to that of his son, the hero of Crécy and Poitiers. The play, therefore, seems to fall between two kinds. There is enough attempt at unity to make it fit uneasily into the class of chronicle plays, but not enough unity is achieved to allow it to rank with the History play as developed by Marlowe and Shakespeare.

Tucker Brooke ascribed the whole play to Peele. Comparison with his other plays is difficult because only *The Arraignment of Paris* exists in an adequate text. The opening lines of *David and Bethsabe* are as fine in their way as anything in *Edward III*, but the way is quite different. *Edward I* is much nearer to *Edward III* in theme, but its style is more Marlovian, and it contains few sustained passages of poetry. Tucker Brooke suggests that *Edward III*, although finer than any of Peele's known works, was potentially within his grasp:

A few more years of practice, a free hand, and the change from the dry threshed husks of Biblical narrative to the full and stimulating garners of native history might have performed a far greater transfiguration.

The dates of Peele's other plays are mostly uncertain, but some of them were probably written no earlier than *Edward III*. Nothing we know of his career suggests that he would in his later years have had the opportunity of escaping from the unsatisfactory conditions of a hack-writer, or of rising so far above his accustomed level. If Peele had a hand in the play we might explain its characteristics by an hypothesis similar to the one advanced by some critics concerning *Titus Andronicus*—that Shakespeare revised a play by Peele, rewriting the Countess scenes, and making extensive alterations in Act IV. But critics of Elizabethan drama have a tendency to ascribe to Peele any anonymous plays of the period for which no suitable author can be found; and the evidence for his hand in *Edward III* is very slight.

4

Timon of Athens
and the Cash-Nexus [1]

'O William! we receive but what we give.'

This line was addressed by Coleridge to Wordsworth in a draft of
Dejection. It might equally well be said by any critic to Shakespeare: for it is unfortunately true that almost everyone finds in
Shakespeare what he brings. The case of *Hamlet* is the most
notorious. Coleridge, for example, painted an admirable self-
portrait and labelled it with the Prince's name; an eminent
psychoanalyst inevitably diagnosed a case of Oedipus complex;
the theologically minded C. S. Lewis discovered that Hamlet was
nothing less than man burdened with original sin: the Southamp-
ton fans argue that Hamlet was more or less a portrait of Essex;
and Landauer, a social-democrat, proclaimed that Hamlet was a
great democrat.

Political prejudice, indeed, is particularly liable to warp the
judgement. A Marxist regards Falstaff as a satire on a degenerate
aristocracy; but the Conservative Warwick Bond, ignoring Sir
John's title, argues that he is a portrait of the British worker. The
Marxists, of course, disagree amongst themselves. Mr. Jackson
thinks that Shakespeare was 'a healthy, well-poised, sceptical,
melioristic' humanist, 'somewhat to the left of the centre of
advanced bourgeois opinion'. Smirnov more or less concurs in
this testimonial: Shakespeare for him was an exponent of 'the
heroic ideals of bourgeois humanism'. But Professor Spassky
maintains that Shakespeare 'regarded the beginnings of the capitalist age with a scathing contempt which at times took the form of
bitter hatred'.

Tolstoy and Shaw were certain that Shakespeare was neither
Tolstoyan nor Shavian, and Godwin lamented that Shakespeare

1. From *Modern Quarterly Miscellany*, i (1947).

was incapable of depicting a hero—that is to say, a man actuated by ideals. But these three writers, having a passion for reforming the world, put ideas above poetry. It is very rare to find a critic fully conscious of Shakespeare's greatness who does not discover that the poet shares his views. The radical Hazlitt managed to avoid this. He pointed out that Shakespeare admired arbitrary power and was attacked by the Tory reviewers for the honesty of this admission. But, in spite of Hazlitt, it must be said that the temptation to enrol Shakespeare in one's own party is almost irresistible.

It is only possible to do this, without falling into manifest absurdity, by ignoring much of the evidence. The negative capability possessed by Shakespeare made his opinions fluid. His mind, as Keats said of his own, was 'a thoroughfare for all thoughts—not a select party'. It is difficult to point to any opinions in his dramatic work which were certainly his own. Miss Spurgeon, indeed, proved that Shakespeare disliked flatterers, dogs, bad smells, treachery, meanness, and ingratitude; and that he loved generosity and loyalty. Apart from the dogs—and the description of the hounds in *A Midsummer Night's Dream* shows that Shakespeare approved of dogs in their proper place—every one of these likes and dislikes is shared by every sane person. Miss Spurgeon proved merely that Shakespeare did not qualify for Bedlam or Berchtesgaden. His readers had suspected as much.

I

This introduction was necessary to show that I am fully aware of the dangers inherent in my title; but the purpose of this essay is not to prove that Shakespeare was a proleptic Marxist; it is rather to show that Marx (in a sense that will become apparent) was a Shakespearian.

To argue whether Shakespeare was progressive or reactionary is meaningless. In the plays written in the sixteenth century, he seems to have accepted what has been called the Elizabethan World Picture.[2] Generally speaking, this differed very little from the medieval conception of the universe. It was believed that the visible world was the manifestation of God; that the stars and the

2. By E. M. W. Tillyard, in his book of that title.

animals were made for man; and that man was the link between the angel and the animal. Man, being rational, could rise above the animals and comprehend God. As Theodore Spencer puts it:

Everything in the world was part of the same unified scheme, and the body and soul of man, each a reflection of the other, and both an image of the universal plan, were the culmination and final end of God's design.[3]

This theological conception was combined, in the ordinary Englishman's mind, with a wholesome fear of civil war. The Tudor historians contrasted the strong government of their own times with the chaos of the previous century. The Wars of the Roses provided a well-remembered lesson of the horrors of civil war; and the religious strife of the reigns of Edward VI and Mary, together with the wars still raging in France, reinforced the theological insistence on Order.

Shakespeare absorbed the views of his own time and used them for dramatic purposes. In his English histories, he dealt with what was thought to be the key period of English history—the causes of the Wars of the Roses, the wars themselves, and the restoration of Order through the union of York and Lancaster.[4]

Tillyard pointed out that Shakespeare was the only writer of historical plays who regularly made use of these interrelated theological and political ideas. Tillyard, I believe, is unjust to Marlowe in this connection; but, roughly speaking, his analysis is sound. Shakespeare makes clear that though Richard II and John were bad kings, it was wrong to rebel against them; and that even though Henry IV was a usurper, rebellion against him was likewise a sin. *The powers that be are ordained of God.* On the other hand, Richard III was a usurping tyrant, 'a monster for whose case the ordinary rules do not hold good'. As the Tudors had gained the throne by rebellion against Richard, it would have been tactless to have condemned Richmond's act. With this exception, Shakespeare stands on the side of order and submission. It is noteworthy that the patriotic Falconbridge remains loyal to the

3. *Shakespeare and the Nature of Man*, p. 20.
4. And, if we are to believe Tillyard, a suggestion that the Tudors were also the descendants of King Arthur. See *Shakespeare's History Plays*, to which I also refer in the next paragraph.

tyrant John, even when he believes him to be the murderer of Arthur.

Spencer has shown how the received ideas of the universe underwent a series of shocks. The Reformation broke up the unity of Christendom and put a greater emphasis on individual choice; Copernicus proved that the earth was not the centre of the universe;[5] Montaigne cast doubt on man's superiority to the other animals; and Machiavelli shook the belief that laws were equally binding on king and subjects. Spencer proceeds to argue that it was the impact of these disintegrating ideas on his former conception of the nature of man that moved Shakespeare to write his great tragedies. Whether one agrees with this simplification or not, one can hardly fail to notice a change at the turn of the century in Shakespeare's attitude to order.

Until 1600 or so Shakespeare frequently uses *order* in the heavily charged theological sense, signifying, not merely political order, but the whole range of correspondences in the universe. A few examples will suffice. In *King John*, the King of France begs Pandulph to impose 'some gentle order'. The Papal Legate replies:

> All form is formless, order orderless,
> Save what is opposite to England's love.

When Northumberland, at the beginning of the second part of *Henry IV*, hears the news of Hotspur's death, he cries:

> Let heaven kiss earth! Now let not Nature's hand
> Keep the wild flood confin'd! Let order die,
> And let this world no longer be a stage
> To feed contention in a ling'ring act;
> But let one spirit of the first-born Cain
> Reign in all bosoms, that, each heart being set
> On bloody courses, the rude scene may end,
> And darkness be the burier of the dead.

In *Henry V* the Archbishop delivers a long speech about bees, beginning:

> Therefore doth heaven divide
> The state of man in divers functions,
> Setting endeavour in continual motion;

5. Shakespeare was closely connected with Digges—the leading English Copernican. See Hotson's *I, William Shakespeare*.

To which is fixed as an aim or butt
Obedience; for so work the honey bees,
Creatures that by a rule in nature teach
The act of order to a peopled kingdom.

In *Troilus and Cressida* we get the last and greatest of these speeches on order, where Ulysses discourses eloquently on the necessity of order in human affairs as in the universe:

The heavens themselves, the planets, and this centre
Observe degree, priority, and place,
Insisture, course, proportion, season, form,
Office, and custom, in all line of order;
And therefore is the glorious planet Sol
In noble eminence enthron'd and spher'd
Amidst the other . . .

Order in the state, as in the universe, is founded on degree:

Take but degree away, untune that string,
And hark what discord follows!

In this speech Shakespeare expounds the orthodox Tudor doctrine, partly as an analysis of the lack of unity in the Greek army, but dramatically as a preparation for Troilus's speech on his discovery of Cressida's faithlessness:

O madness of discourse,
That cause sets up with and against itself!
Bifold authority! where reason can revolt
Without perdition, and loss assume all reason
Without revolt.

The bonds of heaven are slipp'd, dissolv'd, and loos'd;
And with another knot, five-finger-tied,
The fractions of her faith, orts of her love,
The fragments, scraps, the bits, and greasy relics
Of her o'er-eaten faith, are bound to Diomed.

After the way Shakespeare has built up the conception of order, the expression of chaos in this speech is enormously impressive. Order has been shattered by the faithlessness of a woman, and it will be remembered that Othello declares later:

When I love thee not
Chaos is come again.

After *Troilus and Cressida* Shakespeare does not again refer to order in this sense, except possibly in Time's speech in *The Winter's Tale*, where he says

> Let me pass
> The same I am, ere ancient'st Order was,
> Or what is now receiv'd.

We still have references to the idea of order (as for example in Macbeth's description of order in the world of dogs) but we no longer have the word. The reason is simple. Shakespeare dissociates political order from metaphysical order. When he speaks of political matters he tends to use the word *Authority*; and when he is discussing order in the universe he often uses *Nature* or one of its derivatives. Statistics are notoriously unreliable, but there seems to be some significance in the fact that in the eleven plays written by Shakespeare in the seventeenth century (omitting the doubtful *Pericles* and *Henry VIII*) nature and *natural* are used three hundred times, including forty times in *King Lear* alone. In eleven plays written in the sixteenth century (nine histories, and four early comedies to make up the quota) the words are used only seventy-one times. The average for the plays written before 1600 is 5·5; the average for the plays written after that date is 23·1. If the word *unnatural* is included the averages become 6·3 and 24·8 respectively. It is reasonable to suppose from these figures that in the seventeenth century Shakespeare was more concerned than he had been to consider the fundamental nature of man and to question the position of man in the universe. This may be due to a greater awareness of original sin; it may have been stimulated by his reading of Montaigne; or it may have arisen simply from the fact that he was writing tragedies which demanded more obstinate questionings.

For our present purpose Shakespeare's increased use of the word *authority* is especially significant. Whereas in the sixteenth century he had accepted the idea of order—the hierarchy of ruler and ruled as part of the divine ordering of the universe—he now became more concerned with the shortcomings of authority. In *Troilus and Cressida* he had analysed the upsetting of order by the feebleness of Agamemnon, and the jealousies of the Greek chiefs. But in *Hamlet* the praise of order is put into the mouth of Rosencrantz and Guildenstern:

> The single and peculiar life is bound
> With all the strength and armour of the mind
> To keep itself from noyance; but much more
> That spirit upon whose weal depends and rests
> The lives of many. The cease of majesty
> Dies not alone, but like a gulf doth draw
> What's near it with it. It is a massy wheel,
> Fix'd on the summit of the highest mount,
> To whose huge spokes ten thousand lesser things
> Are mortis'd and ajoin'd; which when it falls,
> Each small annexment, petty consequence,
> Attends the boist'rous ruin. Never alone
> Did the king sigh, but with a general groan.

The apologists for Claudius (of whom there have been several in the last few years) have supposed that these lines are intended as choric commentary rather than as the utterance of a professional flatterer. But even if we are as critical of Hamlet as L. C. Knights, we must surely admit that the conventional doctrine of order, when used to buttress a lecherous, treacherous, fratricidal usurper, has at least an undertone of irony.

The unworthiness of authority receives greater emphasis in *Measure for Measure*. It does not affect the argument that Angelo is only the Duke's deputy and that he shares his authority with Escalus; for the purpose of the play he possesses autocratic power, and throughout the play the corruption of power is vehemently attacked. The wretched Claudio, condemned for fornication, remarks bitterly:

> Thus can the demigod Authority
> Make us pay down for our offence by weight
> The words of heaven: on whom it will, it will;
> On whom it will not, so; yet still 'tis just.

In the first great scene between Angelo and Isabella, the word *authority* is iterated throughout. The most famous of Isabella's speeches contains a superb invective against tyrannical authority:

> Could great men thunder
> As Jove himself does, Jove would ne'er be quiet,
> For every pelting petty officer
> Would use his heaven for thunder, nothing but thunder.
> Merciful Heaven,
> Thou rather, with thy sharp and sulphurous bolt

> Splits the unwedgeable and gnarled oak
> Than the soft myrtle. But man, proud man,
> Dress'd in a little brief authority,
> Most ignorant of what he's most assur'd,
> His glassy essence, like an angry ape,
> Plays such fantastic tricks before high heaven
> As makes the angels weep; who, with our spleens,
> Would all themselves laugh mortal.

A little later Isabella continues:

> Because authority, though it err like others,
> Hath yet a kind of medicine in itself
> That skins the vice o'th' top.

Angelo himself, left alone on the stage, is forced to admit that

> Thieves for their robbery have authority
> When judges steal themselves.

But, in a later scene, after he has fallen, he boasts that even if Isabella accuses him, she will not be believed:

> For my authority bears a so credent bulk
> That no particular scandal once can touch
> But it confounds the breather.

King Lear was written soon after *Measure for Measure*, and here Shakespeare criticized authority through the mouths of Kent and the Fool—although, of course, they remain loyal to the King —and still more in the speeches of Lear in the third and fourth acts of the play. Lear's prayer for the poor naked wretches concludes with a lesson for authority:

> O, I have ta'en
> Too little care of this! Take physic, pomp;
> Expose thyself to feel what wretches feel,
> That thou mayst shake the superflux to them,
> And show the heavens more just.

These sentiments are universalized by the parallel prayer of the blinded Gloucester:

> Heavens, deal so still!
> Let the superfluous and lust-dieted man
> That slaves your ordinance, that will not see
> Because he does not feel, feel your power quickly;
> So distribution should undo excess,
> And each man have enough.

and by the pity felt by both Lear and Gloucester for Edgar in his disguise as Poor Tom. In the mock trial of Regan and Goneril, Lear accuses the false justicer of letting the criminals escape. The judges in this trial consist of a fool, a madman, and a serving-man. The counsel for the prosecution is a mad king. So authority is turned on its head. But the great attack on authority comes in Act IV when the mad Lear instructs Gloucester on the world's injustice:

See how yond justice rails upon yond simple thief. Hark, in thine ear; change places and, handy-dandy, which is the justice, which is the thief? Thou hast seen a farmer's dog bark at a beggar? . . . And the creature run from the cur? There thou mightst behold the great image of authority: a dog's obey'd in office.
Thou rascal beadle, hold thy bloody hand.
Why dost thou lash that whore? Strip thy own back;
Thou hotly lusts to use her in that kind
For which thou whip'st her. The usurer hangs the cozener.
Through tatter'd clothes small vices do appear;
Robes and furr'd gowns hide all. Plate sin with gold,
And the strong lance of justice hurtless breaks;
Arm it in rags, a pigmy's straw does pierce it.
None does offend, none—I say none; I'll able 'em.
Take that of me, my friend, who have the power
To seal th'accuser's lips. Get thee glass eyes,
And, like a scurvy politician, seem
To see the things thou dost not.

Successful men are hypocrites; or else, through the power of their money, their vices are concealed. Justice is merely an instrument of the strong and wealthy to oppress the poor and weak. But since all are equally guilty, none does offend; since they are human beings, all have an equal right to be forgiven. It may be argued that this analysis of authority was put by Shakespeare into the mouth of a madman and that we are therefore not intended to take it as a serious criticism of society; but few readers will accept so comfortable a conclusion. It is, after all, merely a development of the eminently sane speeches of Isabella. Lear has come to realize that a king is merely a man, and that he has been betrayed by flattery:

They flatter'd me like a dog, and told me I had white hairs in my beard ere the black ones were there. To say 'ay' and 'no' to everything that I said! 'Ay' and 'no' too was no good divinity ... Go to, they are not men o' their words. They told me I was everything; 'tis a lie—I am not ague-proof.

Lear, at the beginning of the play, is incapable of disinterested love, for he uses the love of others to minister to his own egotism. His prolonged sufferings free his heart from the bondage of the selfhood, and he learns disinterestedness. At the same time he acquires humility and a new sympathy with the outcasts of humanity. The old authoritarian Lear dies in the storm; he is resurrected as a fully human being. He discovers for the first time the riches of his own soul.

If the attitude to authority in *Measure for Measure* and *King Lear* is compared with the attitude to order in the histories, it will be apparent that Shakespeare's position had shifted. Order is still necessary, but it is dissociated from its political corollary. Shakespeare was still fully conscious of the dangers of disorder, but he was now more concerned with the evils of power. It might be said, in Hegelian terms, that the praise of order and the analysis of authority are the thesis and antithesis of the Shakespearian dialectic.

II

The bitterness of *Timon of Athens*, written soon after *King Lear*, has been ascribed by some critics to Shakespeare's sympathy with the riots in Warwickshire against the enclosures, and by others to a more personal cause. The late Caroline Spurgeon showed that the iterative image is the triple one of flatterers-dogs-sweets; and the natural deduction to make from this fact is that Shakespeare conceived the theme as the betrayal of Timon by flatterers. This interpretation is supported by the fable of Fortune put into the mouth of the Poet, and intended by Shakespeare as a pointer to the meaning of the play:

> When Fortune in her shift and change of mood
> Spurns down her late beloved, all his dependants,
> Which labour'd after him to the mountain's top
> Even on their knees and hands, let him slip down,
> Not one accompanying his declining foot.

Later in the play—in a passage, however, which is thought by some critics to be un-Shakespearian—the Poet proposes to write a satire against the softness of prosperity, with a discovery of the infinite flatteries that follow youth and opulency.

It would be hazardous to deny that this was the main theme of the play; but Shakespeare in his mature plays rarely confines himself to a single theme, and the iterative image throws light on only one aspect of each play. Even so, one hesitates to believe that 'Shakespeare is both presenting and refusing a set of feelings about Dog as a metaphor, making it in effect a term of praise'.[6] In spite of Mr. Empson's oblique defence of Apemantus, the popular view is surely correct: Apemantus is inserted in the play as a foil to Timon. Both are cynics and misanthropists; but whereas Apemantus is a natural snarler, incapable of generosity, Timon represents the ruin of a magnanimous man, turned to misanthropy by the betrayal by his friends. This interpretation is supported by the sources of the play, whether or not Shakespeare read Boiardo's *Timone*, as Warwick Bond suggests.

Miss Spurgeon, in a footnote, unjustly disposed of Wilson Knight's essay on *Timon of Athens*; for though she was perfectly right to say that there is no gold imagery in the play, she was wrong to brush aside the two hundred references to gold. As the essential nature of an image is that it should throw light on an idea or object by means of a comparison, it was impossible for Shakespeare to use gold as the basis of his imagery. But gold-symbolism is used throughout the play. Wilson Knight claims that it is used as a symbol of Timon's golden heart; but its significance is surely not this. He is nearer the truth when he suggests that there is 'a contrast between gold and the heart's blood of passionate love of which it is a sacrament: the association of the metaphorical value of gold and the value of love'. Gold is also a symbol of man's greed and of the economic basis of society. It is a symbol of the way in which the means of generosity corrupt the recipient, and of the way in which gross inequality in society destroys disinterestedness in love. It is not only Timon's friends who are corrupted by the wealth he dispenses. Timon himself is prevented from being fully human by the weight of his own riches, as Lear was by the weight of Authority. Timon tried to buy love with gold and was himself guilty, to a lesser extent, of the fault for which he blamed his friends.

6. *The Structure of Complex Words* (1951), p. 176.

Some critics have supposed that the sex nausea apparent in some of Timon's speeches, for example the soliloquy when he departs from Athens and the lines addressed to Alcibiades' harlots, signifies an intrusion of Shakespeare's personal feelings, and that the play is a comparative failure because the dramatist could not maintain the balance and impersonality of great art. There may be an element of truth in this—it is certainly truer of *Timon of Athens* than of *Hamlet*[7]—but there is a more dramatic reason for the railings against venereal disease. Timon's love of his fellow men is warped and poisoned by their ingratitude and, assuming unconsciously that all love has a sexual basis, he avenges himself by calling down the appropriate plague. In one of his early works, Marx declares:

The endless degradation, in which man exists simply for himself, is expressed in the relation to the woman as booty and as the servant of the general lust. For the secret of this relationship finds its unambiguous, clear and revealed expression in the relation of man to woman, and in the way in which the immediate and natural relation of the species is regarded. *The immediate, natural and necessary relationship of one human being to another is that of man to woman.* From the character of this relationship can be seen how far man has come to be, and to regard himself as, a creature of a certain kind. The relationship of man to woman is the most natural of one human being to another: *in it is revealed how far the natural behaviour of man has become human* (i.e. how far his human nature has become natural to him); in it is revealed how far the needs of man have become human needs, that is to say, *how far another person has become one of his needs as a human being, how far existence has become mutual being.*[8]

In Athens, it is clear, love is a commodity like everything else. The only women we see are masquers and harlots. The sex nausea of Timon is an appropriate criticism of a society which is dominated by the acquisitive principle, a society which is bound together by what Marx calls the cash-nexus.

Lear's ravings about sex have been naturally associated with the curses of Timon. It is true that the Elizabethans were aware that madness often led to an upsurge of thoughts which before would

7. Cf. T. S. Eliot on *Hamlet*: 'full of some stuff that the writer could not drag to light, contemplate, or manipulate into art'.
8. *Nationaloekonomie und Philosophie* in *Der Historische Materialismus. Die Frühschriften* (edited Landshut and Meyer), i, p. 294.

have been suppressed. Lear, moreover, harps on the lechery which
is common to the gilded fly and the fine lady because his mind is
obsessed with the idea that the mother of his children must have
been unfaithful to him:

> If thou should'st not be glad,
> I would divorce me from thy mothers tomb
> Sepulchring an adultress. . . .

And he is obsessed, too, with the thought that ungrateful children
are created by the act of sex:

> Is it the fashion, that discarded fathers
> Should have thus little mercy on their flesh?
> Judicious punishment! 'twas this flesh begot
> Those Pelican daughters.

But it is significant that the mad Lear proceeds directly from his
invective against the simpering dame to analyse the corruption of
society through the power of gold. As Eliot has pointed out, each
one of Shakespeare's plays throws light on all the others. *King
Lear* and *Timon of Athens* are inter-illuminating.

   Timon of Athens was probably written in 1607–8, just after
Volpone and two or three years before *The Alchemist*—the two
plays in which Jonson so superbly satirized the avarice which is
the motive-force of an acquisitive society. It is possible that
Timon was partly suggested by *Volpone*; but whereas Jonson was
sufficiently detached to treat the theme, though with considerable
bitterness, satirically, Shakespeare could only deal with it in a
tragic spirit. Some twelve years before, in *King John*, Shakespeare
had incidentally treated the same theme. The difference of
attitude is striking.

> That smooth-fac'd gentleman, tickling commodity,
> Commodity, the bias of the world—
> The world, who of itself is peised well,
> Made to run even upon even ground,
> Till this advantage, this vile-drawing bias,
> This sway of motion, this commodity,
> Makes it take head from all indifferency,
> From all direction, purpose, course, intent—
> And this same bias, this commodity,
> This bawd, this broker, this all-changing word,
> Clapp'd on the outward eye of fickle France,

Hath drawn him from his own determin'd aid,
From a resolv'd and honourable war,
To a most base and vile-concluded peace.
And why rail I on this commodity?
But for because he hath not woo'd me yet;
Not that I have the power to clutch my hand
When his fair angels would salute my palm,
But for my hand, as unattempted yet,
Like a poor beggar raileth on the rich.
Well, whiles I am a beggar, I will rail
And say there is no sin but to be rich;
And being rich, my virtue then shall be
To say there is no vice but beggary.
Since kings break faith upon commodity,
Gain, be my lord, for I will worship thee.

Falconbridge is, of course, making himself out to be more cynical and self-seeking than he is in fact. The last twelve lines were added by him as an afterthought lest his attack on the naked pursuit of self-interest should be thought priggish or self-righteous. But his half-humorous railing is very different in spirit from the bitter curses of Timon. The contrast is partly due, of course, to the characters who speak the lines; but most readers would agree that Shakespeare himself had come to feel more deeply on the subject in the intervening years. He could no longer treat the acquisitive instinct so tolerantly.

Some of the most impressive speeches in the play describe the overthrowing of order by the power of gold. Shakespeare chooses as his hero, not a king, a statesman, or a great warrior, but a man whose eminence depends entirely on his wealth, and whose power vanishes with his wealth. It is as though he realized, at the beginning of the capitalist era, that power was shifting from one class to another and that authority was decreasingly invested in the nominal rulers. It is for this reason that the play may be said to continue the debate on order and authority. Money, the new basis of authority, is the destroyer of order. The intricate and all-embracing idea of order, inherited from the medieval world, may have been undermined by Luther, Copernicus, and Machiavelli; but Hooker's conception of order differs very little from that of pre-Reformation thinkers, the new astronomy substituted a new order for that which it disproved, and Machiavelli, though his influence on political morality was disintegrating, was primarily concerned with the maintenance of order in the State. Shakespeare, even though he may have accepted Copernican theories with his mind, continued to assume the Ptolemaic system in his poetry.[9] He could reject Machiavellianism as a temporary aberration. But the new domination of money was clearly a threat to the conception of order Shakespeare shared with his contemporaries: it substituted for it an order divorced from morality, an authority without responsibility, a power animated entirely by self-interest.

III

When Timon, digging for roots, discovers gold, he exclaims:

> Gold? Yellow, glittering, precious gold? No, gods,
> I am no idle votarist. Roots, you clear heavens!
> Thus much of this will make black white, foul fair,
> Wrong right, base noble, old young, coward valiant.
> Ha, you gods! why this? What, this, you gods? Why, this
> Will lug your priests and servants from your sides,
> Pluck stout men's pillows from below their heads—
> This yellow slave
> Will knit and break religions, bless th'accurs'd,
> Make the hoar leprosy ador'd, place thieves
> And give them title, knee, and approbation,
> With senators on the bench. This is it
> That makes the wappen'd widow wed again—
> She whom the spital-house and ulcerous sores
> Would cast the gorge at this embalms and spices
> To th'April day again. Come, damn'd earth,
> Thou common whore of mankind, that puts odds
> Among the rout of nations, I will make thee
> Do thy right nature.

There follow the scenes with Alcibiades and Apemantus. Just before the latter goes out, Timon again addresses the newly found gold:

> O thou sweet king-killer, and dear divorce
> 'Twixt natural son and sire! thou bright defiler
> Of Hymen's purest bed! thou valiant Mars!

9. Even Milton, a generation later, though certainly a Copernican, continued to make use of Ptolemaic conceptions in his poetry.

Thou ever young, fresh, lov'd, and delicate wooer,
Whose blush doth thaw the consecrated snow,
That lies on Dian's lap! thou visible god,
That sold'rest close impossibilities,
And mak'st them kiss! that speak'st with every tongue
To every purpose! O thou touch of hearts!
Think thy slave man rebels, and by thy virtue
Set them into confounding odds, that beasts
May have the world in empire!

In the work from which I have already quoted, *Political Economy and Philosophy*, Marx quotes both the above passages, together with these lines from *Faust*:[1]

Was Henker! freilich Händ' und Füsse
Und Kopf und H——, die sind dein;
Dock alles, was ich frisch geniesse,
Ist das drum weniger mein?
Wenn ich sechs Hengste zahlen kann,
Sind ihre Kräfte nicht die meine?
Ich renne zu und bin ein rechter Mann,
Als hätt' ich vierundzwanzig Beine.[2]

Marx then provides the following analysis and commentary:

I am what I possess. I am the owner of money, and my power is as great as the power of my money. The qualities of money—the owner's qualities and essential powers—are mine. What I am, and what I can do are not determined by my individuality. I may be hideous, but I can buy the most beautiful women: therefore I am not really hideous, for the effect of hideousness—its power to repel—is destroyed by money. I may be lame, and yet money can get me twenty-four legs. I may be wicked, dishonest, conscienceless, and unintelligent; but money is honoured, and so its owner is honoured too. Money is the highest good. It raises me above the trouble of being dishonourable, for I seem to be honourable. I may be unintelligent; but since money is the real mind of things, how should its owner be unintelligent? And, besides, he can buy intelligent people; and is not he who has power over the intelligent more intelligent than they? Since I can do everything the heart can desire through the power of money, have I not all human capacities at my disposal? Does not money, then, transform all my incapacity into its opposite?

1. Op. cit. i, pp. 356–60.
2. *Faust*, ed. Betsch (1926), lines 1820–7.

If money is the link which binds me to human life, to society, to nature and to other men, is it not the link of links? Can it not loose and bind all ties? So is it not also the universal means of separation? It is the true coin of separation and the true means of alleviation—it is the alchemy of society.

Shakespeare singles out two special characteristics of money: First, it is the visible divinity, the transformer of all human and natural qualities into their opposites, the universal transmuter and changer of things, which turns impossibilities into brothers. Secondly, it is the universal whore—the universal bawd of men and peoples. The power to change and transmute all human and natural qualities—the divine power of money—lies in its power of alienation, estrangement and externalisation of the specific essence of man. It is the alienation of human capacity. What I, as a man cannot do—what my individual and essential powers are incapable of doing—I can accomplish through money. So that money turns every essential power into something which it is not of itself, that is, into its opposite.

If I desire a certain food, or want to use the post because I am not strong enough to cover the ground on foot, money will provide me with both food and postal-service: it lifts my wishes out of the world of idea; it translates them out of an ideal and imaginary existence into the real, physical one—out of imagination into life, out of imagined being into real being. All this mediation is true creative power.

Of course demand exists also for the man who has no money. But his demand is a mere creature of the imagination, which has no effect on me, on himself, or on any third person. It has no real existence. . . . The difference between the effective demand—based on money—and the ineffective one—based only on my need, passion or desire—is the difference between being and thinking, between an objective idea, external to me and under my control, and an idea which merely exists in my mind.

If I have no money to travel, I have no need to: that is, I have no need which is real or realizable. If I have a vocation to study, but have not the money for it . . . I have no effective and true vocation. On the other hand, supposing I have actually no vocation to study but have the will and the cash, then I have an effective vocation to do so. Money . . . is the objective and universal means for turning idea into reality and reality into a mere idea. It can just as easily turn the real, natural and essential powers of men into abstract ideas, and so into imperfections, into torturing phantoms of the mind, as it can turn real imperfections and phantoms of the mind—the powerless powers which exist only in the imagination of the individual—into actual essential powers and capacities. And so we see it is the general converter of individualities, which transforms them into their opposites and adds to their qualities others which conflict with them.

In its role as a converting power, money is hostile to the individual and to the social bonds which are claimed to be essential in themselves. It turns loyalty into disloyalty, love into hate, hatred into love, virtue into vice, vice into virtue, slave into master, master into slave, stupidity into intelligence, intelligence into stupidity. Since money, as the existing and active conception of value, interchanges and metamorphoses everything, it is the universal transformation and confusion of things; it is the topsy-turvy world; it is the muddle and transmogrification of all natural and human qualities. The coward who can buy pluck is plucky. Since money is not exchanged for a definite quality or object but for the whole world of man and nature, it exchanges (from its owner's point of view) any quality for any other, even for its opposite. It makes brothers of impossibilities. It compels contradictions to kiss each other.

But if you regard a man as a human being and his relationship to the world as a human one, you can only exchange love for love, trust for trust, and so on. If you want to enjoy art, you must be a person educated in art; if you want to influence other men you must be a man who is effective in stimulating others and challenging them. Every one of your relationships to men and to nature must be a definite one corresponding, in its expression of your real individual life, to the object of your will. If you love without response ... your love is powerless and a misfortune.

Marx goes on to show that on the assumptions of the political economists and in a capitalist society a worker is merely a commodity: his wages are merely a necessary cost of capital and he is dehumanized by the system.

I have quoted this passage at length partly because it seems to have been ignored by Shakespearian commentators and partly for its intrinsic interest. It provides an effective commentary on Timon's diatribes about the power of gold and throws a useful sidelight on one aspect of the play.

Political Economy and Philosophy was written by Marx in 1844, left in an unfinished and fragmentary state, and not published until 1932. The two editions (published in Germany and Russia) differ somewhat in their arrangement of the text, and there has not so far been an English translation. But the work is of great interest because it shows the mind of Marx at work at the turning-point of his life, when he was finally converted to Communism. It provides the philosophical basis of Communism which he assumed in his more famous works.

Marx analyses the philosophical implications of the main terms of political economy. He shows that in the industrial system of Adam Smith human labour is represented as the essence of private property, and private property as the essence of all human industry. Here the fundamental paradox of bourgeois society is revealed. For, the more clearly human labour is recognized as the essence of private property, the more self-contradictory must appear the inhumanity of the conditions of a society based on private property. It is this contradiction which reaches its height in the existence of capital and labour. Although capital *is* labour, the capitalist can live without labouring, while the labourer can hardly live at all. The resolution of this conflict in Communism (Marx argues) represents the next step that mankind must take in order to restore its humanity. For man fulfils himself in society: only in his social activities is he fully man. That is why, in a society based on private property, man is in a state of self-estrangement. Neither his wants and needs, nor their possible fulfilment, are truly human. Even his senses are not human; they would become so only if their objects were related to him in a human way. But this depends on the conditions in which man carries on the job of producing his material existence; and these conditions are, today, in contradiction to his humanity.[3]

Private property (Marx declares) has made us so dumb, dull and inactive, that we regard the object as ours only when we possess it, only when it exists for us in the form of capital, or when we own it, eat it, drink it, wear it, live in it, in short, when we use it. In place of all physical and intellectual senses there has been substituted the self-alienation of all of them—the sense of possession. Man's essence had to be reduced to this, its absolute poverty, so that it could be allowed to bring forth its inner wealth. The abolition of private property is therefore necessary to the freeing of all the senses and attributes of man.

Only by this means can the senses themselves become really human:

The eye becomes a human eye when that which it sees has become socially human—an object made by man for man. It is as though the senses themselves had now become, in their own practice, human philosophers; for they contemplate the object for its own sake. But

3. I am indebted for this paragraph to an unpublished essay by Karl Polanyi, the author of *Origins of our Time*.

that object has now entered into an objective and human relationship, which involves both the object and the man.[4]

Marx uses the quotations from *Timon of Athens* to support his criticisms of an acquisitive society. One might go further and say that some of these criticisms were suggested by Shakespeare, and that Shakespeare was one of the spiritual godparents of the *Communist Manifesto*. Marx would doubtless have become a Communist even if he had never read *Timon of Athens*, but his reading of that play helped him to crystallize his ideas.

Years later, when he wrote *Capital*, Marx made use of the same quotation from *Timon of Athens* in a footnote to a passage which is a condensation of his former commentary:

Since money does not disclose what has been transformed into it, everything, whether a commodity or not, is convertible into gold. Everything becomes saleable and purchasable. Circulation is the great social retort into which everything is thrown, and out of which everything is recovered as crystallised money. Not even the bones of the saints are able to withstand this alchemy; and still less able to withstand it are more delicate things, sacrosanct things which are outside the commercial traffic of men. Just as all the qualitative differences between commodities are effaced in money, so money on its side, a radical leveller, effaces all distinctions. But money is itself a commodity, an external object, capable of becoming the private property of any individual. Thus social power becomes a private power in the hands of a private person. That was why the ancients denounced money as subversive of the economic and moral order of things. Modern society which, when still in its infancy, pulled Pluto by the hair of his head out of the bowels of the earth, acclaims gold, its Holy Grail, as the glittering incarnation of its inmost vital principle.[5]

4. Op. cit., p. 299.
5. Everyman ed., i. 112–13. In a sequel to this essay, published in *Shakespeare in a Changing World* (ed. A. Kettle, 1964), I tried to show that Shakespeare was not guilty of the easy utopianism of Gonzalo's ideal commonwealth. He did not believe in the withering away of the state, nor in repudiating civilization, nor even in the natural goodness of primitive man. Caliban does not represent the noble savage dispossessed by the ignoble white man. In *The Tempest* was at last resolved the conflict between the need for order and the corruption of authority. The treachery against Prospero succeeded because he had neglected wordly ends and thereby enabled his brother to seize the dukedom of Milan. But by the end of the play his spiritual wisdom and power, which had been a political weakness, proves to be his ultimate strength. The ghost of Machiavelli had been laid.

5

The Conclusion of
The Winter's Tale[1]

I

Charlotte Lennox in *Shakespeare Illustrated* (1753) spoke of the statue scene in *The Winter's Tale* as 'a mean and absurd contrivance':

for can it be imagined that Hermione, a virtuous and affectionate wife, would conceal herself during sixteen years in a solitary house, though she was sensible that her repentant husband was all that time consuming away with grief and remorse for her death: and what reason could she have for chusing to live in such a miserable confinement when she might have been happy in the possession of her husband's affection and have shared his throne? How ridiculous also in a great Queen, on so interesting an occasion, to submit to such buffoonery as standing on a pedestal, motionless, her eyes fixed, and at last to be conjured down by a magical command of Paulina.

Mrs. Lennox concludes that Greene's novel 'has nothing in it half so low and improbable as this contrivance of the statue', and that the play is 'greatly inferior to the old paltry story that furnished him with the subject of it'.

A German critic, Heinrich Bulthaupt (1889) makes a similar complaint. He finds it incredible that the Hermione of the first part of the play would consent to 'this farce of a statue' and he declares that every charm 'is put to flight by the ever-recurring dense, rationalistic preparation of the scene';

Instead of using some means full of the miraculous, Shakespeare lets Paulina play Providence. Thus the scaffolding creaks in all its joints; human passion and grandeur are inconceivably mingled with the affectation of a comedian. Our tragic sympathy, our moral indignation has been quickened,—but she, whom we commiserated, trifles away

1. From *The Morality of Art*, ed. D. W. Jefferson (1969).

our sympathy with a living statue which she represents, and the man, for whom we wished the heaviest punishment, garners the fairest harvest of indulgent fate. A plot which should have been treated only as a tragedy, is, without justification, conducted to a superficial end of reconciliation.

A number of critics have likewise complained of the penultimate scene of the play in which the discovery of Perdita's birth is reported in ornate prose instead of being displayed on the stage. Dr. Johnson remarked: 'It was, I suppose, only to spare his own labour that the poet put the whole scene into narrative.' Hartley Coleridge suggested that Shakespeare was in a hurry; that he could compose this sort of dialogue with the least aid from inspiration; and Gervinus said that Shakespeare wisely reported the recognition of Perdita, 'otherwise the play would have been too full of powerful scenes', to which Q retorted:

If we really prefer this sort of thing, . . . then Heaven must be our aid. But if, using our own judgement, we read the play and put ourselves into the place of its first audience, I ask, are we not baulked? In proportion as we have paid tribute to the art of the story by letting our interest be intrigued, our emotion excited, are we not cheated when Shakespeare lets us down with this reported tale?

Lytton Strachey, it will be remembered, had declared that Shakespeare, while he was writing his last plays, was bored with both life and drama; and T. S. Eliot, putting it more positively, remarked that Shakespeare had ceased to be interested in character as such: he had gone 'beyond the dramatic'.

The two main complaints made by critics of the denouement of *The Winter's Tale* are that the reported recognition of Perdita is undramatic and lazy, and that the statue scene is both incredible in itself and false to the character of Hermione. Let us first consider the second complaint. It is significant that the complaints were made by readers rather than spectators. Spectators, even when they saw only eighteenth-century adaptations, did not share the disapproval of many of the critics. Mrs. Inchbald, who foolishly included Garrick's adaptation in her collection of the *British Theatre*, admitted that when Mrs. Siddons played Hermione, the statue scene was 'far more grand in exhibition than the reader will possibly behold in idea'; and Thomas Campbell, the poet, replying to Mrs. Lennox remarked dryly: 'Mrs. Lennox says, that the statue scene is low and ridiculous. I am sure Mrs. Siddons used to make it appear to us in a different light.' Campbell had the advantage of being Mrs. Siddons's biographer; and in describing her performance he said:

Mrs. Siddons looked the statue, even to literal illusion; and, whilst the drapery hid her lower limbs, it showed a beauty of head, neck, shoulders and arms, that Praxitiles might have studied. This statue scene has hardly its parallel for enchantment even in Shakespeare's theatre. The star of his genius was at its zenith when he composed it; but it was only a Siddons that could do justice to its romantic perfection. The heart of everyone who saw her when she burst from the semblance of sculpture into motion, and embraced her daughter, Perdita, must throb and glow at the recollection.

There are more detailed accounts of performances of the statue scene by Macready and Helen Faucit in 1847. Helen Faucit herself gave a full account of the performance in her book *On Some of Shakespeare's Female Characters*[2] and there are long reviews in contemporary newspapers. Helen Faucit's performance was described as 'the finest combination of Grecian sculpture, Italian painting and British acting, that has in our day been seen on the stage'. Another reviewer said 'It was the most entrancing thing we ever remember to have seen—actually suspending the blood, and taking the breath away. It was something supernatural almost.' Hermione has a long period in which she does not speak, and in the space of 160 lines she had only one short speech, addressed not to Leontes but to Perdita. In Euripides' play, when Herakles brings back Alcestis from the grave, she remains completely silent for the rest of the play; and although there is no evidence that Shakespeare had read *Alcestis*, he seems to have shared Euripides' dramatic tact in this particular. But it is nevertheless difficult for the actress playing Hermione. It is a great strain on the nerves and muscles, as Helen Faucit observed, to stand motionless for so long, when even a movement of the eyelashes would destroy the illusion. Helen Faucit was helped by the fact that her arm was resting on a pedestal. But when music sounded, and she turned her head to let her eyes rest on Leontes, this had 'a startling, magnetic effect upon all'. She moved down

2. Helen Faucit, *On Some of Shakespeare's Female Characters* (1891), pp. 337–92.

the steps from the dais and paused at a short distance from Leontes. 'At first he stood speechless, as if turned to stone; his face with an awe-struck look upon it.' When Paulina says 'Nay, present your hand', Leontes advanced, hesitantly, and touched the hand held out to him. Then he cried, 'O, she's warm!' These words were deleted from many acting versions, for fear they should raise a laugh, but the tone in which they were spoken impressed critics of both Macready and Gielgud. Helen Faucit had been warned, at one of the rehearsals, to be prepared for something extraordinary—but it was not until the first performance before an audience that she realized the point of the warning. Macready's joy at finding Hermione alive seemed uncontrollable. 'Now he was prostrate at her feet, then enfolding her in his arms.' The veil covering her head and neck fell off. Her hair came unbound and fell over her shoulders and Macready kissed and caressed it. The change in Macready was so sudden and overwhelming, that Helen Faucit cried out. Macready whispered to her 'Don't be frightened, my child! Don't be frightened! Control yourself'. As this went on, the audience were tumultuously applauding, with a sound like a storm of hail. When Perdita and Florizel knelt at her feet, Hermione looked, she was told, 'like Niobe, all tears'.

I have described this performance at some length to show that, however much the scene might be criticized in the study, it created a tremendous effect in the theatre; so much so, that at one performance, at Edinburgh, when Hermione descended from her pedestal, 'the audience simultaneously rose from their seats, as if drawn out of them by surprise and reverential awe at the presence of one who bore more of heaven than of earth about her'. As one Scottish critic said:

When she descended from her pedestal, with a slow and gliding motion, and wearing the look of a being consecrated by long years of prayer and sorrow and seclusion, it seemed to us as if we looked upon a being almost too pure to be gazed on with unveiled eyes;

and an Irish critic said

We think not then of the symmetry of form, the perfection of outline, so far beyond the rarest achievements of art. For the spirit which breathes from the face, where grief has long grown calm, and suffering brightened into a heavenly pity, in the pure world of thought—the spirit which bears within it so much of heaven, with all that is best of earth, alone possesses our every faculty.

These critics, in some ways typically Victorian, express themselves in a rather sentimental way; but they illustrate the impact of the scene on the spectators, and they show that Shakespeare had triumphantly overcome the improbabilities of his fable. The methods by which he achieved this triumph were well analysed in a preface written by Granville-Barker in 1912, but not included in his collected prefaces. He shows that Shakespeare prepares the audience:

through Paulina's steward, almost to the pitch of revelation, saving just so much surprise, and leaving so little, that when they see the statue they may think themselves more in doubt than they really are whether it is Hermione herself or no. He prepares Leontes, who feels that his wife's spirit might walk again: who is startled by the strange air of Hermione that the yet unknown Perdita breathes out; who, his egotism killed, has become simple of speech, simple-minded, receptive.

Barker goes on to speak of the way in which the previous scene postpones the revelation, and of the way in which, from the moment the statue is disclosed, 'every minor contrast of voice and mood that can give the scene modelling and beauty of form, is brought into easy use'. Music is used, as so often in the last plays, to create the appropriate atmosphere; and the alarm and scepticism of Camillo and Polixenes contrast with the rapture of Leontes. Above all, Shakespeare avoids what lesser dramatists would have indulged, any speeches of noble forgiveness. Robert Greene, for example, in *James IV*, makes his Dorothea forgive her erring husband in words which illustrate what Barker describes:

> Shame me not, Prince, companion to my bed.
> Youth has misled—tut! but a little fault.

The 'little fault' had consisted of attempted murder.

The actors taught the critics that the statue scene, far from being absurd, could be overwhelmingly effective on the stage; and no critic during the past hundred years has echoed Mrs. Lennox's complaints, with the sole exception of Robert Bridges. But, of course, a scene could be immensely effective on the stage without being satisfying to the reader, and without being great drama.

II

The first critic of *The Winter's Tale*, the astrologer, Dr. Simon Forman, who witnessed a performance at the Globe on 15 May 1611, mentions the fact that Perdita is restored to her father after sixteen years and he gives a description of Autolycus—from whom he deduced the moral that one should 'beware of trusting feigned beggars or fawning fellows'. But, oddly enough, he does not mention the statue scene or the restoration of Hermione. This has led some critics to suppose that in its original form Shakespeare's play was closer to its source, Greene's *Pandosto*, and though it is unlikely that he made Leontes fall in love with Perdita and commit suicide when he realized that she was his daughter, it is possible that Hermione was not restored to life. This receives some support from the fact that Hermione appears to Antigonus in a dream; this is not, of course, decisive, even though it leads the audience to assume that Hermione is dead. But if in the play, as Dr. Forman saw it, Hermione was not restored—and her restoration is not hinted at by the oracle—Shakespeare must have attempted to round off his tragi-comedy with the restoration of Perdita to her father, and the reconciliation of Leontes and Polixenes through the marriage of their children. The reconciliation would have been less satisfying than that in *Cymbeline* and *The Tempest*; and, on the whole, I think that the restoration of Hermione must have been part of Shakespeare's original plan.

By his jealousy Leontes has brought on himself a sixfold tragedy.[3] 1. He has lost his beloved wife. 2. He has lost his best friend. 3. He has lost his son and heir. 4. He has lost his newborn daughter. 5. He has lost his faithful councillor Camillo. 6. He has lost his faithful servant, Antigonus. At the end of the play he regains his wife, his friend, his daughter, and his councillor; he obtains a son-in-law, who will rule in Sicilia instead of Mamillius; and only Antigonus, pursued by a bear, is not restored. The pattern of reconciliation fits in with that of the other Romances. In *Pericles*, the hero is reunited in the last act with his wife and daughter, and the daughter marries. In *Cymbeline* Posthumus is reunited to the wife he thought dead; Cymbeline recovers his

---

3. Cf. R. G. Moulton, *The Moral System of Shakespeare* (1903), p. 84.

lost daughter and her brothers. In *The Tempest*, Prospero is
reconciled with his enemies, and the reconciliation is cemented
by the marriage of Ferdinand and Miranda. In both *The Tempest*
and *The Winter's Tale* the marriage of the children unites two
thrones. But the denouement of *The Winter's Tale* differs from
that of the other plays. In *Pericles* we have seen how Thaisa is
restored to life by the medical skill of Cerimon, and we do not
share Pericles' delusion that both Thaisa and Marina are dead. We
know, therefore, that all may come right in the end. In *Cymbeline*
we know that Pisanio has refused to obey his master's orders and
that he has spared Imogen; and even when Fidele apparently dies,
only a few minutes elapse between her funeral and her recovery
from the drug. But in *The Winter's Tale* the audience is not let
into the secret. News is brought by Paulina that Hermione is
dead:

> O Lords,
> When I have said, cry woe: the Queen, the Queen,
> The sweet'st, dear'st creature's dead: and vengeance for't
> Not dropp'd down yet . . .
> I say she's dead: I'll swear't. If word, nor oath
> Prevail not, go and see: if you can bring
> Tincture, or lustre in her lip, her eye
> Heat outwardly, or breath within, I'll serve you
> As I would do the Gods.   (III. ii. 200–8)

Leontes asks Paulina to take him to the dead bodies of Hermione
and Mamillius: 'One grave shall be for both.' In the last scene
Leontes says of his wife:

> I saw her
> (As I thought) dead: and have (in vain) said many
> A prayer upon her grave.   (v. iii. 139–41)

In between these passages there are many references to Hermione's
death. More significant is Antigonus' account of his vision of the
ghost of Hermione: he says to the babe on the coast of Bohemia:

> thy Mother
> Appear'd to me last night: for ne'er was dream
> So like a waking. To me comes a creature,
> Sometimes her head on one side, some another,
> I never saw a vessel of like sorrow,
> So filled, and so becoming: in pure white robes

Like very sanctity she did approach
My cabin where I lay: thrice bow'd before me
And (gasping to begin some speech) her eyes
Became two spouts; the fury spent, anon
Did this break from her. 'Good Antigonus,
Since Fate (against thy better disposition)
Hath made thy person for the thrower-out
Of my poor babe, according to thine oath,
Places remote enough are in Bohemia;
There weep, and leave it crying: and for the babe
Is counted lost for ever, Perdita
I prithee call't: For this ungentle business
Put on thee by my Lord, thou ne'er shalt see
Thy wife Paulina more'. And so, with shrieks,
She melted into air. Affrighted much,
I did in time collect myself, and thought
This was so, and no slumber. Dreams are toys,
Yet for this once, yea superstitiously,
I will be squar'd by this. I do believe
Hermione hath suffer'd death.   (III. iii. 17–42)

The vision behaves as a ghost, chooses a name for her daughter, and prophesies Antigonus' death. I think there can be no doubt that even if Shakespeare did not intend Hermione to be dead at this point in the play, he intended us to think so. For this he has been taken to task by Professor B. Evans. Shakespeare does not normally deceive his audience. If he had written Jonson's *Silent Woman* he would have revealed early in the play that the supposed woman was a boy, as he lets us know, but not the characters on the stage, that Ganymede is Rosalind, that Fidele is Imogen, that Cesario is Viola, that Sebastian is not dead, that Marina is not dead, that the learned doctor is Portia, that the Friar in *Measure for Measure* is the Duke.

Why then does Shakespeare in *The Winter's Tale* violate his normal principles of dramaturgy and leave us to suppose that Hermione is dead and buried? Some critics blame the influence of Beaumont and Fletcher, who put up a much higher value on surprise than Shakespeare ever did.

There is, of course, plenty of evidence that Beaumont and Fletcher were acquainted with Shakespeare's plays, and some slight evidence that Shakespeare knew Beaumont and Fletcher's. They wrote, after all, for the same company; and Fletcher and

Shakespeare collaborated in *The Two Noble Kinsmen* and *Cardenio*, if not in *Henry VIII*. There are obvious resemblances between *Philaster* and *Cymbeline*; but as we don't know the exact dates of the plays, we don't know which dramatist was the imitator. If Shakespeare was imitating Beaumont and Fletcher, as Thorndike and others have argued, he transformed the material he borrowed. This can be seen from the fact that whereas in all the romances from *Pericles* to *The Tempest*, Shakespeare was concerned with reconciliation and reunion, and, in the three plays for which he was wholly responsible, with forgiveness, the tragi-comedies of Beaumont and Fletcher, though theatrically effective, have no such theme. The difference can be seen equally clearly, if one compares short passages which are clearly related to each other. A character in *Philaster*, for example, addresses a bank covered with wild flowers:

> Bear me, thou gentle bank,
> For ever, if thou wilt. You sweet ones all,
> Let me unworthy press you: I could wish
> I rather were a corse strewed o'er with you
> Than quick above you.   (IV. i)

In the fourth act of *The Winter's Tale*, Perdita ends her flower-catalogue with the words:

> O, these I lack
> To make you garlands of, and my sweet friend,
> To strew him o'er and o'er.   (IV. iv. 127–9)

Florizel asks 'What, like a corse?' and Perdita replies:

> No, like a bank for love to lie and play on;
> Not like a corse; or if, not to be buried,
> But quick and in mine arms. (IV. iv. 130–2)

The character in *Philaster* would rather be dead than alive; and his death-wish is contrasted with Perdita's wish to have Florizel very much alive in her arms.

It would be wrong, then, to blame Beaumont and Fletcher for any characteristics of *The Winter's Tale*; for Beaumont and Fletcher used the tragi-comic form as an escape from the logic of tragedy; and Shakespeare, whatever else he was doing, was clearly not doing that.

A number of critics have argued that Shakespeare was writing a kind of immortality myth; and if the 'resurrection' of Hermione was to convey that kind of impression, it was necessary for the audience, as well as the characters, to suppose that she had actually died in Act III. Such critics can refer to Paulina's willingness to swear that Hermione was dead.

Professor J. A. Bryant (to take an extremist) argues that the play embodies 'something of the Christian view of the redemption of the human race' and that Shakespeare undertook to suggest 'the miraculous aspect of divine mercy that has always made Christian teaching about the subject seem "foolishness to the Greeks" '. To bring back Hermione after sixteen years was his own idea. Mr. Bryant goes on:[4]

Consequently many readers have regarded the play as a whimsical though lovely fairytale with serious overtones here and there. From the Christian point of view, however, *The Winter's Tale* makes the hardest possible sense . . . as having ended in the only possible way for a play designed to suggest not only man's utter folly and helplessness but also his only hope of salvation. Here in the end those who survive are 'precious winners all', as Paulina calls them; and they are that because the dead has miraculously come to life and they have been granted grace to see the resurrection.

Professor Wilson Knight, more cautiously, remarks that the resurrection of Hermione is 'the crucial and revealing event to which the whole action moves'.[5] To S. L. Bethell,

The restoration of Hermione, her coming back as from the dead, is a carefully prepared symbol of spiritual and actual resurrection, in which alone true reconciliation may be attained.

But, Bethell adds, 'Hermione's is not a genuine resurrection'.[6]

Professor Adrien Bonjour is surely right to point out[7] that Shakespeare calls attention to Hermione's wrinkles and to the fact that Paulina two or three times a day visited the house where Hermione was hidden. It is wrong to assert that Shakespeare does

---

4. J. A. Bryant, Jr., *Hippolyta's View* (1961), p. 222.
5. G. Wilson Knight, *The Crown of Life* (1947), p. 76.
6. S. L. Bethell, *The Winter's Tale: A Study* (1947), p. 103.
7. A. Bonjour, 'The Final Scene of *The Winter's Tale*', *English Studies*, xxxiii (1952), 15–16.

not explain the mystery in realistic terms. Bonjour quite convincingly suggests that

> The reanimation of Hermione's statue may thus be considered as a symbol of the redeeming power of true repentance which may win again a long lost love and atone for the disastrous consequences of a past crime.

At this point we must turn to the penultimate scene of the play, which, as we have seen, has been criticized more frequently than the statue-scene.

III

If Shakespeare were merely saving himself trouble by reporting, instead of representing, the discovery of Perdita's birth, we could cheerfully throw him to the wolves. Nor can we seriously defend him on the grounds that the play would otherwise be too full of powerful scenes. But it may nevertheless be true that if he had dramatized the recognition of Perdita as powerfully as he did the restoration of Hermione, the emphasis of the play would be changed. Hermione has been absent from the stage for the best part of three acts, and another long scene with Perdita would have made it more difficult to restore Hermione, not merely to life, but as the central character of the play. A mere resurrection would be child's play compared with this feat of dramaturgy.

If we look at *Pericles* we see that Shakespeare was faced with a similar problem, but that he solved it differently. The reunion of Pericles and Marina is presented in a long scene of 265 lines; the reunion of Pericles and Thaisa and of Thaisa with Marina is presented in less than a third of the space. There were two good reasons for this. Shakespeare was probably not the author—and certainly not the original author—of the early scenes in which Thaisa appears before the birth of Marina; and secondly his imagination was chiefly engaged by the story of Marina. He had shown the recovery of Thaisa by means of the skill of Cerimon and this, no doubt, was one of the reasons why he did not in *The Winter's Tale* show us another good physician restoring Hermione after her supposed death.

So again, when he wrote *The Winter's Tale* he did not wish to repeat himself too closely. He could not hope to surpass the great Marina-Pericles scene; this is the climax of it:

> Tell thy story;
> If thine consider'd prove the thousandth part
> Of my endurance, thou art a man, and I
> Have suffered like a girl: yet thou dost look
> Like Patience gazing on king's graves, and smiling
> Extremity out of act. What were they friends?
> How lost thou them? Thy name, my most kind virgin?
> Recount, I do beseech thee: come, sit by me.

MAR. My name is Marina.

PER.   O, I am mock'd,
And thou by some incensed god sent hither
To make the world to laugh at me.

MAR.   Patience, good sir,
Or here I'll cease.

PER.   Nay, I'll be patient.
Thou little know'st how thou dost startle me,
To call thyself Marina.

MAR.   The name
Was given me by one that had some power,
My father, and a king.

PER.   How! a king's daughter!
And call'd Marina?

MAR.   You said you would believe me:
But not to be a troubler of your peace,
I will end here.

PER.   But are you flesh and blood?
Have you a working pulse? and are no fairy?
Motion? Well; speak on. Where were you born?
And wherefore called Marina?

MAR.   Called Marina,
For I was born at sea.   (v. i. 135–58)

I have said that Shakespeare always avoided too close a repetition of scenes he had written earlier. This can be seen by comparing scenes which might almost have been identical. For example, Julia in *The Two Gentlemen of Verona* is disguised as a page and sent by Proteus, whom she loves, to visit her rival, Silvia. In the same way Viola, disguised as Cesario is sent by Orsino, whom she loves, to plead his love with Olivia. The situation is superficially identical, but it is treated so differently in the two plays that no one watching *The Two Gentlemen* is likely to be disturbed by memories of *Twelfth Night*. Another example may be given. Sir Toby Belch extracts money from Sir Andrew

Aguecheek, his dupe, by promising him the hand of Olivia, his niece. In the same way Iago extracts money from his dupe, Roderigo, by promising to further his suit with Desdemona. Sir Toby persuades Sir Andrew to fight with his supposed rival, Cesario; as Iago persuades Roderigo to fight with his supposed rival, Cassio. Once again, despite the similarity between the situations, no one is likely to feel that Shakespeare was merely repeating himself.

It will be recalled that when Keats abandoned *Hyperion* because he found it impossible to eliminate the influence of Milton, he said that he wished to devote himself to other sensations. This, I am sure, was the attitude of Shakespeare when he completed each play. Each new play had to be something different. That is why all attempts to define Shakespearian Tragedy have been unsuccessful. There is, indeed, no such thing as 'Shakespearian Tragedy'— there are only Shakespearian tragedies.[8]

Shakespeare must have been aware of the similarity of theme of the four romances; all of them end with reunions, in three out of four voyages play a significant part, in three out of four the action covers two generations, in three out of four the climax is an act of forgiveness, and in two of them the parents are reconciled by the marriage of the children. Precisely because of these similarities, it was important to make the plays differ as much as possible in other ways. In two plays the wrong committed is caused by jealousy: but in one the jealousy is self-generated and in the other it is aroused by the cunning of a villain. In *The Winter's Tale* the central character is the jealous husband, the wife being banished from the stage during the central acts. In *Cymbeline* the central character is the wronged wife; and in *The Tempest* the wronged hero. In *Pericles* and *The Winter's Tale* there is a gap of sixteen years. *The Tempest* begins sixteen years after the commission of the crime which brought Prospero to the enchanted island.

Secondly, the assumption of literary critics that the scene is ineffective on the stage is quite unfounded. In every production I have seen, both professional and amateur, the scene has been very successful; and my experience has been confirmed by that of Professor Nevill Coghill (in his article defending the stagecraft of the play in *Shakespeare Survey*).[9]

8. Cf. p. 2 above.
9. N. Coghill, 'Six Points of Stage-craft in *The Winter's Tale*', *Shakespeare Survey 11* (1958), p. 39.

'In practice', says Coghill, 'this scene is among the most gripping and memorable of the entire play. Whoever saw the production of it by Peter Brook at the Phoenix Theatre in 1951–2 will remember the excitement it created. I know of at least two other productions of the play in which this scene had the same effect, and generated that mounting thrill of expectation needed to prepare us for the final scene.' As with the final scene, it looks as though the actors can sometimes teach the critics.

Coghill goes on to disagree with Bethell, who had suggested that in the penultimate scene Shakespeare was having his final fling at court jargon:

There may be a case to be made against the Metaphysicals and their wit, but I do not believe that Shakespeare was here making it; we, if we admire Donne and Crashaw, should not gird at the conceits of the three gentlemen. Let us consider their situation; never in the memory of court-gossip has there been so joyful and so astounding a piece of news to spread; they are over the edge of tears in the happy excitement and feel a noble, indeed a partly miraculous joy, for the oracle has been fulfilled; so far as they can they temper their tears with their wit. What could be a more delightful mixture of drollery and tenderness, or more in the best 'Metaphysical' manner than

'One of the prettiest touches of all and that which angled for mine eyes, caught the water though not the fish, was when, at the relation of the Queen's death, with the manner how she came to't gravely confessed and lamented by the King, how attentiveness wounded his daughter; till, from one sign of dolour to another, she did, with an "Alas", I would fain say, bleed tears, for I am sure my heart wept blood'.

Could Donne [Coghill asks] have found a better hyperbole than 'wounded', or Crashaw a more felicitous conceit for eyes and tears?

Coghill, I believe, is partly right and partly wrong. He is right in his general account of the tone of the scene; but he is wrong to compare the conceits to those of the metaphysicals. Although a study remains to be written on the influence of the Metaphysicals on Jacobean Drama, and of the influence of the dramatists on the Metaphysicals, the style of this scene is purely Arcadian. Compare, for example, the passage in which Sidney describes his heroine wounding the cloth with her needle. It was appropriate that Shakespeare should use the Arcadian style in this play, for his main

source, *Pandosto*, was one of Greene's best 'Arcadian' novels; and
it is significant that in the one play which used *Arcadia* as a source,
King Lear, Shakespeare should write in the Arcadian style, when
another anonymous gentleman describes the way in which
Cordelia receives the news of her father:

> Patience and sorrow strove
> Who should express her goodliest. You have seen
> Sunshine and rain at once; her smiles and tears
> Were like, a better way; those happy smilets
> That played on her ripe lip seemed not to know
> What guests were in her eyes; which parted thence,
> As pearls from diamonds dropped. In brief,
> Sorrow would be a rarity most beloved,
> If all could so become it.   (IV. iii. 18–26)

There are two other observations I should like to make on this
scene. First, beneath the artificial language, we can see careful
preparation for the final scene and hints of the symbolical meaning
of the play. When Leontes and Camillo, for example, are shown
the proofs of Perdita's parentage, 'they looked as they had heard
of a world ransomed, or one destroyed'. This links up with the
language of redemption in the last scene.

The other point I want to make has been discussed by Leslie
Bethell. The second gentleman says that 'such a deal of wonder is
broken out within this hour, that ballad-makers cannot be able to
express it. . . . This news (which is called true) is so like an old
tale, that the verity of it is in strong suspicion'. Later on the third
gentleman says 'Like an old tale still'. Bethell thinks this is a
deliberate attempt on Shakespeare's part to alienate the audience
in a Brechtian sense:[1]

Such internal comments upon the nature of a story always remind us of
its unreality, breaking through any illusion which may have been
created. Thus they combine with the deliberately old-fashioned technique to insist that it is after all only a dramatic performance that the
audience have before them.

I doubt whether this is true. When, after the murder of Caesar,
Brutus says:

> How many ages hence
> Shall this our lofty scene be acted o'er . . .

I do not think the illusion of reality is destroyed so that the audience are suddenly conscious that they are watching a play; and when Cleopatra is afraid that she will be represented on the stage, and that an actor will boy her greatness in the posture of a whore, Shakespeare risked this reminder of the stage because he knew that he had convinced his audience of Cleopatra's reality. In the same way, the continual references in *The Winter's Tale* to the incredible nature of the story have the paradoxical effect of undercutting the audience's scepticism.

IV

Our consideration of the last two scenes of *The Winter's Tale* should lead us to two main conclusions. In spite of the many crimes committed in Shakespeare's name during the past three hundred years by actors and producers, it is only fair to say that they sometimes demonstrate in performance that Shakespeare was wiser than his critics. The other conclusion I have not had time to develop. It is this: that Shakespeare, although he lived in the age of Spenser, never indulged in allegory as such; but nevertheless in many of his plays, and particularly in the last romances, there are allegorical undertones. It is impossible to believe that Shakespeare was writing these tragi-comedies merely to emulate the successes of Beaumont and Fletcher and Heywood. He was concerned with such basic human questions as the necessity of forgiveness; and I think there is no doubt that in *The Winter's Tale* he was attempting, among other things, to reinterpret the story of Proserpine. Perdita refers herself to the Proserpine story; she is playing the role of the goddess Flora in the sheep-shearing scene; she refers to Whitsun-pastorals; she is described by Leontes as a goddess, welcome as the Spring to the Earth.[2]

2. Cf. K. Muir, *Last Periods of Shakespeare, Racine and Ibsen* (1961), pp. 39 ff.

6

This Side Idolatry[1]

Ben Jonson told William Drummond of Hawthornden that 'Shakespeare wanted art'. A few years later, when he was invited to write a commendatory poem for the First Folio, he admitted not merely that Shakespeare equalled all the Greek and Latin dramatists rolled into one, but that he was not without art. His final verdict in *Discoveries* a year or two later was that Shakespeare ought to have revised his work. To the players who boasted that Shakespeare 'never blotted out line', Jonson retorted 'Would he had blotted a thousand!' Then he used the phrase which has provided me with a title: 'I lov'd the man, and doe honour his memory (on this side Idolatry) as much as any.' The parenthesis implies that even so early there was a Shakespeare cult; but during the next hundred years critics of Shakespeare were mainly concerned with his alleged lack of art and with the task of deciding which things in his work were admirable and which were to be deplored. Dryden's spokesman in the *Essay of Dramatic Poesy* confessed that he could not say of Shakespeare that he was everywhere alike: 'Were he so, I should do him injury to compare him with the greatest of mankind.' Elsewhere he complained of a number of faults and showed by his adaptation of *Troilus and Cressida* what he considered some of those to be.

Shakespeare's violation of the three unities came to be gradually accepted, although late in the eighteenth century Garrick rewrote *The Winter's Tale* so as to eliminate the fifteen-year break in the action. The critics found it more difficult to accept the mingling of tragedy and comedy and Pope tried to protect Shakespeare's reputation by rejecting as spurious the Porter's speeches in *Macbeth*. Dr. Johnson, however, defended the mingling of comedy and tragedy on the grounds that life itself has a similar mixture,

1. The Byron Memorial Lecture, delivered at the University of Nottingham, 24 October 1975.

in which, at the same time, the reveller is hasting to his wine, and the mourner burying his friend; in which the malignity of one is sometimes defeated by the frolick of another.

But Johnson balanced his splendidly phrased eulogy with the customary list of faults. These included a lack of moral purpose, the quibble, the fatal Cleopatra for which he lost the world and was content to lose it, and the frequent impropriety of his diction —not so much the indecencies as the unpoetical words which disfigure some of his most famous speeches—Lady Macbeth's blanket of the dark, the word 'peep', the epithet 'dunnest', and the butcher's implement 'knife', and Hamlet's bare bodkin with which he contemplated suicide. No one, I suppose, would now agree that Shakespeare's diction was mean; and we are suspicious of direct didacticism; but there are still many critics who deplore Shakespeare's puns—despite the fact that the Christian Church was founded with a pun.

After Johnson came the age of bardolatry, culminating in Coleridge. He demanded a reverential attitude from a critic of Shakespeare. He thought that Shakespeare wrote one detestable play, *Measure for Measure*, but generally speaking he was able to safeguard the poet's reputation by blaming interpolations on actors. The nicest example of this is to be found in his comments on the Porter's speech. He agreed with Pope that Shakespeare was not responsible for it; but observing that 'the primrose way to the everlasting bonfire' was too good for anyone but Shakespeare, he argued that the words were added by Shakespeare to the interpolation.

The bardolatry continued throughout the nineteenth century, although it was derided by Bernard Shaw, who pointed out that the actor-managers who paid lip-service to Shakespeare's perfection showed by their alterations that they thought he was a very incompetent dramatist. The bardolatry was also attacked at the beginning of the present century by a number of critics. Robert Bridges blamed the groundlings, those wretched beings (he called them) whose bad taste prevented the greatest of poets from becoming the greatest of artists. (When one considers that the most popular play of the Elizabethan period was *Hamlet*, and the longest-running play of our time is *The Mousetrap* one is hardly in a position to cast stones at Shakespeare's original audience.) Bridges complained of Shakespeare's obscenity, of his faulty characterization, of his huddled endings. Edgar Elmer Stoll similarly argued, but without condemning Shakespeare for it, that the Elizabethan theatre required exciting situations, but not consistency of characterization, and critics such as Bradley who regarded Shakespeare as a great psychological realist were reading subtleties into the plays which simply were not there.

This canter through what is now called the critical heritage, superficial and selective as it has inevitably been, reveals a disturbing fact: that each generation of critics levels new complaints against Shakespeare's plays, while the complaints of their predecessors come to seem unimportant, or are dropped altogether. That the complaints were ever made rebounds on the critics, as when Mr. Eliot spoke of *Hamlet* as certainly an artistic failure.

Take, for example, the alleged lack of poetic justice in Shakespeare's tragedies. To depict a world in which the good are always victorious and the innocent never suffer is to be guilty of sentimentality, satisfying to Miss Prism, who explained that in her novel, 'the good end happily and the bad unhappily: that is what fiction means'. Washington Irving apparently thought that Shakespeare was an author of this kind. When he visited Stratford-upon-Avon, he wrote 'Praised be the bard, who gilded the harsh realities of life with innocent illusions'—an odd eulogy for the author of *King Lear*. It would be nice to think that Cordelias are never hanged, that Macduff's family is not murdered, that Cressidas are not really unfaithful.

Dryden's complaint of Shakespeare's excessive use of metaphor must seem equally strange to a generation that has absorbed *The Wheel of Fire*, *Seven Types of Ambiguity*, the numerous studies of imagery, or indeed, read modern poetry and its apologists. Complaints about the structure of the plays have diminished ever since it was realized that they were written for a particular playhouse. There are few books of criticism which seem more dated than William Archer's *The Old Drama and the New*, in which he argued for the superiority of Pinero, Jones, and Galsworthy to all the dramatists of the sixteenth and seventeenth centuries.

I set out this evening to discuss Shakespeare's faults, and you may be feeling that I am trying to show that his faults were imaginary; but I am merely suggesting that we should take warning from the great critics of the past who have been so greatly mistaken and not condemn faults which our children will regard as merits.

I want, therefore, to consider the modern strategies which have been adopted to excuse Shakespeare's shortcomings. One method is to blame the conditions of the Elizabethan theatre, for which plays were hurriedly written, and often altered by the players; and, if they were published, disfigured by misprints, not all of which can be remedied. Another excuse, related to the first, is to suggest that Shakespeare inherited lines and motivations from source-plays: that *Hamlet*, for example, is a kind of palimpsest, with Kyd's crudities showing through Shakespeare's final conceptions. But surely, it is as much to be deplored in a dramatist if he incorporates crude work by others, as if he writes it himself. By using source-material, he made himself responsible for it.

The favourite defence, however, of Shakespeare's shortcomings in recent years has been that the plays were scripts to be performed, not poems to be read; and that discrepancies brought to light in the study are entirely irrelevant to a consideration of the dramatic quality of the plays. There is some justification for this line of defence. The plays *were* written to be performed; and they come alive only in the theatre, where actors, for better or worse, provide an extra dimension. It is true, too, that for the last two hundred and fifty years the novel has superseded the drama as the most popular form of literature, and the novel, on the whole, is more naturalistic than poetic drama; but we should not demand of a play, even from a prose play by Ibsen, the same kind of verisimilitude we expect from a novel by Jane Austen or George Eliot. We cannot stop a scene to check whether what has been said in Act II conflicts with something uttered in Act I. The tape is irreversible. Nevertheless I am a little uneasy with this apologia for Shakespeare's flaws. Once the plays were published, and half of his plays were published in his lifetime, they ceased to be merely theatrical scripts: and once an officious editor has called attention to discrepancies, all undergraduates and most schoolchildren will be aware of them.

As Maurice Morgann properly insisted, 'we have no right to call upon Shakespeare for explanations upon points which he means to obscure'; but we ought to distinguish, or attempt to distinguish, between deliberate and unintentional obscurities and discrepancies.

In considering Shakespeare's shortcomings we ought to distinguish the plays he wrote before the age of thirty, and those he wrote afterwards. He was a late developer. Whereas the plays of Marlowe, Congreve, and Sheridan were all written in their twenties, Shakespeare's important work was still to come when he reached the age of thirty. It is easy to point to immaturities in the plays written before that date. Some of the weaknesses, indeed, may be due to the gap of thirty-five years between performance and publication of some of the plays. Prompt-books may be altered to suit the persistent substitutions by actors; scenes may be rewritten for revivals in the middle of rehearsals; some pages may be devoured by rats or made illegible by an overturned tankard. Other weaknesses may be due to the inefficiencies of collaboration. I believe that Shakespeare was wholly responsible for the second and third parts of *Henry VI*, but I think that a single author can hardly have written Part I, for there are some scenes which appear to be written in ignorance of others. If one looks at the various references to Falstaff's cowardice—not the Falstaff of *Henry IV* but his namesake—it is obvious that two dramatists were writing independently, and unknown to each other, of the same incident.

In *The Two Gentlemen of Verona*, there are some minor confusions which could easily have been cleared up. Its latest editor, Clifford Leech, lists some forty questionable points, most of which pass unnoticed in performance. But it is disturbing to have the two gentlemen travelling from Verona to Milan, and for characters then to speak of Milan as Verona and Padua. Much more serious—and the reason why this otherwise charming comedy is seldom revived—is the preposterous denouement. Proteus, you will remember, having been repulsed by Silvia, attempts to rape her; Valentine who loves her arrives in the nick of time to save her from a fate worse than death; Proteus says he is sorry; whereupon Valentine offers to hand over the woman he loves to the man she detests. If the scene is meant to be a serious treatment of the rival claims of love and friendship, it is absurdly ineffective, since Silvia is not consulted; if it is meant to exemplify the duty of forgiveness, it is equally absurd, since Proteus's repentance is perfunctory; and if it is meant to satirize the two gentlemen, the satire misfires. It is difficult to believe that any tolerably good poet (which even his enemies would allow Shakespeare to be) could perpetrate Valentine's couplets, before and after Proteus's speech of repentance:

> The private wound is deepest. O time most accurst!
> Mongst all foes that a friend should be the worst!
> PROT. My shame and guilt confounds me.
> Forgive me Valentine; if hearty sorrow
> Be a sufficient ransom for offence,
> I tender't here; I do as truly suffer
> As e'er I did commit.
> VAL.   Then I am paid;
> And once again I do receive thee honest.
> Who by repentance is not satisfied
> Is nor of heaven nor of earth, for these are pleas'd;
> By penitence th'Eternal's wrath's appeas'd.
> And, that my love may appear plain and free,
> All that was mine in Silvia I give thee.

Whereupon Julia, not unnaturally, swoons; and Silvia is stricken dumb. These lines would have been on the last page of the prompt-book and one would like to think it had been damaged, and that someone other than Shakespeare tried to repair what Racine called the irreparable ravages of time.

A different sort of problem may be illustrated from another early comedy. In some ways *The Comedy of Errors* is masterly; it is much more ingenious than the Plautine comedy on which it is based. But editors have been worried by the ages of the twins. We learn in the first scene that Antipholus of Syracuse had left home at the age of eighteen, and that his father had been travelling for five years since that time. In the last scene, however, the father says that it is seven years since they parted: in other words two years elapsed between Antipholus's departure and his own. This would make the twins twenty-five years of age. In the same scene the Duke declares that he has been patron to Antipholus of Ephesus for twenty years, and it is mentioned that he had been brought to Ephesus by the uncle of the Duke, and there is nothing to suggest that he was only an infant at the time. When the two Antipholuses are reunited to their mother, she says:

> Thirty-three years have I but gone in travail
> Of you, my sons.

If one adds nine months of actual pregnancy to the twenty-five years of the sons' age, one still gets only twenty-six; yet the thirty-three years suit the Duke's testimony, since he would have become Antipholus's patron, not when he was five, but when he was thirteen.

I doubt whether this discrepancy has ever been noticed in the theatre: the action is too swift to allow such calculations. It is probable that Shakespeare knew what he was doing, and that he wished to achieve particular effects in the two contexts. In the first scene it was important for us to believe that Antipholus went in search of his twin as soon as he reasonably could, and therefore eighteen years of age was more suitable than twenty-six. In the last scene it was necessary to stress the length of time the Duke had known Antipholus of Ephesus, and twenty years was better than twelve. This meant that Æmilia's 'travail' had to be extended to thirty-three years.

Shakespeare's early plays are not seriously damaged by flaws of this kind. What does damage them, at least in comparison with his later work, is that he had not yet learnt to differentiate one character from another, not by what they *do*, or even by what they *say*, but by how they say it. It is often said that if all the speech-prefixes were lost, it would still be possible to allocate the speeches to the right characters. This is perhaps partially true of the mature plays, such as *Twelfth Night* or *Hamlet*, but it is manifestly untrue of the early comedies and histories. It is comparatively easy to differentiate the style of characters who speak in prose, as Launce and Speed are beautifully distinguished in the *Two Gentlemen of Verona*. It is much more difficult in verse; and the effect of the comparatively regular verse of the early plays is to make everyone talk alike. In *Henry VI*, for example, lords and ladies, kings and commoners, servants and masters, adopt the same style, and it is a style which is too far removed from the language actually used by men. This does not matter in epic poetry, but it is fatal to drama. We get the impression that actors are declaiming eloquent speeches, not that the characters are talking or thinking. Take, for example, these lines from *2 Henry VI*:

> The gaudy, blabbing, and remorseful day
> Is crept into the bosom of the sea;
> And now loud-howling wolves arouse the jades
> That drag the tragic melancholy night;
> Who with their drowsy, slow, and flagging wings
> Clip dead men's graves, and from their misty jaws
> Breathe foul contagious darkness in the air.

The words are spoken by a sea-captain, but there is nothing in the language to characterize the speaker. One is relieved when in the very next scene the deplorable Jack Cade comes on to speak his racy prose:

There shall be in England seven halfpenny loaves sold for a penny; the three-hooped pot shall have ten hoops; and I will make it a felony to drink small beer. All the realm shall be in common, and in Cheapside shall my palfrey go to grass.

I am not suggesting, as so many critics have done, that the fault of the early plays is that they are rhetorical and that Shakespeare was converted from the use of rhetoric, as Berowne forswore 'taffeta phrases, silken terms precise'. Nothing could be further from the truth. To the end of his career, Shakespeare continued to use all the resources of rhetoric, but in his later plays he used them with the art which (we are told) conceals art.

Already in *3 Henry VI*, Shakespeare had evolved a characteristic style for the most dynamic and evil of his early characters, Richard, Duke of Gloucester. Any actor playing the part has merely to follow the score. In the plays which followed more and more characters are individualized. The contrast between the styles of Richard II and Bolingbroke in the abdication scenes, or the contrast between the verse of Oberon and Titania and that of Theseus and Hippolyta in *A Midsummer Night's Dream* (somewhat blurred in Brook's brilliant production because he doubled the parts) are examples of Shakespeare's increasing skill in this respect. At about the same time, perhaps in the same year, he created Mercutio and Juliet's Nurse. The Nurse was the most significant advance, for in her first appearance she speaks in verse so natural and colloquial, and so garrulous, that the compositor printed it as prose.

These three plays, *Richard II*, *A Midsummer Night's Dream*, and *Romeo and Juliet*, are particularly interesting because alongside scenes which everyone admires, there are other scenes which have been variously deplored. English audiences, despite the heroic drama of the seventeenth century which was never more than a minority taste, have always been rendered acutely uncomfortable by rhymed verse. But we should remember that in 1595 rhyme was not yet a lost cause; Sidney's sister approved of it; blank verse could still be regarded as an innovation; Shakespeare had written three narrative poems and numerous sonnets in stanza form. Yet critics would like to believe that Shakespeare was not responsible for the rhyming scenes, or that if he was, they were written long before and were unwisely retained when the play was revised. One such scene is the one in the last act of *Richard II* when Aumerle gallops to court to beg pardon for his treason, pursued by his father who begs for his execution, pursued in turn by his mother, who begs for his forgiveness. It is certainly difficult to take the scene seriously. The henpecked York, praying for the death of his son, the Duchess praying for his pardon, and all three kneeling to Bolingbroke, make a farcical scene, and the farce is underlined by the rhyming:

DUCH. Say 'Pardon' King; let pity teach thee how.
The word is short, but not so short as sweet.
No word like Pardon for kings' mouths so meet.
YORK. Speak it in French, King; say *pardonne moy*.
DUCH. Dost thou teach pardon, pardon to destroy?
Speak pardon as tis current in our land;
The chopping French we do not understand.

Shakespeare, I presume, could not help noticing the element of absurdity in Holinshed's account of this episode; and he may have wished to use it for comic relief. But even when it is played for laughs, as it was at Stratford last year, the audience seemed somewhat embarrassed. We must write it down as one of Shakespeare's mistakes.

Some of the rhyming in *A Midsummer Night's Dream* is equally controversial, since a good poet (De La Mare) and a famous editor (Dover Wilson) have both argued that some of the dialogue of the lovers was written earlier than the rest of the play, and probably written by another poet. At least Shakespeare was guilty of incorporating the feeble lines in his own play. But these passages in Act III (to which Dover Wilson refers) should not be considered in isolation, but in connection with other rhymed passages in the play—the ritualistic stichomythia in the first scene gives place at the end to Helena's rhymed couplets which have the effect of making Helena's love faintly absurd, as Edith Evans in the 1920s and Vanessa Redgrave in the 1960s both appreciated. All the passages in III. 2. to which exception has been taken are spoken after Puck has begun to anoint the eyes of the lovers. The awkward rhyming suggests that they are bewildered puppets, manipulated by Puck:

> Do not say so, Lysander, say not so.
> What though he love your Hermia? Lord, what though?
>
> Alack, where are you? Speak, an if you hear;
> Speak, of all loves! I swoon almost with fear.
>
> No? Then I well perceive you are not nigh.
> Either death or you I'll find immediately.

In most recent productions of the play, the actors have extracted plenty of fun from the bad rhymes, and if (which I doubt) the lines were written earlier than the rest of the play, Shakespeare may have seen how their crudity could be turned to good account, as the badness of the Pyramus and Thisbe playlet is part of the fun.

A scene in *Romeo and Juliet* which everyone deplores is the one where Juliet's apparently lifeless body is discovered, and four characters indulge in a ritual lament:

NURSE. She's dead, deceased, she's dead, alack the day!
LADY C. Alack the day, she's dead, she's dead, she's dead!
NURSE. O woe! O woeful, woeful, woeful day!
Most lamentable day, most woeful day,
That ever, ever I did yet behold!
O day! O day! O day! O hateful day!
Never was seen so black a day as this:
O woeful day, O woeful day!
CAP. O child! O child! my soul, and not my child!
Dead art thou! Alack, my child is dead;
And with my child my joys are buried!

It has been suggested that as the audience knew that Juliet was not really dead, it would have been wrong to arouse their grief at this point; and that to have done so would have detracted from her actual death-scene. That doubtless is why the emotion of the characters was distanced in this ritual mourning. But, unfortunately, the lines remind us of Pyramus and Thisbe. Perhaps, as Charles B. Lower has recently argued, the characters should speak all together.

Less excusable are the lines Romeo speaks when he is banished. He complains that carrion flies may touch Juliet's hand:

This flies may do, when I from this must fly.

This is the kind of line that gives puns a bad name.

After 1595, we do not meet this kind of badness in Shakespeare's work, although there are lapses even in some of his best plays. *The Tempest*, for example, is so magnificent as a whole, that we ignore some intermittent patches of bad writing. In the last scene, Prospero is given these lines to speak, if he can:

> at pick'd leisure,
> Which shall be shortly, single I'll resolve you,
> Which to you shall seem probable, of every
> These happen'd accidents; till when, be cheerful
> And think of each thing well.

If we came upon such lines in the writing of any other dramatist, should we not deplore the contorted and unnatural syntax? It cannot be explained, as some of the extraordinary speeches of Leontes can, as being a deliberate and successful means of showing the conflict in the mind of a character.

Some of the most interesting attacks on Shakespeare in the present century have been concerned with his characterization. It has been argued by Stoll and others that Elizabethan dramatists were not bothered by the need to make their characters consistent, that their integrity was always subordinated to the demands of the plot. This line was a natural reaction against the subtle analysis of A. C. Bradley, which (Stoll argued) was alien to the spirit and conditions of the Elizabethan theatre. Stoll is, I believe, very nearly right:

> Oh, the little more, and how much it is!
> And the little less, and what worlds away!

Let us, then, consider a handful of places where Shakespeare's characterization has been called in question. The first is the character of Margaret in *Much Ado About Nothing*. She is Hero's waiting-gentlewoman, whose conversation with Borachio leads to Hero's repudiation in church. Why does she allow herself to be called by Hero's name? What kind of explanation could Borachio have used to persuade her? Why does she not attend the marriage of her mistress? Obviously she could not attend the ceremony without bringing the play to a premature conclusion. But, apart from this, it is difficult to reconcile the Margaret whom we see on the stage with a woman who apparently dotes on Borachio. In the last act of the play Borachio swears that she

> Knew not what she did when she spoke to me,
> But always hath been just and virtuous
> In anything that I do know by her.

Leonato says that

> Margaret was in some fault for this,
> Although against her will, as it appears
> In the true course of all the question.

Kirschbaum, not surprisingly, called these lines 'meaningless verbiage'. Borachio had promised that Don Pedro and Claudio would 'see me at her chamber window, hear me call Margaret Hero, hear Margaret term me Claudio'. Why on earth should Margaret be persuaded to call Borachio Claudio? The difficulty may not be noticed in the theatre, but it is clear that Margaret's character has been sacrificed to the demands of the plot. It would not do to have Margaret an accomplice in the plot against Hero's honour, so she has to engage blindly in an improbable and unexplained charade. Yet in the rest of the play she is witty and sensible, unlikely to be attracted by a drunkard, and far too shrewd to fall in with his plans.

Improbabilities with minor characters in comedies do not greatly detract from our enjoyment of the play, as a guilty and punished Margaret would; but what of improbabilities which undermine the credibility of a tragedy? Ever since Rymer called *Othello* a bloody farce, there have been critics to point out its deficiencies. There are, we are told, two major flaws. As Desdemona and Cassio travel to Cyprus on different boats, and Othello's marriage is not consummated until the night after he and Desdemona arrive in Cyprus, Cassio and Desdemona could not have committed adultery. It is absurd for Iago to pretend that they had done, and Othello must have been insane to believe it. The other flaw is that Iago's plot depends on a series of lucky chances—that Desdemona drops the handkerchief, that Bianca arrives at the crucial moment—and on improbable psychology: that Emilia would not confess earlier that she had picked up the handkerchief, that Othello would not accuse Desdemona openly and give her a chance of clearing herself. Stoll adds that the noble

Othello of Act I would never become the jealous maniac of Act III.

Must we agree with Byron, who remarked in a letter 'I do not think Shakespeare without the grossest faults'? Or is it possible to put forward a reasonable defence, at least in this case? We may dismiss Stoll's complaint that the Othello of Act I is not the sort of man to become a jealous maniac, because this (in a sense) is the point of the play. How does a noble hero come to kill the wife he loves? The greater the contrast between the man and his actions the more tragic, and the more intense, the action is likely to be. The same thing is true of Macbeth. Shaw described Macbeth as a literary gentleman, rather like Shakespeare himself, who would never have committed a murder. But nineteenth-century ideas about human behaviour seem now somewhat naive, more naive than the writers on psychology known to Shakespeare, Dr. Timothy Bright, for example, or that great self-analyser, Montaigne.

For the same reason we may dismiss the accusation that in real life the jealous husband would have confronted his wife with the evidence, or that a woman who had stolen from her mistress would confess to her misdeed, as soon as she realized that it was the cause of the husband's jealousy. But these charges are, of course, less important than the obvious fact that Cassio and Desdemona could not have committed adultery. The answer, I think, is that Iago's original suggestion is not that they had committed adultery, but that they had had a love-affair in Venice at the time when Othello was wooing Desdemona, and Cassio was acting as a go-between. Only when Othello has been hooked, when he is no longer able to reason, does Iago invent the dream and mention the handkerchief. His temptation is geared to the victim's receptivity.

In any case the audience is cunningly confused about the time scheme. On the one hand, the action seems to be extremely rapid, with Desdemona murdered less than two days after the consummation of her marriage; on the other hand, there are indications of a much longer time having elapsed. Bianca claims that Cassio has not visited her for a week; and news of the dispersal of the Turkish fleet has to travel to Venice, and Lodovico has then to sail from Venice to Cyprus.

This device of double-time (as it has been called) was never noticed by audiences until it was pointed out to them. It could be regarded as a fault only by those who have been steeped in the heresy of naturalism—either because poetic drama was out of fashion, or because naturalistic methods of staging made it easier to spot violations of verisimilitude. (Bernard Shaw never made this kind of mistake; and his attacks on bardolatry were accompanied by a keen appreciation of what Shakespeare did provide—which was a good deal closer to opera than to the novel.)

Of course Iago is a stage-villain; but as a posthumous book by Stanley Hyman made abundantly clear, we can find in the text of the play plenty of evidence that Iago was also a Satanic figure, choosing evil as his good, and hating Othello and Desdemona for their goodness. We can also find evidence that he is motivated by professional jealousy, that he is a malcontent, that he wants to infect Othello with the jealousy from which he himself suffers, and even that he is in love with Desdemona. This multiplication of personae, far from making Iago seem unreal, is a means of impressing his three-dimensional reality on an audience.

It is nearly always possible to find reasonable explanations—not excuses, but justifications—of the points of dramaturgy which have been most criticized. It is no longer necessary to defend *Cymbeline* against the charge brought against it by Dr. Johnson that it displayed unresisting imbecility, for everyone now realizes that the extraordinary mixture of legendary Britain with ancient Rome and renaissance Italy, of pastoralism and folk-lore with Holinshed and Boccaccio (with some references to James I's foreign policy and the Tudor settlement thrown in for good measure) was designed to prevent us from looking for historical verisimilitude, when the poet's purpose was quite other.

No-one now imagines that Shakespeare was careless in transposing Sicilia and Bohemia in *The Winter's Tale*, thus crediting Bohemia with a coast-line; for Princess Elizabeth and her betrothed, the ruler of Bohemia, were in his original audience. If this was madness, there was method in it.

No-one now, no-one we are likely to meet, expresses concern at Shakespeare's anachronisms. They are either very trivial (such as the clock in *Julius Caesar*) or they are deliberately introduced to make his audience see the relevance of a historical event set in the remote past. T. S. Eliot, who lacked most qualities necessary for the writing of satisfactory plays, made *Murder in the Cathedral* much more interesting than Tennyson's play on the same subject, because he made the audience realize, by the rather crude speeches of the knights at the end of the play, that they could not shrug off the murder of Becket as something that happened in the distant past. Elizabethans and Jacobeans were very ready to see contemporary significance, even where none was intended: Haywood was carpetted for his prose history of Henry IV, the unfortunate Daniel got into similar trouble for *Philotas*, Greville burnt his play on Antony and Cleopatra, and the Essex conspirators foolishly believed that a subsidized performance of *Richard II* would be useful propaganda for their cause.

Shakespeare was not interested in writing of 'old forgotten far-off things / And battles long ago'. The Scottish king-killer was made relevant to a Jacobean audience because one of his victims was the ancestor of James I, but much more by the current interest in demonology, and by its reminders of the Gunpowder Plot—what a character calls 'dire combustion'—and the trials that followed, notably of the equivocator who could not equivocate to heaven.

I would like, finally, to consider objections to the so-called problem plays, which still find hostile critics. We need not take too seriously the objections to their obscenity: the City fathers of Oxford who tried to ban a performance of *Measure for Measure*; the Vicar of Stratford who protested about a performance at the Memorial Theatre; the lady who wrote to *The Gloucestershire Echo* to say that her sense of decency and cleanliness were outraged by the play, though (as she claimed) 'I am no prude'; and, as late as 1937, the Vicar of Buxton who objected to a performance in the town because the play was 'disfigured by a persistent and exaggerated use of the sex motive'. In all these cases, as in similar complaints of *Troilus and Cressida*, the critics were offended by a more realistic treatment of sex than in the romantic comedies.

A more serious complaint is that we cannot be sure how we ought to take the plays. In *All's Well*, the nominal hero is so dreadful that we cannot believe that Helena's prize was worth having. Moreover his lines of repentance are perfunctory and feeble. When he realizes that he has been tricked into fathering Helena's child, he says:

> If she, my liege, can make me know this clearly,
> I'll love her dearly, ever, ever dearly.

Shakespeare never wrote worse than this, even in his prentice days.

And there are serious criticisms which can be levelled against *Measure for Measure*, notably that the first half of the play is one of Shakespeare's finest achievements, and the reader, if not the spectator, feels let down in the second half, which is mostly in prose.

There are, however, two criticisms which are often made of *Measure for Meassure* which I do not regard as valid.

1. That parts of it are more or less allegorical, or parabolic; and other parts are extremely naturalistic, and the two parts do not blend. Sometimes we think of the Duke as a representative of the Deity, and at other times as an interfering busybody, vain, touchy, and deceitful, who chooses as his deputy a man he knows to be a hypocrite. Sometimes we think of Isabella as a saint, and sometimes, as she has been alliteratively described, as a 'Pietist in her religion, a Pedant in her talk, a Prude in her notions, and a Prig in her conduct'.

It seems to me important that we should keep our minds suspended between the two interpretations, that the ambiguity was intentional, and that we should condemn those directors who try to make things easier for us by suppressing the evidence that conflicts with their chosen interpretation, as for example in the last three productions of the play at Stratford.

2. The other stumbling-block in both *Measure for Measure* and *All's Well* is the bed-trick, the substitution of one woman for another in a man's bed without his knowledge. We may pass over the well-authenticated cases in real life because (as Aristotle implies) art should be more probable than life.

The bed-trick is a means of showing symbolically the blindness of the sexual instinct, the way in which (as Helena puts it)

> lust doth play
> With what it loathes for that which is away.

(I am reminded of Dr. Johnson's remark, on the only occasion when he talked to Boswell about sexual intercourse: 'Were it not for imagination, Sir, a man would be as happy in the arms of a Chambermaid as of a Duchess')—in the arms of Helena as of Diana, in the arms of Mariana as of Isabella. In *Measure for Measure* the bed-trick is used with greater subtlety. Mariana's consent to take Isabella's place has the effect of saving Isabella and of redeeming Angelo. But it is also the climax of several substitutions, some of them gratuitous. It is first proposed to execute

Barnardine and send his head in place of Claudio's; but when Barnardine refuses to oblige, Ragozine (who has conveniently died in prison) provides the necessary head, and the Duke exclaims:

> O! 'tis an accident that heaven provides!

It has been suggested that if the part of the Duke was played by Shakespeare himself, the audience would appreciate that it was an accident provided not by God, but by the dramatist. The introduction of a second substitute was not because Barnardine had endeared himself to his creator, but simply to call attention to the theme of substitution. And, as James Black has pointed out, there is a reference by Isabella to the central substitution of her faith:

> Why, all the souls that were, were forfeit once,
> And he that might the vantage best have took,
> Found out the remedy.

Of course the bed-trick was an integral part of the plot of *All's Well*, and necessary to the plot of *Measure for Measure* if it was to be a play about forgiveness rather than a tragedy; but as so often Shakespeare made a virtue of necessity.

I set out to lecture on Shakespeare's faults. I came to bury Shakespeare not to praise him; but, as you will have noticed, I have ended by acting for the defence. Indeed, I must confess that Dr. Johnson's remark that Shakespeare never wrote six consecutive lines without some fault or other seems to me to be absurd; and that in producing his plays I have always come to regret the cuts and alterations I have made in the brashness of youth or the vanity of age.

Of course there are numerous imperfections in Shakespeare's plays: some of them due to the way the texts have been transmitted, some to the terrifying pressures of a repertory theatre, and some to inexperience, not merely of Shakespeare himself, but of all the playwrights of the 1590s. But all great writers sacrifice certain perfections, as a chess-master sacrifices his queen to win a game.

The art of the dramatist—apart from some technical accomplishments not too difficult to acquire, if we judge by those popular playwrights who do acquire them—lies in his power of becoming all his characters, from hero to second gentleman, from grandee to grave-digger. He convinces us of the reality of his characters not merely by finding a style and an idiom to suit each one, not merely by a super-ventriloquism, but by setting going in our minds contradictory impressions, so that there is an apparent opposition between our rational understanding of a scene, or a character, and what we are made to feel about them. This, you will remember, is one of Maurice Morgann's points. Everyone recognizes the difference between Macbeth's outward actions and his inner life; and the whole play of *Hamlet* depends on a similar contrast: between the man who lugs the guts of Polonius off stage, and the man who soliloquizes.

It is, of course, absurd to discuss those aspects of a character which the poet deliberately left in obscurity—what, to take an improbable example, was the subject of Hamlet's postgraduate study at the University of Wittenberg. It was this kind of illegitimate curiosity that led to the spoof title 'How many children had Lady Macbeth?' But it is nevertheless true that the intense reality of Shakespeare's principal characters is such, that we are made to feel that we know them more intimately than we do our own friends. Max Beerbohm, writing on *Hamlet*, remarked that

To his acquaintances a man may seem to be this or that kind of man, quite definitely. That is only because they know so little about him. To his intimate friends he is rather a problem. To himself he is an insoluble problem.

As Morgann says, when Shakespeare makes a character act or speak from traits which have not actually been portrayed, but which we can infer, this seems to carry us beyond the poet to nature itself. 'A felt propriety and truth from causes unseen I take to be the highest point of poetic composition.'

7

Some Freudian Interpretations of Shakespeare[1]

In a general survey of the Shakespearian criticism of the present century,[2] I touched briefly on psychoanalytical interpretations of Shakespeare; and in introductions to *Macbeth*[3] and *King Lear* I have referred to Freud's interpretations of those plays. I propose in this essay to consider the main contributions of Freud and his followers to the criticism of Shakespeare, and to offer some general observations on the validity of such criticism.

Freud himself made several brief excursions into the field of Shakespearian criticism. As early as 1900 he suggested that the Oedipus complex was the cause of Hamlet's delay:[4]

Hamlet is able to do anything but take vengeance upon the man who did away with his father and has taken his father's place with his mother —the man who shows him in realisation the repressed desires of his own childhood. The loathing which should have driven him to revenge is thus replaced by self-reproach, by conscientious scruples, which tell him that he himself is no better than the murderer he is required to punish.

Freud goes on to claim that 'it can, of course, be only the poet's own psychology with which we are confronted in *Hamlet*'. These hints were afterwards expanded by Ernest Jones in *The Problem of Hamlet and the Oedipus Complex* (1911), in *Hamlet and Oedipus* (1949), and in his edition of the play.

Jones argues that Hamlet's repression of infantile Oedipus wishes arouses unconscious resistances against the killing of Claudius, and that he cannot 'bring himself to take action against

1. *Proceedings of the Leeds Philosophical and Literary Society* (1952).
2. *Shakespeare Survey 4* (1951).
3. p. lxvi.
4. *The Basic Writings of S. Freud*, ed. A. A. Brill (N.Y., 1938), p. 310.

the man whose crime coincides with his own unconscious wishes'. He cannot kill his uncle without killing himself; and he is only able to kill his uncle when he knows his own end is near, and when, as his mother is dead, his action is disinterested. Hamlet's behaviour throughout the play is suicidal:[5]

The course of alternate action and inaction that he embarks on, and the provocations he gives to his suspicious uncle, can lead to no other end than to his own ruin.

When Hamlet says that he is prompted to his revenge by heaven and hell, he means, unconsciously perhaps, that he wants to kill Claudius as a hated rival, as well as the murderer of his father. He may rather be alluding to the possibility that his father's spirit was the Devil in disguise.

Jones goes on to suggest that the only other way out of Hamlet's dilemma is for him to kill his mother; and he has to caution himself before going to the interview with Gertrude not to be a Nero, to 'speak daggers to her, but use none'.

Lastly, Jones argues that Hamlet's Oedipus complex is a reflection of Shakespeare's own. He quotes Ella Freeman Sharpe's remark that 'the poet is not Hamlet. Hamlet is what he might have been if he had not written the play.' He repeats Freud's suggestion that Shakespeare rewrote *Hamlet* 'while he was still under the influence of the thoughts stirred by his father's death'.[6] He points out traces of the Oedipus situation in other plays, notably in *Julius Caesar* and *Coriolanus*. He discusses the significance of the story of the *Sonnets* and of the alterations made by Shakespeare in the Hamlet story:[7]

When the double betrayal by his friend and his mistress broke over him like a thunder-cloud he was unable to deal with it by any action, but it aroused the slumbering associations in his mind, and he responded by creating Hamlet, who expressed for him what he could not express for himself—his sense of horror and failure. In this transformation Shakespeare exactly reversed the plot of the tragedy.

Whatever we may think of such speculations about Shakespeare's life, the Freudian theory of *Hamlet* is an attractive one,

5. Jones, op. cit., p. 88.
6. But Freud came to believe that Shakespeare was not the author of the plays.
7. Op. cit., pp. 155–6.

more attractive certainly than the clinical terms used by Jones to describe Hamlet's state: 'a severe case of hysteria on a cyclothymic basis'. It goes far to explain the impression that the play has made on purely literary critics, and it seems to have been the basis of T. S. Eliot's essay[8] in which he complained that

Hamlet, like the sonnets, is full of some stuff that the writer could not drag to light, contemplate, or manipulate into art.

Even C. S. Lewis's theory, that Hamlet is a kind of Everyman, may find some support from the Freudian interpretation, for, as Jones himself admits,[9] the conflict in *Hamlet* 'is an echo of a similar one in Shakespeare himself, *as indeed it is to a greater or lesser extent with all men*'.

Here, perhaps, is the key to the whole problem. Shakespeare, being a dramatist to his fingertips, was able to utilize and magnify the infantile Oedipus wishes which are common to us all. In real life and in an ordinary man such repressed wishes would doubtless reflect an unresolved Oedipus complex; but as they have been segregated and intensified by the poet for the purposes of his play, we cannot assume that he himself suffered from the neurosis he depicted in his hero. There are other plays as great as *Hamlet*, though Jones regards it as his masterpiece; and it is clear that *Macbeth, Othello, King Lear* cannot be explained in terms of the Oedipus complex, and would give us no hint that Shakespeare suffered from it.

Frederic Wertham's *Dark Legend* (1946) is a remarkably well-written book about a boy of nineteen in a New York slum, who murdered his mother by stabbing her thirty-two times with a bread-knife. She had taken several lovers after her husband's death, including the boy's uncle, but the crime was not committed until some years later when she had turned over a new leaf. Wertham shows that Gino did not really kill his mother as a punishment for her sins, as he had imagined at the time, but because he felt that she had been false to him. He had little temptation to kill any of her lovers; and from the fact that his feelings of guilt were actually lifted by the crime, Wertham assumes that the repressed incestuous feelings were more terrible to the boy than matricide itself. Gino found it difficult to tell his mother what he

8. *Selected Essays* (1932), p. 144.
9. Jones, op. cit., p. 101.

thought of her, as his intelligence was rather below average, and as he was proud of his obedience to her: 'I took her life away; but no one can say I ever disobeyed her.'

Wertham compares Gino with Hamlet, who could unpack his heart with words and speak daggers to his mother, but use none. He argues that both the boy and Hamlet suffered from an Orestes complex. The characteristics of this complex are excessive attachment to the mother image, and hostility towards the mother image (as revealed in the closet scene), a general hatred of women (as displayed in the Nunnery scene), homosexual potentialities as displayed in his attitude to Horatio, ideas of suicide as revealed in the soliloquies, and emotional disorder based on profound feelings of guilt:

O what a rogue and peasant slave am I!
What should such fellows as I do crawling between earth and heaven?

Wertham's most effective evidence is to be found in the third act of the play. Just before the scene with his mother, Hamlet exclaims:

> Now could I drink hot blood,
> And do such bitter business as the day
> Would quake to look on.

Then he pulls himself up, and continues:

> O heart, lose not thy nature, let not ever
> The soul of Nero enter this firm bosom;
> Let me be cruel, not unnatural—
> I will speak daggers to her, but use none.

Nero, of course, murdered his mother; and it is revealing that Hamlet has to caution himself not to be guilty of matricide. Immediately afterwards, Hamlet finds Claudius praying; and just as Gino had refrained from killing his uncle on the excuse that he could not fire the gun because of the safety-catch, so Hamlet spares his uncle on the excuse that he did not want to send him to heaven by killing him at his prayers. Commenting on the closet-scene Wertham asserts that

it is an unavoidable psychological conclusion that the torrent of erotic pictures which Hamlet hurls at his mother indicate unconscious fantasies on his own part in which he is not only the accusing spectator, but also the active participant.

Wertham seizes with avidity on a later passage, where Hamlet says to his uncle, 'Farewell, dear mother'. He assumes that this is a slip which reveals the unconscious mind of the Prince. It may equally well be a piece of feigned madness; for Hamlet's explanation seems to be the motive of his remark rather than a forced explanation to explain a slip of the tongue.[1]

According to Jones,[2] Wertham has since withdrawn from his position that Hamlet's matricidal impulses were the sole explanation of his dilemma:

Actually matricidal impulses ... always prove to emanate from the Oedipus complex ... for which they are an attempted solution.

But this seems to be implied in Wertham's book.

Both Jones and Wertham have written books which are learned and intelligent. Jones in particular seems to have read everything that has ever been written about the play, and his criticisms of his predecessors are often excellent. Here and there he relies too much on romantic biographies; but he builds up an astonishingly good case. It is only when we recollect that Coleridge's Hamlet was very like Coleridge, Murry's was very like Murry, Schopenhauer's like Schopenhauer, C. S. Lewis's prince weighed down by the burden of original sin as we might expect from the author of *The Screwtape Letters*, that we are apt to wonder whether it is an accident that the disciple of Freud should diagnose an Oedipus complex and that the propagandist for the Orestes complex should find one in Hamlet.

Freud stresses the importance of the theme of childlessness in *Macbeth*.[3] There is only one way by which the hero can disprove the prophecy relating to Banquo, namely, to have children himself who can reign after him. At first he expects them, as in his injunc-

---

1. Jones (op. cit., p. 99) makes a similar comment on this passage. Wertham and Jones both believe that Hamlet's words to Ophelia, 'Those that are married already, all but one, shall live' are not a threat to the eavesdropping King, but an involuntary threat to Gertrude. Wertham is guilty of one or two slips. He declares that until the Fortinbras scene Hamlet always mentions the sexual guilt of his mother first, and his father's murder second; but in the soliloquy at the end of Act II there is an attack on Claudius, but no reference to Gertrude. Hamlet does not speak of his mother's incestuous pleasure, but of his uncle's.

2. Op. cit., p. 98.

3. *Collected Papers*, iv (1934), pp. 328 ff.

tion to his wife before the murder of Duncan to bring forth men children only;[4] but by the first scene of the third act, Macbeth reveals in a key soliloquy that his motive for murdering Banquo is the fact that his own childlessness will lead to the fulfilment of the prophecy with regard to Banquo's heirs.[5] Macduff's words, 'He has no children', 'lay bare the essential motive' which forces Macbeth to violate his own nature by indiscriminate murder. Freud suggests that

It would be a perfect example of poetic justice in the manner of the talion if the childlessness of Macbeth and the barrenness of his Lady were the punishment for their crimes against the sanctity of geniture— if Macbeth could not become a father because he had robbed children of their father and a father of his children, and if Lady Macbeth had suffered the unsexing she had demanded of the spirits of murder. I believe one could without more ado explain the illness of Lady Macbeth, the transformation of her callousness into penitence, as a reaction to his childlessness, by which she is convinced of her impotence against the decrees of nature, and at the same time admonished that she has only herself to blame if her crime has been barren of the better part of its desired results.

He thinks it is impossible to guess what motives could have turned the hesitating ambitious Macbeth into an unbridled tyrant, and 'his steely-hearted instigator into a sick woman gnawed by remorse'; but he suggests that 'together they exhaust the possibilities of reaction to the crime, like two disunited parts of the mind of a single individuality'.[6]

Once again Freud has called our attention to a comparatively neglected aspect of the play, though it has been touched on by Wilson Knight in *The Imperial Theme*, by Cleanth Brooks in *The Well Wrought Urn*, and by Roy Walker in *The Time is Free*. But it is not the central theme of the play, and on that Freud throws no light.

In one of his essays, Freud has an interesting discussion of the casket scenes in *The Merchant of Venice*.[7] He argues from Bassanio's address to the leaden casket:

Thy paleness moves me more than eloquence

4. I. vii. 72.   5. III. i. 47–71.
6. See also L. Jekels, 'Shakespeare's *Macbeth*' in *Imago*, v (1918).
7. *Collected Papers*, iv (1934), pp. 244 ff.

that lead is both pale and dumb, and that dumbness and pallor are dream-symbols of death. The very fact that lead reminds him of the grave makes Morocco pass hurriedly to the other caskets. Freud suggests that the caskets represent three women, and that the leaden casket represents the goddess of death:

Man rebelled against the recognition of the truth embodied in the myth and constructed a substitute in which the third of the sisters is not death but the fairest and most desirable of women ... Nor was this substitution in any way difficult—it was prepared for by an ancient ambivalence, it fulfilled itself along the lines of an ancient context which could at that time not long have been forgotten. The Goddess of Love herself, who now took the place of the Goddess of Death, had once been identified with her.

By means of this myth, man is able to pretend that he *chooses* death; he does not have it forced upon him against his will.

Just where in reality he obeys compulsion, he exercises choice; and that which he chooses is not a thing of horror, but the fairest and most desirable thing in life.

There is no reason to believe that Shakespeare intended the caskets to have any such significance; but it is possible, if unprovable, that the scenes obtain some of their effect because of their connection with an archetypal myth.

In the same essay, Freud discusses the opening scene of *King Lear*, and he argues that the King's choice between the three has the same significance as the choice of the caskets. Lear is an old and dying man who is unwilling to renounce the love of women. He insists on hearing from his daughters how much he is loved. Cordelia, who masks her true self and is as unassuming as lead, and whose silence is contrasted with the volubility of her sisters, represents Death.

Eternal wisdom, in the garb of the primitive myth, bids the old man renounce love, choose death, and make friends with the necessity of dying ... One might say that the three inevitable relations man has with women are here represented—that with the mother who bears him, with the companion of his bed and board, and with the destroyer. Or is it the three forms taken on by the figure of the mother as life proceeds—the mother herself, the beloved who is chosen after her pattern, and finally the Mother Earth who receives him again. But it is in vain that the old man yearns after the love of women as once he had it from his mother; the third of the Fates alone, the silent goddess of Death, will take him into her arms.

The opening sentence in this passage has been quoted with approval by George Orwell[8] and by Empson;[9] and it is certainly one of the leading themes of the play. But few would agree that Cordelia symbolized death, or that Goneril and Regan could be interpreted in Freud's way. 'There is something both beautiful and suggestive in this', as Lionel Trilling[1] remarks, 'but it is not *the* meaning of *King Lear* any more than the Oedipus motive is *the* meaning of *Hamlet.*' There is, perhaps, more truth in Maud Bodkin's interpretation of the three sisters. To a parent the child may be 'both loving supporter of age and ruthless usurper and rival';[2] and this ambivalent attitude is distributed between the good and evil children of King Lear.

Miss Ella Freeman Sharpe's interpretations of Shakespeare are more extravagant than those of Freud and Jones, and they illustrate the dangers of the Freudian method. She has a brief essay on *Hamlet*, but her most substantial literary essay[3] attempts to show that *The Tempest* and *King Lear* 'are linked together in a cycle of inner experiences, a cycle which seems characteristic of creative artists'. *Timon of Athens*, which comes between the other two plays, represents the nadir of the revolutionary cycle. Miss Sharpe refrained from calling her article 'The Role of Regression in Manic-Depression'; but she argues that the storm in the play represents 'the rage before the onset of depression', and that *The Tempest* represents the 'readjustment to reality'. We might, perhaps, object that *King Lear* faces reality more squarely than *The Tempest*; but Miss Sharpe is only expressing in Freudian terms a widely held view of Shakespeare's development. It is when she comes to examine *King Lear* in detail that she jumps to somewhat extravagant conclusions.

She thinks that Shakespeare was dramatizing a conflict of childhood and infancy, and that he regressed to the loves and hates of early childhood. The three daughters 'represent three different aspects of one mother'; and the poet, through Lear, 'reveals

8. *Shooting an Elephant* (1950), pp. 33 ff.
9. *The Sewanee Review* (Spring 1949), pp. 179–80.
1. *The Liberal Imagination* (1951), pp. 34–57.
2. *Archetypal Patterns in Poetry* (1934), pp. 15–16.
3. *Collected Papers on Psycho-Analysis* (1950), pp. 214 ff.

emotional reactions to the mother of his childhood and, more hidden and complicated, those experienced towards his father'. The cause of the storm is mother-Goneril's pregnancy, and Miss Sharpe on rather slender evidence thinks that the child Shakespeare lapsed into incontinence at the age of two and a half, just before the birth of his brother Gilbert in October 1566, and that he ran away from home at the age of five in the late summer— because of the seasonal indications given in Act IV—during his mother's next pregnancy. Unfortunately for this ingenious theory, Joan Shakespeare was born in April, and his mother would not be noticeably pregnant in the late summer of the previous year. Ann, however, was born in September 1571, when Shakespeare was seven—rather old, that is, for the kind of infantile conflict Miss Sharpe describes.

Whatever we may think of Miss Sharpe's general theory, we may be permitted to question some of her assumptions. It is difficult to believe that Shakespeare's incontinency was dramatized in the quarrel about the knights, who symbolized fæces; that

the decision to stay with each daughter a month in turn is the outcome of the complexity of emotional reactions concerning phantasies arising in childhood from the observations of signs of the mother's menstruation:

for, apart from the impossibility of proof, Shakespeare would have found this decision in one of his numerous sources; that the line, 'Goneril with a white beard', tells 'of repressed knowledge of menstruation, bandage, and pubic hair'; that Lear is driven into the hysterical pretence of *being his mother* because he complains of the well-known disease, *hysterica passio*; that 'folds of favour' symbolize the mother's breasts; and that 'Pray you, undo this button' represents 'the symbolic surrender to the father'. Miss Sharpe argues that when the father-figure, Kent, replies 'Oh! let him pass':

Father's heart is melted, he does not hate him. In that button undone, and the symbolic 'passing' is clear enough the psychical homosexual retreat from the Oedipus conflict.

It is hazardous to assume that Mrs. John Shakespeare displayed emotional stupidity in dealing with her son's incontinence; that (except in a very general sense) Shakespeare had experienced distraught states of mind in early childhood; that he resented the fact that he was sent to use an outside lavatory while his little sister was 'condoned for messing';[4] that Lear's ravings reveal 'repressed childhood observations concerning the female genitals';[5] and that 'the retreat in depression and the re-emergence to life' is the 'psychological representation ... of our primitive forefathers seeking the actual underground shelter from the wrath of the gods manifested in the elements overhead'. It is possible, on the other hand, to find some substance in Miss Sharpe's suggestion that the inner meaning of the division of the kingdom is that Lear gave up the government of himself.

Many of the incidents on which Miss Sharpe relies are to be found in Shakespeare's sources; and one would have thought that it would be safer to rely for evidence only on those incidents for which no source has been discovered. The most one can say is that the play reflects a profound spiritual or psychical disturbance; and, if one accepts the main principles of psycho-analysis, one might assume that the origins of the disturbance should be sought in early childhood. Shakespeare may have been attracted to the Lear story because it could be made to symbolize an early conflict forgotten by his conscious mind, but it is difficult to see how we can hope to discover the nature of that conflict from the evidence available. It may likewise be true, as Miss Sharpe suggests, that the power which the play exerts over our hearts is due to the fact that we all resent banishment from the Eden of infant phantasy to a world of reality, and that we therefore sympathize with Lear, whose expulsion into the storm symbolizes this early banishment.

It would have been unnecessary to examine Miss Sharpe's essay in detail if it had not been introduced by Ernest Jones and described by a rash reviewer as the best criticism of Shakespeare ever written. Miss Sharpe was a teacher of English before she became a successful lay analyst, but in her application of psycho-analysis to literature she became the victim of her own ingenuity.[6]

4. Op. cit., pp. 234-5. This is based on the Fool's words: 'Truth's a dog that must to kennel' ... etc.

5. Shakespeare found some of the material for these speeches in Harsnett's *Declaration*. Cf. *R.E.S.* (January 1951), pp. 11–21.

6. Trilling, op. cit., refers to an interpretation of *Henry IV* by Franz Alexander. 'In the development of Prince Hal we see the classic struggle of the ego to come to normal adjustment, beginning with the rebellion against

There are some critics who argue that as Freud's theories were not propounded until three hundred years after Shakespeare began to write, it is absurd for us to attempt to interpret the plays in the light of psychoanalysis. The only psychology that can reasonably be applied to Shakespeare's characters is that of his own time; and even though the psychological books of the day were confused and contradictory, we may be certain from verbal parallels that Shakespeare at least knew Timothy Bright's *Treatise of Melancholy*, and that he read that work before writing Hamlet.[7]

---

the father, going to the conquest of the super-ego (Hotspur), then to the conquest of the *id* (Falstaff), then to the identification with the father and the assumption of mature responsibility.' Two other articles may be mentioned. In a study of *The Tempest* (*International Journal of Psycho-analysis* (1923), pp. 43 ff.) Hans Sachs suggests that Caliban represents Shakespeare's predecessors, Stephano and Trinculo the actors, and Ferdinand the poet's successor. Shakespeare started with the question, how soon would his own unmarried daughter marry and he lose her? Sachs suggests, too, that by not erasing entirely the incestuous relationships in *Pericles* and *A Winter's Tale*, Shakespeare showed that he preferred his own daughter to his aged wife; and that like Leontes, he had to take the guilt for the death of his son on his own head. There seems to be little evidence for these theories. R. Eisler in 'Der Fisch als Sexualsymbol' (*Imago*, 1914) argues that Caliban is a Phallic Demon.

7. Cf. *P.M.L.A.* xli. 667 ff.; J. Dover Wilson, *What Happens in Hamlet*, pp. 309 ff.; Lily Campbell, *Shakespeare's Tragic Heroes* (1930), *passim*; Ruth L. Anderson, *Elizabethan Psychology and Shakespeare* (1927), *passim*; L. C. T. Forest, *P.M.L.A.* (1946), p. 672; and R. Heppenstall and Michael Innes, *Three Tales of Hamlet* (1950), pp. 17–19, 22 ff. Bright distinguished between the fears engendered by a bad conscience, and the neurotic fears of the melancholy man. 'Whatsoeuer molestation riseth directly as a proper obiect of the mind, that in that respect is not melancholicke, but hath a farther ground then fancie, and riseth from conscience, condemning the guiltie soule of those ingrauen lawes of nature, which no man is voide of, be he neuer so barbarous. This is it, that hath caused the prophane poets to haue fained Hecates Eumenides, and the infernall furies; which although they be but fained persons, yet the matter which is shewed vnder their maske, is serious, true, and of wofull experience . . . ' 'On the contrarie part, when anie conceit troubleth you that hath no sufficient grounde of reason, but riseth onely vpon the frame of your brayne, which is subject . . . unto the humor, that is right melancholicke, and so to be accompted of you. These are false points of reason deceaued by the melancholie braine, and disguised scarres of the heart, without abilitie to worke the pretended annoyaunce: neither do they approch the substaunce, and the substantiall and soueraigne actions of the soule, as the other doeth' (op. cit., pp. 193–5).

There are several possible answers to this argument. First, critics of every age have applied the latest psychological theories to Shakespeare's characters. Secondly, it is obvious that Hamlet is not merely the melancholy man of Bright's treatise. As Shakespeare created life-like characters we should expect them to reveal aspects of human nature of which the professional psychologists were then ignorant. Just as people suffered from appendicitis before Edward VII had his appendix removed, so people suffered from unresolved Oedipus complexes before Freud discovered them. Presumably they suffered from them in the time of Sophocles. Thirdly, if Shakespeare created his characters partly by infusing them with his own spirit, and not merely by objective observation of his neighbours, he may unconsciously have revealed his own character and complexes.

The sceptic may point out that we cannot possibly analyse a long-dead patient because we lack the necessary knowledge, and cannot ask him the necessary questions—such ghosts do not come to us in a 'questionable shape'. Moreover, it may be urged that the greater the poet, the more impersonal and inscrutable he is likely to be. To this the Freudian might reply that a great poet is a fit subject for scientific analysis because he is infinitely more articulate than the average man, that great poetry is created by the collaboration of the conscious mind with the unconscious, and that however classical and objective a poet may be he is liable to reveal himself in the subjects he chooses, in his deviations from his sources, and perhaps in his use of imagery.

Dover Wilson has denied the possibility of diagnosing the complexes of a character in a play:[8]

A fundamental misconception vitiates this and most previous attempts of the kind: that of treating Hamlet as if he were a living man or a historical character, instead of a single figure . . . in a dramatic composition . . . Apart from the play, apart from his actions, from what he tells us about himself and what other characters tell us about him there is no Hamlet.

To this Ernest Jones[9] retorted that Dover Wilson himself interpreted what he supposed to be going on in Hamlet's mind throughout the play; that no dramatic criticism of the characters

8. Ed. *Hamlet*, pp. xliv ff.
9. Jones, *Hamlet and Oedipus*, pp. 18–19.

in a play is possible 'except under the pretence that they are living people'; that 'in so far and in the same sense as a character in a play is taken as being a living person, to that extent must he have had a life before the action in the play began'; and that he was perfectly aware that Hamlet was only a figment of Shakespeare's mind. One feels nevertheless that Jones sometimes tends to blur the distinction between art and life, and that there is a real danger of substituting a case-history of Prince Hamlet for a genuine criticism of the play itself.

Freudian criticism has been most useful as a method of counter-attacking those 'realist' critics who have sought to explain Shakespeare in terms of his contemporaries. Stoll and Schücking have both emphasized the survival of primitive techniques in Shakespeare's plays and, in reaction against Bradley, they have tried to show that his characters are psychologically impossible. The Othello depicted in the first act of the play could not have murdered Desdemona; Macbeth could not have murdered Duncan; Iago is melodramatic; and many of the plays are partially spoilt for us by conventions, such as that of the 'calumniator believed', which now strike us as absurd. Against such views, J. I. M. Stewart has argued brilliantly in *Character and Motive in Shakespeare* (1949) that the characters only seem to be impossibly inconsistent if they are considered in the light of an outmoded psychology. With the new light thrown on the unconscious mind and on the irrationality of human behaviour by Freud and others, the very inconsistencies of the characters help us to believe in their reality. The strange behaviour of Othello, Leontes, and Lear may be paralleled in the case-books of the psychiatrists. There are more things in heaven and earth than were dreamt of in the philosophy and psychology of the nineteenth century.

This line of argument seems to me to be valid, though pressed too far it might convert the tragic heroes into a gang of psychopaths.[1] It is at least a useful second line of defence of Shakespeare's psychological realism.

This is not the place to discuss the Adlerian and Jungian criticisms of Shakespeare; but the very fact that they differ completely from those of Freud, and that they conform, as do those of

1. See, for example, H. Somerville, *Madness in Shakespearian Tragedy* (1929).

Freud, to the general theories of their authors should warn us against accepting any of them without reserve. Adler, for example, regards *Hamlet* as a play dealing with the morality of revenge:[2]

So far as we can see there is only one case in which killing can be justified, and that is in self-defence, when our own life or the life of another person is in danger. No one has brought this problem more clearly under the purview of humanity than Shakespeare has done in *Hamlet*, although this has not been understood.

This interpretation, however, is very close to that of the pacifist critics: Middleton Murry, Max Plowman, and Roy Walker.[3]

2. *Social Interest* (1938), p. 106.
3. J. Middleton Murry, *Shakespeare* (1936); Max Plowman, *The Right to Live* (1942), p. 161; Roy Walker, *The Time is out of Joint* (1948).

8

The Singularity of
Shakespeare[1]

The theme for today is Shakespeare as an International Presence.
But I think you will agree that the holding of this Congress, with
delegates from the four imagined corners of the world, makes it a
work of supererogation to enlarge on this theme; and I may add
that the editor of a Shakespeare journal earns an adventitious
popularity with his philatelist colleagues. But I want nevertheless
to call attention to one curious fact about Shakespeare's international presence. I have seen performances of Shakespeare's
plays in Moscow, Prague, and Dubrovnik as well as Kozintsev's
great films and the Japanese *Throne of Blood*. The curious thing is
that the *Hamlet* which ran for a dozen years in Moscow, the
performances in the state theatres of Germany, the wonderful
Othello in Dubrovnik were, of course, not Shakespeare precisely,
but Boris Pasternak's *Hamlet*, or Schlegel-Tieck's *Macbeth*, or a
Serbo-Croat version of *Othello*. It is curious, because those who
share Shakespeare's language, and those who are truly bilingual,
must regard the plays thus robbed of their authentic poetry as
Hamlet without the Prince of Denmark. One is not surprised that
readers of Shakespeare's poetry should lose themselves in
superlatives—that A. C. Bradley, for example, should say in a
letter that the appreciation of Shakespeare was 'the whole duty of
man', although the elders of the Kirk in Glasgow would have been
startled to hear this piece of heresy. One expects Emily Dickinson
to say that while 'Shakespeare remains, literature is firm'. It is a
little more surprising to read an inscription by Bernard Shaw, the
scourge of the bardolators, in his facsimile of the First Folio, 'one
of the great books of the world'; and most surprising to find

1. The Annual Lecture of the Shakespeare Association of America,
delivered at Washington, D.C., 24 April 1976.

Flaubert saying 'What a man Shakespeare was! How small all the other poets are beside him . . . I think that if I were to see Shakespeare in the flesh, I should perish with fear'. Another great novelist, Turgeniev, wrote to Flaubert about Zola: 'I believe that he hasn't read Shakespeare: that is an indelible stain in him, which can never be washed away.' Yet another great novelist, Stendhal, thought that Shakespeare was far and away the greatest of poets, and even declared that he was the Unknown God. It is significant, however, that after calling him divine, he added, 'and yet to me he is almost in prose'.

I am far from undervaluing the translators, even though none can hope to provide an adequate substitute for the original. Yet, it is odd that in the 1950s and 1960s there were more professional productions of Shakespeare in Germany and the Soviet Union than in the United States or England. Indeed, some years ago it was suggested by a nameless Philistine that since the language of the translators was more accessible to modern audiences than Elizabethan language could be, a modern poet— Sir Osbert Sitwell was incredibly suggested—should be persuaded to translate the plays into a modern idiom. We can guess from some modern versions of the Bible what disasters would ensue. (Although there is no truth in Kipling's intriguing story, 'Proofs of Holy Writ', that Shakespeare put the finishing touches to the King James version, it may be argued that on strictly literary grounds we could deduce that that version alone was dictated by the Holy Ghost!)

What, therefore, I wish to share with you today are some thoughts on this question—if we strip Shakespeare of his poetry, does enough remain to justify his position as the greatest of dramatists? It is not an easy question to answer, for two main reasons. First, because a good translator can convey *some* of the poetic effect of the original. Although Pasternak oddly supposed that the repetition of sickness imagery in *Hamlet* was a stylistic fault caused by haste in composition and lack of revision, a translator can faithfully reproduce Shakespeare's iterative imagery. He can likewise, as Flatter tried to do, copy the metrical irregularities of the Folio texts, and differentiate between the style of the Dido speeches in *Hamlet* and that of the soliloquy which follows—'O! What a rogue and peasant slave am I!'—where the brutal realism contrasts with the inflation of the epic style. He can differentiate, too, between Hamlet's colloquial exchanges with Ophelia and the rhymed couplets of *The Murder of Gonzago*. Nevertheless, however devoted and cunning the translator, much will inevitably be lost: and, of course, the greater the poet the greater the loss. We get a much better idea of *Le Misanthrope* in Wilbur's translation than we do of *Phèdre* in Lowell's, although, I suppose, Lowell would generally be regarded as a more important poet than Wilbur.

The second of the difficulties to which I have referred is of much greater importance: the inseparability of Shakespeare's gifts as poet and dramatist. Let me try to sharpen this point by supposing that the young Shakespeare received, by some mistake of the Post Office or some shift in the space–time continuum, the letter Rilke wrote to a young poet:

Time doesn't enter into it. A year doesn't count; ten years are nothing. To be an artist is not to count and calculate; it is to grow like the tree which does not hurry its sap, which confidently resists the great winds of Spring, without doubting that Summer will come. Summer does come: but it comes only for those who know how to wait, as patient, confident and receptive as if they had eternity before them . . . Patience is all.

Shakespeare would have smiled to receive such advice; but, being notoriously polite, he would perhaps have replied:

I thank you from my heart for your advice, free and honest as it is, for the betterment of my poetry. But I fear that you are ignorant of the hard conditions under which I work. I am not, alas, a full-time poet. I am by profession a Player, and most of my time is taken up with the learning of lines, sometimes inferior to my own, with interminable rehearsals and time-consuming performances. I am much in demand for kingly and ducal roles. It is true that my fellows accept the two plays I provide each year as my main contribution to the affairs of the company; but even in this I enjoy only a limited freedom. I have to provide long and impressive parts for the leading actors, and smaller parts within the capacities of the others. I spend many precious hours in a desperate search for stories to turn into plays and, although I try and map out the plots of the next two plays during my annual visit to my family in the country, the dialogue is hardly finished before the first rehearsals. Indeed, I have often been persuaded, against my better judgement, to make alterations during rehearsals. You will appreciate that in these circumstances I smile at your statement that ten years are nothing.

> At my back I always hear
> Time's winged chariot hurrying near.

I cannot wait for ten years, for during that period I must endeavour to write another twenty plays—poor things, but my own. So, my honoured sir, I cannot pretend to be an artist. You rightly compare poetry to the sap of the tree; but the process is less protracted than you describe. Our poesy is as a gum, which oozes from whence 'tis nourished. The fire in the flint

> Shows not till it be struck: our gentle flame
> Provokes itself, and like the current flies
> Each bound it chafes. It does not take ten years.
> Perhaps it takes less in this my workaday world
> Because I have not, unlike you, a bevy
> Of wealthy flattering ladies to coddle me
> While I am lying fallow.

In some such way Shakespeare might have replied—though I confess he would not have anticipated Andrew Marvell—but if he sometimes regretted that he was dyed in the colours of his trade, and did not always appreciate the advantages of the hurly-burly in which he had to write, these at least preserved him from the damaging detachment which separates some dramatists from their audiences, and some poets from their fellow-men. He was, he was compelled to be, a man speaking to men.

Consider, for example, the effect on Shakespeare of his profession. An actor, first of all, spends much of his time in observing other people, so that when the appropriate part comes along, he can incorporate in his performance characteristics he has observed. (As Laurence Olivier watched the behaviour of West Indian immigrants and introduced their mannerisms, brilliantly if disastrously, into his portayal of Othello.) An actor who is also a dramatist does not merely utilize gestures and facial expressions, he picks up tricks of speech: the malapropisms of Dogberry, the anecdotage of Justice Shallow and Juliet's Nurse, the Old Testament flavour of Shylock's speech. Even more importantly, the actor-playwright comes to know instinctively what an audience will take, and the qualities and limitations of his fellow-actors. Most important of all, he knows that *Hamlet* and *King Lear* are merely scripts, which come to life fully only when they are performed. By which, of course, I don't mean that they are scripts which should be hacked about to suit the whims of a director, but rather, as Bernard Shaw was always insisting, musical scores, spoken by actors who bring to life the characters they represent. Each time this happens, the dramatist rewitnesses Pygmalion's miracle. Richard Burbage deserved the legacy in Shakespeare's will with which to purchase a memorial ring.

Everyone realizes how much a dramatist owes to the response of his audience, whether positive or negative. Although *Troilus and Cressida* is a particularly subtle and fascinating play, one should perhaps be glad that its comparative failure on the boards made Shakespeare devote himself to other sensations: to the writing of *Othello* and *King Lear*.

Keats's phrase recalls another more famous one: that the poet has as much delight in depicting an Iago as an Imogen. It is equally true that the actor has as much delight in playing Iago, as today an actress has in playing Imogen. I am not sure whether anyone has pointed out that what Keats described as Negative Capability—'when a man is capable of being in uncertainties, mysteries, doubts, without any irritable reaching after fact and reason'—is a quality which is demanded equally of an actor. It is obvious that an actor playing the role of a villain must (for the time being) play it from that character's point of view. There is a case to be made for Edmund, and Goneril, even for Regan, but woe betide the director who allows that evil trio to quench our sympathy for Lear. Even Rosencrantz and Guildenstern, as Tom Stoppard neatly demonstrated, are not quite what Hamlet makes us think they are.

You will recall that Una Ellis-Fermor in her British Academy lecture (which was afterwards incorporated in *Shakespeare the Dramatist*) argued that the quintessential dramatic gift, which Shakespeare possessed more abundantly than any other dramatist, was the power of giving life to all his characters, not merely to his protagonists. Of course there is a difference between the characterization in depth of Angelo and Isabella on the one hand, and that of Barnardine and Froth on the other: but within the limits of Barnardine's 112 words and Froth's 57 we are given extraordinarily vivid portraits, very much more alive than the minor characters of other dramatists. There are, of course, many minor characters in the early plays who are not fully individualized, and I think perhaps that Una Ellis-Fermor considered too curiously when she took as one of her examples an anonymous sentry in

Antony and Cleopatra. But her main argument seems to me to be sound. It is, indeed, fairly common for a dramatist to make a character memorable by tricks of speech or by the repetition of catch-phrases: the oaths of Bob Acres, the malapropisms of Mrs. Malaprop, the clichés of Boniface, the nautical imagery of Ben Sampson in *Love for Love*; the similitudes of Witwoud, or the fashionable twittering of Belinda in Congreve's first comedy, *The Old Bachelor*, when she encounters Araminta:

Lard, my Dear! I'm glad I have met you—I have been at the Exchange since, and am so tir'd ... Oh, the most inhumane, barbarous Hackney-Coach! I am jolted to a Jelly. Am I not horridly touzed?
ARAM. Your Head's a little out of order.
BEL. A little! O frightful! What a furious Fiz I have! O most rueful! Ha, ha, ha, O Gad, I hope nobody will come this way, till I have put myself a little in Repair! ... Good Dear, pin this ... very well—So, thank you my Dear—But as I was telling you—Pish, this is the untoward'st Lock—So, as I was telling you—How d'ye like me now? Hideous, ha? Frightful still? Or how?

It would be wrong to undervalue such a passage. It illustrates Congreve's wonderful ear—not, as used to be said, for vowel music, but for capturing the different speech cadences of a wide variety of people. But such ventriloquism, superb as it is, is surpassed in dramatic effectiveness by sudden strokes which seem at first to be absurdly out of character but which *by that very fact* convince us of its truth to life. It is unnecessary before such an audience to give examples of this from Shakespeare, but I hope you will allow me to refer to a single example, the recruiting scene in *2 Henry IV*. We have been laughing with Falstaff at the senility of Shallow, at the passing of bribes, and at Falstaff's cruelly funny comments on the countrymen lined up for his inspection. Feeble, the woman's tailor, is apparently the most unsuitable of all the recruits. His trade and his name are both against him. He is the butt of Falstaff's jokes and obscenities. But after he has been enlisted, he has the following speech:

By my troth, I care not; a man can die but once; we owe God a death. I'll ne'er bear a base mind. An't be my destiny, so, an't be not, so. No man's too good to serve's Prince: and, let it go which way it will, he that dies this year is quit for the next.

Feeble's dignified acceptance of the situation, his religious resignation, makes us see him (and the whole scene) with different eyes; and some members of the audience will remember Falstaff's reply in Part I when he is reminded by Hal that he owes God a death: 'Tis not due yet.'

The point I am making about Shakespeare's method of characterization may be made clearer if I describe briefly the very different method of three great dramatists—Molière, Racine, and Ibsen—whose characters are, compared with Shakespeare's, remarkably unambiguous. It is almost as though the poets had based them on lucid, well-considered, character sketches, in which every stroke was entirely consistent.

There can hardly be any disagreement about Molière's major characters. Although Tartuffe does not actually appear until the beginning of Act III, he is the focus of attention throughout the earlier scenes, and there is no ambiguity in his portrayal. He is shown in all his hypocritic turpitude (to use Blake's phrase), and every member of every audience agrees about him, including even the devout who wanted the play banned. We watch him from the outside—we are never allowed inside his mind—and he is given no redeeming characteristics. A greedy, avaricious, sensual con-man, he deliberately uses the cloak of piety to further his criminal schemes—and we rejoice in his downfall. Alceste, in *Le Misanthrope*, is a more complex character and audiences and readers are divided into those who regard him as a self-righteous and humourless prig, and those who regard him as a nearly tragic hero, greatly superior to the society in which he lives. Notice, however, that the different reactions to the character are not due to any real ambiguity: they merely reflect the views and temperaments of different members of the audience—whether they agree with the compromiser Philinte or not. In the same way some people find Milton repellent and Shelley a cad, using the same evidence as those who think that Milton was noble and Shelley a secular saint.

If we turn now to Jean Racine, we find the same refusal to blur the outlines of his characters. We could describe the characters and motivation of Andromache, Agrippine, Bérénice, Phèdre, or Athalie in a few sentences, as school texts do, and no-one would disagree with the summaries. No-one, I think, could write a good book about Racine's tragedies which concentrated attention on the characters as Bradley did in *Shakespearean Tragedy*.

The greatest of the moderns, Ibsen, is also careful to guide the responses of his audience: though in *The Master Builder* and

John Gabriel Borkman he moved into a more ambiguous realm. In nearly all his plays we gradually learn more and more about the past lives of the characters at the same time as we watch them developing in the present. We learn, for example, how Mrs. Alving in *Ghosts* was driven into a loveless marriage, how she left her husband and was driven back to him by the clergyman she loved; how this led to free-thinking and (at the same time) to a hypocritical pretence that her late husband was a paragon of virtue. In the course of the play, she is compelled not merely to tell Oswald that his father was a diseased debauchee, but also to recognize that Captain Alving's debauchery was partly due to her own sin in marrying him when she was in love with someone else. There are, of course, many subtleties which I have had to omit in this brief summary, but Ibsen leaves us with no excuse for misunderstanding his meaning.

The revelation of the past concurrently with the development of the present is also apparent in *Rosmersholm*; the mystery of Mrs. Rosmer's suicide, hinted at first by Rosmer's refusal to cross by the bridge from which she plunged to her death, the revelation that the suicide was caused by Rebecca West's false confession that she was pregnant; the indication that the murder was politically motivated, so that Rosmer would be free to join the progressive party; Rebecca's later confession that she acted under the influence of a wild, uncontrollable passion; and her last confession in which she describes how under the influence of Rosmer and the Rosmersholm view of life, which kills joy, even though it ennobles, her passion was changed to an unselfish love. Ibsen adds to the portrait of Rebecca several further details: that she was illegitimate and that she had unwittingly committed incest. It is a complex portrait, but one which is not open to diverse interpretations—I say this despite the fact that faced with this story of murder and redemption some members of a youth movement asked Ibsen if the message of the play was not the call to work for mankind.

If we turn now from these admittedly great characters from some of the greatest plays since Shakespeare said farewell to his art, to any of *his* major characters, the differences will be apparent —differences which caused Edgar Elmer Stoll such a lot of needless anxiety. Iago may be taken as an example. A recent book by Stanley Edgar Hyman, published posthumously, has the sub-title

'Some approaches to the illusion of his motivation'. Hyman had no difficulty in showing that Iago could be treated simply as a stage villain; but, equally obviously, there is plenty in the text of the play to show that he is a devil, hating goodness and plotting the damnation of Othello; that he is an image of the playwright in his criminal aspect; that he is a Machiavel; and, less convincingly to me, that he is in love with Othello and Cassio, a love that is turned into hatred 'by the defence mechanism called reaction formation'. Oddly enough, Hyman did not discuss a number of other motivations which are suggested in the course of the play—that Iago is in love with Desdemona (as in Shakespeare's source); that he suspects Othello and Cassio of seducing Emilia; that he is a racist, and that he wants Cassio's job—all of which are at least as significant as those suggested by Hyman.

The case of Hamlet is even more notorious. There are more than a thousand rival interpretations of his character and of the reasons for his delay. To Coleridge he suffered from over-reflective intellectualism; to Madariaga and Rebecca West he was an egotist; to Roy Walker, borrowing Niebuhr's terminology, he was moral man in immoral society; to Goethe he was an oak-tree planted in a costly vase; to Schoepenhauer he suffered from world-weary cynicism; Bradley thought he was unable to act because of the shock of his father's death and his mother's remarriage; Freud, not unnaturally, diagnosed an Oedipus complex; and Wertham, until he was branded as a heretic by his fellow-analysts, diagnosed an Orestes complex. Confronted with these, and many other, contradictory theories, C. S. Lewis suggested first, that all critics saw themselves as Hamlet and attached to him their own prepossessions. Coleridge gave the game away when he said 'I have a smack of Hamlet myself, if I may say so'. Secondly C. S. Lewis argued that Hamlet has no character: he was Everyman, guilty of original sin. This point would be more convincing if we did not know that C. S. Lewis had written several books of popular theology and that, like the critics he complained of, he had read into Hamlet his own prepossessions. I find it difficult to accept the idea of a Hamlet without a character: but it is true that many of the rival theories are supported by selective quotations from the text of the play. This extraordinary state of affairs has been attributed to the fact that Shakespeare was grafting on a play, ten or a dozen years old, the ideas and motivations of his maturity and that this pouring of new wine into old bottles made the play (in Eliot's words) 'most certainly an artistic failure', Eliot later retracted, but Waldock clung to this theory. Yet the varied responses of the critics to the play may properly reflect its complexity and ambivalence. As Norman Rabkin showed in his admirable lecture at the Vancouver Conference, the tendency of critics to find a single, incontrovertible meaning in a play is reductive in its effect:

Yet by the end [he said] we have been through a constantly turbulent experience which demands an incessant giving and taking back of allegiance, a counterpoint of ever-shifting response to phrase, speech, character, scene, action, a welter of emotions and ideas and perceptions and surprises and intuitions of underlying unity and coherence rivalled only by our experience in the real world so perplexingly suggested by the artifact to which we yield ourselves.

I do not know whether Professor Rabkin would agree that this account of our experience of a Shakespearian play would not really fit any of the great plays by other dramatists which I have been discussing. It seems to me that in this respect—and particularly in the matter of characterization—we come close to the singularity of Shakespeare.

I have given two examples of complex characterization—Iago and Hamlet—and if there were time I could give a score of others. I need remind you only of the contrast between the views of Bradley and Leavis on Othello, of Stoll's conviction that the jealous maniac of Acts III and IV is incompatible with the portrait we have of the Moor in Act I and again at the end of the play. Then again, there is the well-known contrast between the prudential motives Macbeth offers in his soliloquy in Act I for not murdering Duncan, and the impression we get from the same soliloquy that he is overcome with horror at the thought of the murder. The overt meaning is 'I won't murder Duncan because of what people will say and do'. The inner meaning, conveyed by the imagery of naked babe and angelic trumpets, is quite different. The imagery is used to reveal the unconscious mind of the protagonist, as it is also with Coriolanus.

The singularity of Shakespeare was pointed out by Strindberg, when he used Shakespeare as a stick to beat Ibsen with, as Professor Ewbank reminds me. In one of his *Open Letters* he discusses Hamlet, Ophelia, Polonius, and Claudius and argues that

Shakespeare describes people, in all their facets, as inconsistent, as contradictory, as torn—and tearing themselves to pieces—as aggressive and as incomprehensible as the sons of men really are.

Strindberg goes on to admit that Shakespeare 'does not always do it, and not completely and exhaustively, for no one could do that!'

Many of you, whether you have read this particular essay or not, will be reminded of a famous eighteenth-century piece of criticism, Maurice Morgann's essay on the Dramatic Character of Sir John Falstaff. It is particularly appropriate that we should celebrate Morgann's genius in the year 1976, although it is only 199 years since it first appeared, for if Morgann's advice had been followed the American colonies would probably not have signed the Declaration of Independence. Morgann was Lord Shelburne's secretary in charge of what was called the 'American desk'. He urged on Shelburne and the British government a conciliatory policy, the repeal of Rockingham's Act, which affirmed Parliament's right to tax the colonies whenever they wished, and the rescinding of the Mutiny Act. It may be added that Morgann advocated the abolition of slavery in the West Indies years before anyone else. (I owe these facts to Daniel A. Fineman's Introduction to his edition.)

It is commonly thought that Morgann's main purpose was to prove that Falstaff was not a coward and that in so doing he ignored the distinction between art and life, thus opening the door to a great deal of bad criticism of Shakespeare—such as *The Girlhood of Shakespeare's Heroines*. But this is totally to misunderstand Morgann's aim. Whether Falstaff was a coward or not is largely a matter of definition; but Morgann was fully aware that the characters in a play are not real people. His real distinction lies in his realization of the method of Shakespearian characterization. He points out that characters 'which are seen only in part, are yet capable of being unfolded and understood in the whole'; that a 'felt propriety and truth from causes unseen' is the 'highest point of poetic composition'; and that, by means of 'secret impressions', Shakespeare contrives to introduce 'an apparent incongruity of character and action' so as to suggest the complexity of people in real life.

Morgann's *Essay* contains on page after page passages of astonishing insight into Shakespeare's method, some of them added after publication. Shakespeare's characters are original, 'while those of almost all other writers are mere imitation'. We can account for their conduct 'from latent motives, and from policies not avowed'. There is one splendid paragraph, clarifying the 1777 text, in which Morgann explains that when our impressions and understanding of a scene may be at variance, the effect may be calculated by the poet. This may seem to foreshadow Stoll's idea of Shakespeare as the great illusionist who tricks us into accepting impossibilities; but Morgann insists not merely that delight may be derived from the apparent opposition between impression and understanding, but that the 'Principles of this Disagreement are really in human Nature'.

This, then, is the grand justification for the conflicting impressions Shakespeare gives us of his main characters: life is like that. In most plays and most novels we are presented with neat, rational, well-organized, and consistent characters. Our friends are not like that, as we can tell from the varying impressions different people have of them, and indeed, our own differing views from year to year, and even from day to day. Shakespeare's characters have the same Protean quality.[2]

I come back to the point from which I started. If Shakespeare is enjoyed in dozens of different languages, despite the over-riding importance of his poetry, what quality or qualities does he possess which enable him to be regarded as the greatest of dramatists, a quality which survives the perils and betrayals of translation? It can hardly be the structural brilliance of the plays, since directors usually make considerable changes in adapting the plays for a modern theatre. It certainly cannot be the profound interpretation of life which can be extracted from the plays, a blend of medieval morality, pious platitudes, and stoical consolation, for the plays are admired by many who reject the whole of the Shakespearian ideology as I do not. Nor can it be his psychological realism since the psychology which formed the basis of Elizabethan characterization is now regarded as obsolete. But, as you will have deduced from the line of my argument, Shakespeare's characters appear to be real—not real people, of course, but convincing on the stage, and even on the page. This is due partly,

2. As Flaubert said, great geniuses produced characters who are both types and new individuals, *who are introduced into the human race.*

as Morgann believed, to the conflicting views of a character which we are asked to assimilate. There is nothing which is more likely to convert a flat character into a round one, as when two pictures seen through a stereoscope merge into one which appears to be solid. It is due also, as Morgann hinted, to the way Shakespeare was able to project himself and his experience into a wide range of characters; and, conversely, to the way he himself learnt from his characters. Can we doubt that Shakespeare emerged from the writing of *Hamlet* or *King Lear*, like a man who had undergone a baptism of fire?

Nor is this all. The reality of the characters depends on a quadruple interaction. First, the conflicting impressions which avoid entanglement with obsolete psychological theories; Secondly, the identification of the poet with his characters, imagining himself in the position of Hamlet or Caliban; Thirdly, the pressures of the actual plot, the deeds which somehow have to be harmonized with the doer of them—and the greater the gap between deed and doer, the greater the intensity of the action. Fourthly, there is the actor who embodies the poet's creations, adding to them, subtracting from them, never quite coinciding with them, and by that very fact lending a penumbra to them, and providing yet another conflicting impression to give the illusion of life.

Critics brought up on a tidier, more rational kind of drama—such as William Archer who greatly preferred Pinero, Jones, and Galsworthy to the great Jacobean dramatists, not to mention Wycherley and Congreve—such critics protested that Hamlet was not the sort of man who would murder Rosencrantz and Guildenstern, that Othello, as depicted by Shakespeare, would never have smothered Desdemona, that the puritanical Angelo is the last person to be guilty of the sin into which he falls. We can see how wrong-headed such critics were, not merely because Shakespeare convinces us that these characters did behave in these ways, but because every discovery of modern psychology has vindicated the truth of Shakespeare's portraits.

This, then, I suggest, is the secret of Shakespeare's continued popularity in languages other than his own. His poetry may be seen through a glass darkly, but the subtlety of his characterization survives the process of translation, the transplanting into alien cultures, and the erosion of time. Not altogether undamaged, however. As Bernard Shaw was always insisting,

The individualization which produces that old-established British speciality, the Shakespearean 'delineation of character' owes all its magic to the turn of the line, which lets you into the secret of its utterer's mood and temperament, not by its commonplace meaning, but by some subtle exaltation, or stultification, or slyness, or delicacy, or what not in the sound of it. In short, it is the score and not the libretto that keeps the work alive and fresh.

And who, Shaw might have added, would bother to read the libretto of *Don Giovanni* or of *The Magic Flute*, if it were not for the music of Mozart.

We often speak of the universality of great poetry, accessible, we like to think, to people of different civilizations, with different beliefs and prejudices. Perhaps one may be permitted to suggest at a Shakespeare Congress that almost the only poet who really satisfies Wordsworth's splendid claim is Shakespeare.

Let me conclude with an eloquent prophesy by Maurice Morgann, appropriate at a congress of Shakespearian scholars, and doubly appropriate in a congress held in Washington at this particular time.

Yet whatever may be the neglect of some, or the censure of others, there are those who firmly believe that this wild, this uncultivated Barbarian has not yet obtained one half of his fame; and who trust some new Stagyrite will arise, who instead of pecking at the surface of things will enter into the inward soul of his composition . . . When the hand of time shall have brushed off his present Editors and Commentators, and when the very name of Voltaire . . . shall be no more, the *Apalachian* mountains, the banks of the *Ohio*, and the plains of *Scioto* shall resound with the accents of this Barbarian: In his native tongue he shall roll the genuine passions of nature; nor shall the griefs of *Lear* be alleviated, or the charms and wit of *Rosalind* be abated by time.

9

Robert Greene
as Dramatist[1]

Robert Greene has had the misfortune to be regarded primarily as one of Shakespeare's predecessors and as the author of the attack on him in *A Groatsworth of Wit Bought with a Million of Repentance* (1592). This is unjust to Greene in two ways: first because his best work was all non-dramatic, and secondly because critics have praised his plays for qualities which they do not possess. It may be worthwhile, therefore, to attempt a reassessment of his dramatic work.

It is probable that all his extant plays belong to the last years of his life: *Alphonsus King of Aragon*, the most immature, must have been written after *Tamburlaine* (*c.* 1587). (J. Churton Collins, by means of dubious parallels, convinced himself it was written after Spenser's *Complaints*, printed 1591.) The 'Address to the Gentlemen Readers' in *Perimides*, published in 1588, would seem to show that Greene had by that date written either an unsuccessful tragedy —which may have been *The Comicall Historie of Alphonsus*— or else some other kind of play. Greene mentions that two poets

had it in derision for that I could not make my verses iet vpon the stage in tragicall buskins, euerie worde filling the mouth like the faburden of Bo-Bell, daring God out of heauen with that Atheist *Tamburlan* or blaspheming with the mad preest of the Sonne.

There are several plays which have been ascribed to Greene, including *Selimus*[2] and *George a Greene*; but as the evidence is, to

1. *Essays on Shakespeare and Elizabethan Drama*, edited by Richard Hosley, University of Missouri Press, 1962.
2. The chief evidence for Greene's authorship of *Selimus* is the ascription to him of two extracts from the play in *Englands Parnassus*; but the editor Robert Allott's ascriptions are notoriously unreliable. When the play was reissued in 1638 it purported to be the work of one T. G. These initials may have been intended to signify Thomas Goffe, who was however in his

my mind, inconclusive, it will be safer to confine this discussion of Greene as dramatist to the four plays of which he was the sole author and *A Looking Glasse for London and England*, written (as the title-page of the first edition claims) by Greene and Thomas Lodge.

No critic has found anything to praise in *Alphonsus* (*c.* 1587), Greene's absurd attempt to rival *Tamburlaine*. It was a failure on its first performance and Greene apparently never wrote the promised sequel. Characterization, construction, and versification are all feeble in the extreme. The induction is pointless. The main theme—the rise of Alphonsus by ruthless means—is interrupted in the third and fourth acts by a series of scenes concerning Amurack, scenes which contrive to be both boring and incredible. An enchantress called Medea—presumably not Jason's wife, though there is a later mention of the golden fleece—makes Amurack talk in his sleep; Mahomet, speaking out of a brazen head, deliberately prophesies falsely; and Fausta, Amurack's wife, banished for no very good reason, has a troop of Amazons at her command. At the end of the play, Alphonsus's father turns up in the guise of a pilgrim to arrange his son's marriage to Amurack's daughter Iphigina. Although he has not had the opportunity of talking with either Alphonsus or Iphigina he has mysteriously acquired knowledge not only of the state of their affections but also of their private conversation.

Two more examples may be given of Greene's carelessness. In the first act Belinus announces that he is going to relieve Naples; Albinius advises him to relieve Naples; and Belinus announces that he will follow this advice, as though he had not already decided on this course. Even more absurd is the speech in which Amurack decides to let his daughter marry Alphonsus. It is intended to display the conflict in his mind, but it is so crudely done that the effect is ludicrous:

---

infancy when the play was first published in 1594. The evidence for Greene's authorship on grounds of style is even flimsier. It may be added that the play contains one undoubted echo of *Astrophel and Stella* (283–4); it was certainly influenced by *The Massacre at Paris* (which may have been written after Greene's death); and Selimus's long speech in seven-line stanzas (232–385) reads like a versification of Marlowe's table-talk, written by someone with little knowledge of the stage, and perhaps not originally intended for the public stage.

Now, *Amurack,* aduise thee what thou sayest:
Bethinke thee well what answere thou wilt make:
Thy life and death dependeth on thy words.
If thou denie to be *Alphonsus* sire,
Death is thy share: but if that thou consent,
Thy life is sau'd. Consent? nay, rather die:
Should I consent to giue *Iphigina*
Into the hands of such a beggers brat?
What, *Amuracke,* thou dost deceiue thy selfe:
Aphonsus is the sonne vnto a King:
What then? then worthy of thy daughters loue.
She is agreed, and *Fausta* is content;
Then *Amuracke* will not be discontent.

A Looking Glasse (c. 1590) is a much more competent piece of work. The verse, though quite undistinguished and monotonously regular, is less clumsy than that of *Alphonsus.* The simple morality structure does not require subtle characterization or strong dramatic scenes. The main plot is concerned with the sins and timely repentance of Rasni, King of Nineveh, who commits incest and adultery and connives at murder. He is not dissuaded from his evil courses by the miraculous deaths of his incestuous bride and of his favourite counsellor, nor even by the apparition of a burning sword; but Jonas succeeds in bringing about his repentance in the space of thirty lines. The episodes of the subplots concerning usury (for which Lodge was doubtless responsible), corruption, drunkenness, and adultery are a more relevant mirror of London vice than Rasni's flamboyant sins; and these scenes, mostly in prose, are written with much greater vigour and some humour.

There are, however, some serious dramatic weaknesses. The warning to London would have been obvious without the choric sermons of Oseas; it is uneconomical to have two prophets, Oseas and Jonas, performing a similar function; the episode of the whale is perfunctorily treated; and the class structure of society in Nineveh strains our credulity.

The divergences between the quarto of *Orlando Furioso* and the Alleyn manuscript of Orlando's part are considerable enough to show that it would be unfair to judge Greene's intentions by the extant text; but it is clear that, although some of the verse is not without eloquence, the characterization is still crude. The madness of the hero is quite unconvincing, and Greene bungles the climax of the play: Sacrepant's confession of his slander of Angelica falls flat because Melissa had already revealed this to Orlando.

It is on the remaining plays that Greene's reputation as a dramatist depends, and it may readily be admitted that *Friar Bacon* and *James IV* mark a great advance. It is possible after reading them to understand Nashe's praise of Greene as a plotter of plays, though some think that he was referring rather to the composition of scenarios than to the structure of the plays for which Greene wrote the dialogue.

If we accept the currently orthodox date of *Doctor Faustus* (1592–3), Greene would have had little time to exploit the interest in necromancy aroused by that play: he may therefore have been the pioneer in using magic as a dramatic theme.[3] So far as one can judge Marlowe's play from the textual ruins of the first two quartos, *Friar Bacon and Friar Bungay* (c. 1589), though inferior to it in poetical and dramatic power, is more competently constructed. Greene uses magic to link together the four plots—the making of the brazen head, the rivalry of the Prince and Lacy for the love of Margaret, the later rivalry of Lambert and Serlsby for her hand, and the competition between Bacon and Vandermast. The idea was a good one. It enabled Greene to preserve a rough unity while providing an attractive variety of incident; and on the whole it was carried out successfully. With a willing suspension of disbelief, we can accept Bacon's magic glass through which the Prince sees Lacy courting Margaret and through which the sons watch the fatal fight of Lambert and Serlsby. We can even accept the transport of Bungay, Vandermast, and Miles by diabolical means. Greene obtains some powerful dramatic effects, as when the Prince steps forward to stab Lacy whom he sees in the magic glass; but he is most successful, perhaps, with Miles's reactions to the brazen head and with his colloquy with the devil in the last act. The killing of the Lamberts and the Serlsbys is less easy to accept, since the death of one member of each family would have been enough to motivate Bacon's renunciation of necromancy.

3. Apart from the difficulty of dating *Doctor Faustus* before the publication of its source (1592), the hero's proposal to wall all Germany with brass must have been imitated from Greene's play or from its source, since it is only a passing reference in *Doctor Faustus* and not an integral part of the play, as Bacon's project is in Greene's.

But in spite of the variety of incident, which was the main factor in the success of the amateur production at Stratford-upon-Avon in 1959, the play will hardly stand up to serious critical examination. For the most part the verse is poor. Much of it reads like a weak imitation of Marlowe, relieved only by occasional effective lines. Greene is too fond of the more artificial figures of rhetoric, such as the ending of successive lines with the same word:

> But now the braues of *Bacon* hath an end,
> Europes conceit of *Bacon* hath an end,
> His seuen yeares practise sorteth to ill end:
> And, villaine, sith my glorie hath an end,
> I will appoint thee to some fatall end.

On the other hand, Miles's racy prose and skeltonic doggerel is often amusing.

Greene has been enthusiastically praised for the characterization of his heroine. Certainly the pastoral descriptions of Margaret in the first scene are delightful and the first impressions we have of her bear out the descriptions. She is represented as a gay and unsophisticated country lass. But at moments Greene seems to forget her English simplicity and makes her acquainted with the classics.[4]

> *Phoebus* is blythe and frolicke lookes from heauen,
> As when he courted louely *Semele* . . .

> Proportioned as was *Paris*, when, in gray,
> He courted *Oenon* in the vale of *Troy*.

In the fine scene (3.1), where Margaret takes the blame for Lacy's disloyalty, she is given some deservedly famous lines:

> Why, thinks King *Henries* sonne that Margrets loue
> Hangs in the vncertaine ballance of proud time?

but we forget we are in Fressingfield when she rejects the Prince's offers in these words:

---

4. The classical allusions could be defended, as Richard Hosley reminds me, as part of the larger poetic structure of the play, providing a kind of 'heroic' tone which sorts well enough with Edward's duty as heir apparent to marry a princess; but it tends to spoil the contrast between court and country and to minimize the gulf between Lacy and Margaret.

> if *Ioues* great roialtie
> Sent me such presents as to *Danae;*
> If *Phoebus* tired in *Latonas* webs,
> Came courting from the beautie of his lodge;
> The dulcet tunes of frolicke *Mercurie,*
> Nor all the wealth heauens treasurie affoords,
> Should make me leaue lord *Lacie* or his loue.

Later in the play, after Margaret is betrothed to Lacy, she foolishly gives Lambert and Serlsby to understand that she will choose one of them. Greene's purpose was twofold. He wished—unnecessarily—to demonstrate Margaret's constancy; and he wished to motivate the quarrel between her two suitors whose deaths were to cause Bacon to renounce necromancy. But Margaret, who is not intended to be stupid, has had her character sacrificed to situation. In the last act, as she is about to enter a nunnery, Lacy arrives in time to inform her that he is not married after all and that he had only pretended to be so in order to try her constancy. Margaret promptly forswears the veil; Lacy does not ask her forgiveness, nor does she utter a word of reproach: because of the Griselda convention neither they nor the author regard Lacy's stratagem as at all reprehensible. Here again character has been sacrificed to plot. Margaret is an uneasy compromise between two conventions; but the critics treat her as though she were as three-dimensional as a character in a novel and praise her for qualities she does not possess.

James IV (c. 1591), though purporting to be a historical drama, is based on a story by Giraldi Cinthio. Greene's dramatization is, on the whole, very skilful. The exposition is particularly fine: by the end of the first scene, James, just married to Dorothea, has employed Ateukin to win Ida's love. The conception of all the chief scenes is excellent, and some of them are well executed—notably Ateukin's two temptations of the King and Ida's refusal to listen to Ateukin's dishonourable proposals. The verse, too, is generally more successful than in Greene's previous plays: the influence of Marlowe is not so marked, there is less literary allusion, and the rhetoric is more controlled and more natural. Rhyme, moreover, when it is used (for example, Ida's moral sentiments in the first scene and her love-scene with Eustace in 2.1), is seen to have a dramatic function. But the play has corresponding weaknesses. Although rash critics have compared Bohan

to Jaques and Aster Oberon to Shakespeare's Oberon and Prospero, the induction and the choric interludes between the acts are
tedious and unnecessary. It is absurd for Bohan's sons to appear as
characters in the play he is presenting before Oberon, especially
as the events are supposed to have taken place in an earlier age; it
is artistically confusing when Slipper is rescued from the gallows
by the intervention of Oberon; and Greene does not explain how
Nano, who takes service with Ateukin in the first act, should be in
Dorothea's service in the second. It may be added that the scenes
in which Lady Anderson falls in love with the disguised Dorothea
are bungled, and nothing is made of Sir Cuthbert's jealousy. The
debate between a Lawyer, a Merchant, and a Divine (5.4), which
was presumably intended to illustrate the evil results of James IV's
misgovernment, is never once brought into focus.

We could overlook these faults, as many critics have done, if
the presentation of Dorothea and her husband were entirely
successful. The main difficulty confronting Greene in dramatizing
the story was that the hero's conduct was so atrocious that a happy
ending was almost unthinkable. Greene tries to minimize James
IV's guilt in various ways. Whereas in the source some years
elapse between Astatio's marriage and his passion for Ida,
Greene's hero is already in love with Ida when he marries
Dorothea for reasons of state. Arrenopia's murder is planned by
Astatio himself; in Greene's play the King is tempted by the
villainous Ateukin. Astatio gives out that Arrenopia had committed adultery; James does nothing to blacken Dorothea's
memory. But in spite of these mitigations, James is hardly a sympathetic character. Greene does not convince us, as he convinced
Churton Collins (*Plays and Poems of Robert Greene*, 1905, 2.34),
that James IV is 'a man in whom the higher and lower nature is in
conflict, and in whom the conscience of a naturally honourable
and even chivalrous man is never asleep'. James repents of his
wickedness only when Scotland is invaded; he offers a reward for
the finding of Dorothea not out of remorse but out of fear of her
father, and his plea for forgiveness, eloquent as it is, comes rather
late:

> Durst I presume to looke vpon those eies
> Which I haue tired with a world of woes,
> Or did I thinke submission were ynough,
> Or sighes might make an entrance to thy soule,

> You heauens, you know how willing I would weep;
> You heauens can tell how glad I would submit;
> You heauens can say how firmly I would sigh.

It is, no doubt, possible to forgive such wickedness, as Imogen forgives her husband and Hermione hers; but both Posthumus and Leontes believe that their wives have committed adultery and both undergo a long purgatorial period before they are forgiven. Dorothea speaks as though she had little to forgive:

> Shame me not, Prince, companion in thy bed:
> Youth hath misled,—tut, but a little fault.

James IV's fault was not little, and no woman could seriously believe that it was. Greene intends Dorothea's lines to express not her real opinion but her huge magnanimity in minimizing her husband's misdeeds; but the effect of the lines is to make her into an incredible paragon. This indeed, is the impression left on us by the character as a whole. When, for example, she is informed of the King's faithlessness, she makes a speech which, in the opinion of many critics, exhibits the nobility of her character. But does it? Or does it not rather destroy the illusion of reality?

> He doth but tempt his wife, he tryes my loue:
> This iniurie pertaines to me, not you.
> The King is young; and if he step awrie,
> He may amend, and I will loue him still.
> Should we disdaine our vines because they sprout
> Before their time? or young men, if they straine
> Beyond their reach? no; vines that bloome and spread
> Do promise fruites, and young men that are wilde
> In age growe wise.

Even if we make due allowances for the belief in the theory of wild oats and for the medieval (and Elizabethan) admiration for patient Griseldas, such facile forgiveness, such inhuman lack of resentment, takes away from the reality of the character. She shrinks into pasteboard. Later in the play, when Dorothea learns that the King has issued a warrant for her death, she has an outburst of grief, but of grief unmixed with the indignation which even the most docile woman might be expected to feel:

> Ah poore vnhappy Queen,
> Borne to indure what fortune can containe!
> Ah lasse, the deed is too apparant now!

> But, oh mine eyes, were you as bent to hide
> As my poore heart is forward to forgiue,
> Ah cruell King, my loue would thee acquite!

When Ross urges her to write to her father to avenge her, she rejects his advice because her love for her husband is apparently undiminished:

> As if they kill not me, who with him fight!
> As if his brest be toucht, I am not wounded!
> As if he waild, my ioyes were not confounded!
> We are one heart tho rent by hate in twaine;
> One soule, one essence, doth our weale containe;
> What, then, can conquer him that kils not me?

Dorothea faints with grief when she hears that the King is deserted by his friends; and when Lady Anderson advises her to return to her father, she replies in a speech which for complacent self-righteousness is unequalled in the whole body of Elizabethan drama:

> Ah Ladie, so wold worldly counsell work,
> But constancie, obedience, and my loue,
> In that my husband is my Lord and Chiefe,
> These call me to compassion of his estate:
> Disswade me not, for vertue will not change.

Lady Anderson may well be astonished:

> If English dames their husbands loue so deer,
> I feare me in the world they haue no peere.

It may plausibly be claimed that the impression such speeches give of self-conscious virtue is due to use of the convention by which characters, speaking out of character, inform the audience of their own virtue or villainy, so that the audience will know what their reactions ought to be. But Greene uses this convention so crudely that Dorothea becomes a mere puppet.

The other three women are only sketched. The Countess of Arran has been compared to the Countess of Roussillon in *All's Well That Ends Well*. Beyond the fact that both women are middle-aged countesses, there seems to be little resemblance. Lady Anderson, 'an honourable woman struggling with a dishonourable passion', is not fully realized. Ida is perhaps the most

successful of the three, and Greene contrives to suggest her virtue
and charm.

The view I have taken of Greene's powers of characterization,
especially of his women, is not the orthodox one. G. P. Baker tells
us (*Cambridge History of English Literature*, 1910, 5.138) that by
infusing into romanticism 'sympathetic and imaginative characterisation', Greene 'transmuted it into the realistic romance that
reaches its full development in Shakespeare's *Twelfth Night*,
Cymbeline and *The Winter's Tale*'. F. E. Schelling (*The English
Drama*, 1914, p. 62) speaks of Greene's heroines as 'three of the
most genuine and charming women in the drama preceding
Shakespeare'—which is not saying very much; Allardyce Nicoll
(*British Drama*, 1927, p. 90) says that Dorothea is 'the best-drawn
woman figure in sixteenth century drama outside Shakespeare's
comedies'. Greene's heroines, he tells us, 'are real; yet they have
some elements in them which seem ideal'. T. M. Parrott and R. H.
Ball (*A Short View of Elizabethan Drama*, 1943, p. 73) write in the
same strain. Greene's heroines (they say) 'form a very charming
trio. More fully realized, lifelike, and credible than the shadowy
women of Lyly's plays, they strike a note of true romance and are
in a sense the forerunners of such romantic heroines as Rosalind,
Viola, and Imogen.' J. M. Robertson (*Elizabethan Literature*,
1914, pp. 104–5) speaks of Greene's power of 'presenting a recog-
nizably real woman, tender and true, the moral superior of the
men around her; and . . . Dorothea . . . forecasts the noblest types
of womanhood in Shakespeare'. Greene's editors are even more
emphatic. Churton Collins assures us that Ida is 'beautifully
drawn, a Miranda nurtured in solitude', and that Dorothea 'would
do honour to Shakespeare; she is the soul of the drama, and as her
presence pervades it, she redeems all the faults of the play'. And
T. H. Dickinson speaks of 'the sweet and simple womanliness of
Greene's gallery'.

Paradoxically enough, these critics do Greene an injustice; for,
in approaching the plays from a Bradleyan standpoint and in
praising the fine powers of characterization displayed in them, they
pass over the real qualities—the liveliness and variety—possessed
by Greene. *James IV* has, of course, a superficial resemblance to
some of Shakespeare's plays—Dorothea, like Imogen, escapes
from the threat of murder by disguising herself as a boy; and,
again like Imogen, she forgives her husband. But this does not

justify an attempt to credit Dorothea with the qualities of a Shakespearian heroine. In reading the critics cited above, one gets the impression that they have confused virtue with verisimilitude. Margaret and Dorothea display an infinite capacity for forgiveness; therefore they are good; therefore they are well drawn.

It may be suggested that Greene's treatment of his own wife conditioned his portraits of wronged and forgiving womanhood. Dorothea may, as Robertson suggests, have been named after Greene's wife; and his deathbed letter expresses hope of the forgiveness which the heroes of his plays and novels invariably received. It is true that lifelike characters can be created on the basis of wish-fulfilments, but Greene was not writing in a convention which demanded realistic characters.

From the semifictional accounts of how he became a playwright in *Francescoes Fortunes* and *A Groatsworth of Wit*, it is apparent that Greene wrote merely 'to mittigate the extremitie of his want'. During the last few years of his life he made great strides as a dramatist, from the puerility of *Alphonsus* to the comparative maturity of *James IV*. But, although in some ways Shakespeare's plays are closer to Greene's than they are to Lyly's, Lyly was much the better artist. Artificial as his plays are, Lyly achieves perfectly what he sets out to do. Greene attempts to bring a wider range of incident and emotion into his plays and it is arguable that, though he is never fully successful, his plays were nearer than Lyly's to those of the greater dramatists who succeeded him. He was right to recognize that the 'vpstart crow' was 'well able to bombast out a blanke verse as the best of' the university wits. He did not realize that this same 'absolute *Iohannes fac totum*' was shortly to leave them far behind.

IO

The Comedies of Calderón[1]

Many recent critics have written on Calderón's tragedies and tragicomedies; but to his comedies, which constitute a third of his work, comparatively little attention has been paid. Yet Calderón is one of the few dramatists who could be used to support Socrates' opinion, expressed in *The Symposium*, that the poet who excels in tragedy should be equally successful in comedy. No one would pretend that *Les Plaideurs* is worthy to stand beside *Phèdre*, admirable as it is, or that *The Mourning Bride* is a tragic masterpiece. But Calderón's comedies, though poetically inferior to the best of the tragedies, are dramatically very effective, and they were used as a quarry by English and French playwrights in the seventeenth century. Even today, one would expect them to be more acceptable to an English-speaking audience than those tragedies which depend on the code of marital honour prevalent in Calderón's day.

In the present essay I shall discuss a representative selection of the comedies, using my own versions.[2] The comedies lose less in translation than the tragedies inevitably do, if only because in them the intrigue is more important than the poetry.

It is useless to expect from Calderón's comedies the same power of characterization displayed in the best Elizabethan comedies or in those of Molière or Congreve. There are no characters in his plays comparable in stature to Rosalind, Shylock, Malvolio, Volpone, Tartuffe, Alceste, or Millamant. His characters have just enough life to satisfy the demands of his plots and characters could often be transferred from one play to another without loss in transit. Calderón, indeed, is so careless or so indifferent to this

1. From *The Drama of the Renaissance. Essays for Leicester Bradner*, ed. Elmer M. Blistein (1970).
2. A translation of *Una casa con dos puertas mala es de guardar* ('A House with Two Doors') was published in the *Tulane Drama Review*, viii (1963), 1–157.

aspect of the art of the dramatist that he uses the same names in play after play. It would be difficult, and pointless, to attempt to distinguish between the dozen characters who are christened Beatriz or Laura or Leonor or Fabio, and the still larger number who are named Don Juan or Ines.

Nor can it be said that Calderón attempts to correct the manners or morals of his age. He does not, like Jonson, satirize avarice; nor, like Shakespeare, self-love or pride; nor, like Molière, hypocrisy or affectation; nor, like Congreve, the coxcombs and the fops. He does not even appear to criticize his jealous heroes and heroines: jealousy is the natural and inevitable result of suspicious circumstances.

Whether Calderón means to criticize the conventions of the age with regard to love and marriage is more debatable. We certainly sympathize with the heroines who manage to evade the vigilance of fathers or brothers, but there is little evidence that Calderón regarded such vigilance as unreasonable. Its function in the plays is generally to prevent the path of true love from being smooth. Yet in *The Phantom Lady* (*La dama duende*), the libertinism of Don Luis is criticized, at least by implication; and there are some plays in which the code of honour appears to be treated with some irony and others in which he is more outspoken. In *The Worst Doesn't Always Happen* (*No siempre lo peor es cierto*), for example, Don Pedro seems to be the poet's mouthpiece when he exclaims, in the second scene of the second act:

> Woe to the first who made so harsh a law,
> A contract so unjust, a tie so impious,
> Which deals unequally to man and woman,
> And links our honor to another's whim.

It must be admitted that the 'cloak and sword' comedies (*capa y espada*) are all very much alike. Whereas the five comedies Shakespeare wrote between 1595 and 1601 differ widely one from the other, Calderón's formula remains remarkably consistent. He presents us always with the love affairs of two or three couples. There is always a father or a guardian to be outwitted—never a mother—and the lovers are aided by their servants of both sexes. When a male visitor arrives at the house of the heroine, she is compelled to retire to her own apartments. When she goes out, she conceals her face and is often taken for another. Fathers, guardians, and brothers live in perpetual fear that their daughters, wards, and sisters will be compromised. The heroes frequently become jealous when they are driven to believe—usually mistakenly—that they have a rival.

One other limitation of Calderón's comedies remains to be mentioned. It would seem that the verse, though perfectly adequate for its purpose, is seldom poetically distinguished, and it is certainly inferior to the poetry of the tragedies. But this is a matter on which an English reader must hesitate to express an opinion. In any case, this is not a serious limitation, any more than it is with Molière. No one reads *Le Misanthrope* or *Tartuffe* for the poetry.

The supreme quality displayed by Calderón in his comedies is his power to exploit a dramatic situation so as to extract from it the maximum of entertainment. His initial assumptions are often simple enough but they suffice for his comic purposes; the causes of misunderstanding—a sliding panel between adjacent rooms, a veiled lady, the borrowing of a friend's house for an assignation —are less important than the variations he plays on them and the complications which result.

The initial situation in *A House with Two Doors is Difficult to Guard* (*Una casa con dos puertas mala es de guardar*) is caused by Felix's fear that his sister will be compromised if people learn that his friend, Lisardo, is staying in their house and meeting his sister. He therefore shuts off part of the house and does not allow Marcela to meet his guest. Not unnaturally, Marcela is consumed with curiosity, and she goes for a walk along a road she knows he will take. They meet and fall in love. Anxious to see him again in order to swear him to secrecy, she arranges a meeting in the house of her brother's fiancée, Laura, pretending it is hers. Lisardo imagines he has fallen in love not with Marcela but with Laura, and he is torn between love and the duties of friendship. Felix, finding that a stranger is visiting Laura's house, becomes violently jealous, and Laura is jealous of his former mistress. After numerous additional complications, Laura's father returns unexpectedly, and he assumes that her honour has been compromised.

The characters are all bewildered, but the audience is fully aware of the truth. In this Calderón's method resembles Shakespeare's, who, as Professor Bertrand Evans has demonstrated,

never leaves the audience in the dark.[3] We know, but Bassanio does
not, that Portia is confronting Shylock; we know, but Orlando
does not, that Ganymede is Rosalind; and we know, but Olivia
and Orsino do not, that Cesario is a girl. So in *The House with
Two Doors* the audience is aware that Lisardo is in love with
Marcela and not with Laura; and when he describes to Felix his
meeting with the mysterious lady, the audience knows it is the
sister that Felix has tried to prevent him from meeting.

Another comedy, *From Bad to Worse* (*Peor esta que estaba*),
also depends on conventions of honour and propriety. The governor's daughter, Lisarda, knowing that everything she does arouses
the comment of her neighbours, goes for walks with her face
covered, accompanied only by her maid. She meets a man who
calls himself Fabio. His real name is Cesar. Having killed a man
in a duel, believing him to be the lover of his mistress, Flerida, he
has fled. Flerida, anxious to prove her innocence, searches for him
in vain and under the name of Laura takes service with Lisarda.
The governor arrests Cesar and sends the veiled lady who is with
him at the time of his arrest to his own house, with instructions
that his daughter look after her. He thinks that the lady is Flerida,
but she is in fact his own daughter, and Lisarda thinks he has
recognized her. This is the situation at the end of the first act.
Before the end of the play, after many misunderstandings, Cesar
marries Flerida, and Lisarda, not without reluctance, agrees to
marry Juan, to whom she had been betrothed. Once again, the
audience is let into the secret of the various disguises, and the
laughter comes from the fact that all the characters on the stage are
deluded. Cesar does not know that Flerida is living in the house of
Lisarda, nor that she is guiltless. Lisarda and Flerida do not know
that Fabio is Cesar. Juan does not know that the woman to
whom he is betrothed is in love with his friend, Cesar. The
governor does not know that he has arrested his own daughter,
and Lisarda does not realize that he does not know.

The best-known of Calderón's comedies is probably *The
Phantom Lady*. The heroine is a young widow, Angela, who is
confined to the house by her brothers. She slips out with her maid
to see the entertainments in the grounds of the palace. There she is
seen but not recognized by one of her brothers, Don Luis, who

3. Bertrand Evans, *Shakespeare's Comedies* (New York, 1960), *passim*.

pursues her. She appeals for help to the first gentleman she encounters, Don Manuel, and the two men fight a duel which is interrupted by Angela's other brother, Don Juan. It turns out that Manuel is an old friend of Juan's and that he is to be his guest. Angela's apartment is separated from that of Manuel by a movable panel, unknown to him. Grateful and attracted, she uses the secret entrance to find out more about him. She and her maid rummage through his luggage, purloin a portrait of a lady, presumably someone he loves, and substitute charcoal for coins in his servant's bag. Angela leaves a note by Manuel's pillow. Cosme, the servant, assumes the room is haunted, while Manuel assumes that the veiled lady is Luis's mistress and that there is a secret entrance to his room. This is the situation at the end of the first act.

In the remainder of the play Calderón exploits the situation for all it is worth. Angela's maid blows out Cosme's candle and leaves Manuel holding a laundry basket, thereby giving him the impression that there has been supernatural intervention. Later on, Manuel, returning to fetch some papers, finds Angela in his room. She pretends to be a ghost, but is forced to confess she is a woman when he offers to run his sword through her. She makes an assignation with him in her own room, which he is tricked into believing is far away, as Tony Lumpkin tricks Mrs. Hardcastle in *She Stoops to Conquer*. In the end Manuel has to fight another duel with Luis, and Angela confesses her identity and her love to Manuel. He agrees to marry her, and Juan marries her cousin Beatriz, whom Luis has been pestering with his attentions behind his brother's back.

Honig is doubtless right in thinking that the play is a criticism of the code of honour and that Angela's stratagem is designed to convert the rule of honour into the rule of love. Her brothers, like Ferdinand and the Cardinal in *The Duchess of Malfi*, want her to remain a widow, wish to confine her to the house, and object when—in the privacy of her own room—she doffs her mourning.[4]

The Phantom Lady is sometimes regarded as Calderón's best comedy and it certainly contains some of his most effective scenes. But the play as a whole is spoiled, as others are not, by a number

4. *Calderón: Four Plays* (New York, 1961), pp. xxii–xxiv. But I doubt whether Honig is right in suggesting that Luis is guilty of incestuous desires: Luis does not know that he is pursuing his own sister.

of loose ends and improbabilities. It is difficult to believe that
Manuel, who deduces that his room has a secret entrance, would
have no suspicion of the movable mirror. Angela finds a portrait
of a lady in his luggage and asks her maid to purloin it, but in a
later scene she goes back to Manuel's room to have another look
at the portrait, and it is never explained whom the picture represents nor to what extent Manuel's affections are free. At the end
of the play he appears to marry Angela to protect her honour
rather than because he loves her, and this is somewhat disturbing
after we have heard Angela's very beautiful confession of love.
Beatriz has quarrelled with her father, but we are not told how she
becomes reconciled with him, nor how she can marry, apparently
without his permission. In the final duel, Manuel disarms Luis,
and instead of handing him his sword, allows him to go off to find
another—a clumsy device to get him off the stage.[5] Lastly, Luis
behaves badly or foolishly throughout the play, but his brother
seems quite unaware of his character, while Manuel speaks of him
in the most flattering terms. It would seem that Calderón, who
wrote an enormous number of plays, was here guilty of some
carelessness.

Another comedy, *The Secret Spoken Aloud* (*El secreto a voces*),
depends on the use of an ingenious code by which two people can
convey a message without those not in the secret being aware of
it. The first words of each line of verse convey the secret message,
while the meaning of the whole lines is quite innocent. This
suggests that the delivery of the verse, here unrhymed, must
have been somewhat formal, the line divisions being distinctly
marked.

One of the best plays, *The Advantages and Disadvantages of a
Name* (*Dicha y desdicha del nombre*), violates the unity of place,
the first two scenes being set in Parma and the remainder of the
play in Milan. Felix offers to take the place of his friend Cesar in
carrying an official letter to the Prince of Urbino at Milan, so that
Cesar can keep a rendezvous with the woman he loves, Violante.
Felix takes Cesar's name, delivers the letter, rescues a woman,
Seraphina, from abduction during the carnival, and is given
hospitality by her father, Lidoro, who knew Cesar's father. Felix

5. If the intention is to show that the sword has been damaged, this is not
made lcear in the dialogue.

does not know that the daughter of the house is the woman he rescued. Nor does he know that the would-be abductor, Lisardo, is determined to kill Cesar, who had killed his brother in a duel. Cesar arrives in Milan and is arrested under the name of Felix, and by the end of the second act Seraphina also arrives, searching for Cesar, who thinks wrongly that she has betrayed him to an ambush. Everything turns out right in the end. The various misunderstandings are cleared up, the fathers agree with some reluctance to the marriage of their daughters, and only the unpleasant Lisardo is deprived both of his vengeance and of his love.

A last example of Calderón's plotting, *The Worst Doesn't Always Happen*, is concerned with the theme of deceptive appearances. Carlos, finding a man hiding at night in Leonor's room, naturally assumes the worst; his friend, Juan, seeing a man leaving his house in the darkness, assumes that his sister Beatriz has a secret lover. The plots are linked by the fact that Carlos, still loving Leonor, has arranged for her to take service with Beatriz and by the fact that Leonor's supposed seducer, Diego, is in love with Beatriz. After many misunderstandings and complications— the arrival of Diego and of Leonor's father, the hiding of Carlos in Juan's house, and what appears to be proof of Leonor's continued guilt—Beatriz and Carlos are persuaded by Leonor's obvious dislike of Diego and by their refusal to marry that appearances were deceptive, that the worst is not always certain.

It is fairly easy to illustrate the ingenuity of Calderón's plotting, though one would have to examine a play scene by scene to demonstrate fully his skill as a playwright; but it is less easy to suggest in translation the liveliness and variety of the dialogue. The humour of his comic servants is a bit repetitive, but in the conversation between his nobly born characters he is remarkably successful. The main difficulty of translating his plays is that they are mostly written in octosyllabic verse, much of it unrhymed; and this is a form which is difficult to naturalize in English. The normal form used by English dramatists in Calderón's day was, of course, blank verse, and this seems the natural medium for a modern translation.

The first passage is taken from the first scene of *A House with Two Doors*, where Marcela encounters Lisardo and neatly mocks at his high-flown compliments by using the same similes:

LISARDO.   Madam, the sun
    Could hardly stop the heliotrope from turning
    Toward its light; the polar star could hardly
    Prevent the magnet from pursuing it,
    Nor would it be less difficult for the magnet
    To stop the steel from being attracted by it.
    Then if your brightness equals that of the sun,
    I'm like the heliotrope; if your indifference
    Is like the polar star's, then my regret
    Is like the magnet's; and if you are harsh
    Even as the magnet, then my eagerness
    Is like the steel's. Then how can I remain
    Contented, when I see my sun depart,
    My polar star, my magnet, I who am
    The heliotrope, the magnet, and the steel.
MARCELA. But sir, the sun each evening disappears
    And leaves the heliotrope; and every morning
    The northern star departs and leaves the magnet;
    Then if the sun and northern star may go,
    You have no better reason to complain
    At my departure. You should tell yourselves
    For consolation, Sir Heliotrope or Sir Magnet,
    That there is night for the sun, day for the star.

Another passage from the third scene of the first act of the same
play is a good example of one of the frequent quarrels between
lovers. Felix tries to explain to Laura that she has no reason to be
jealous of Nise, with whom he had once been in love:

FELIX.   By heaven above,
    Whether you are annoyed or merely jealous,
    You have to hear me now, before I say
    Farewell for ever.
LAURA.   You'll go away at once
    If I do listen?
FELIX.   Yes, I will.
LAURA.   Well, speak
    And then be off.
FELIX.   Should I attempt to deny
    That I loved Nise . . .
LAURA.   Kindly stop at that.
    If you have nothing else to say to me,
    It's useless to proceed. I was expecting

A thousand courteous protestations, true
Or false—for sorrows are consoled by lies—
I thought you'd give a thousand more assurances
Of infinite fidelity, of an attachment
Absolute, exclusive and unalterable,
And then you throw the confession in my face
That you have loved her. Does it not strike you, sir,
That while you think to appease me, you are still
Insulting me?

FELIX.   Why won't you let me finish?

LAURA. What! Sir, you think you can excuse yourself?

FELIX. Without a doubt.

LAURA.   [*aside*] May love permit it!

FELIX.   Hear me!

LAURA. And afterwards you'll go?

FELIX.   Yes.

LAURA.   Very well. Speak
And then be off.

FELIX.   It would be foolish of me
To say I did not love her once; more foolish
For you to imagine that my love for her
Had any likeness to my love for you.
No, it was not a genuine love, but merely
A kind of apprenticeship. I learned with her
How to love you.

LAURA.   But, sir, the science of love
Cannot be learnt; and love does not require
A course of study at the university.
It gets enough instruction on its own,
And of itself knows all it ought to know;
And it can only lose by trying to make
Itself more clever; and therefore, it is said,
Those with the most experience of love
Are always the least capable of loving.

FELIX. I have expressed my meaning very badly . . .

LAURA. No, on the contrary, only too well.

The language of Calderón's gallants is often precious and
absurd, but his heroines, like some of Shakespeare's, expose the
absurdity. When, in the second scene of the first act, Cesar going
under the name of Fabio, compares Lisarda to a sun, whom the
flowers worship, and at her sight burst into bloom, she replies:

                                              I'ld like to think,
Lord Fabio, for politeness, that the flowers
Would tell me pretty things, if they should listen
To you, my flatterer; for your gallantry
Is so refined, that even the very flowers
Would learn love's language from you.

The same couple, later in the same scene, discuss whether it is
possible for Cesar to love Lisarda before he has seen her unveiled.
Cesar argues that a blind man's love is loftier than she allows:

                        The chief object
Of a rational soul is the light of understanding.
That's what I love in you, with that I love you.
If I beheld your beauty's light, that instant
My soul and eyes would have to share my love,
Which therefore would be less, being so shared.
I leave it you to judge if it would be
Proper to rob the soul of half its love
And give it to the eyes.
LIS.   Even though the soul
Should share with the eyes its love, which is its light,
The soul would not love less, but there would be
Merely more love.
CES.   I don't quite understand.
LIS. If when there is a light, another spark
Is brought against it, it communicates
Its flame, but does not thereby cease to burn.
Love is a fire which burns within the soul;
If it's communicated to the eyes,
It does not cease to be as bright a fire
As formerly. The very eyes, which once
Were sad and dull, shine with a sudden radiance
But yet, the fire has entered in the eyes
Without departing from the soul.

Calderón is the least performed of all great dramatists outside
his own country. But the world's repertoire of first-rate comedies is
not so extensive that it can afford to dispense with the dozen or so
masterpieces to be found among his works. Whenever they have
been given a performance in recent years they have been remarkably successful.

II

Congreve on the Modern Stage[1]

I

Some years ago, when my article on Congreve appeared in the Stratford-upon-Avon Studies, I was attacked by the dramatic critic of the *Daily Telegraph* as an academic who had been seduced by the beauty of Congreve's prose into the delusion that he was a good dramatist: if only I had had any experience of the plays in the theatre, I would have known how bad they were. I was provoked into replying that if I was indeed deluded about Congreve's merits as a dramatist, it was not because I had never seen his plays on the stage. Many years before I became an academic, I had seen Edith Evans as Millamant and had myself acted in *The Way of the World*. Later on, I had directed the play at Leeds University and played there to crowded and enthusiastic houses. All this was before I had written a word about Congreve. To this Mr. Darlington replied that, despite this, Congreve was a wretched dramatist; *The Way of the World* deservedly failed in 1700; and the legendary success of Dame Edith as Millamant, or of Sir John Gielgud as Valentine, proved only that great actors and actresses could make silk purses out of sows' ears. It was because of this controversy with Mr. Darlington that I have chosen to speak on the recent stage history of Congreve's plays.[2]

We sometimes forget that the revival of the comedy of manners has been within the lifetime of many of us. Macready, it is true, had put on a bowdlerized version of *Love for Love* in 1842. The nature of the alterations can be judged from a single example.

1. From *William Congreve*, ed. B. Morris (1972).
2. I am indebted to Miss Dorothy Proctor and Mr. Philip Gibbons of the British Theatre Museum for providing me with cast lists of the various productions; to Mr. Latham of the Victoria and Albert Museum for his courteous assistance; to Mrs. Irene Grant and Mrs. S. Carr for help of various kinds; and to various dramatic critics, including some amateurs, whose work I have pillaged.

Scandal's remark—'She is chaste, who was never ask'd the Question' (III. i. 127–8)—was deemed to be scandalous. So he was given the pointless substitute: 'She has never yielded to the temptation of a man's addresses, to whom they were never offered.' In the hey-day of the Victorian period it was no longer possible to present a Congreve play.

In 1904 there were performances of *The Way of the World* by the Stage Society and another production a few years later with Ethel Irving as Millamant. The Stage Society, again, put on *The Double-Dealer* in 1916. *Love for Love* followed in 1917 and was revived by the Phoenix Society in 1921, with some of the earlier cast. All these were performances for members only, and Montague Summers deserves the credit for his pioneering efforts. But the public was still thought to be unready for the plays. My own first introduction to the comedy of manners illustrates this point. The Lena Ashwell players performed in the Public Baths of various South London boroughs and they put on Garrick's adaptation of *The Country Wife*. We had been promised that the play would be quite suitable for the family, and so it proved. Feigned impotence, fornication, and adultery were all removed. The heroine, being Pinchwife's ward, not his wife, was free to marry the blameless young man who was substituted for Horner.

On 7 February 1924, encouraged by the extraordinary popularity of *The Beggar's Opera*, and by the fact that audiences had not objected to the frankness of the dialogue, Nigel Playfair staged his famous production of *The Way of the World*. He assembled a cast uneven in quality but with a Mirabell, a Millamant, and a Marwood who have never been surpassed. The production itself suffered from Playfair's usual tendency to prettify everything. It was, said A. B. Walkley in *The Times*, 'a rattling, jaunty, jigging, almost jazzing revival. The play is fantasticated.' Playfair confessed that, as he thought that the plot was too difficult for an audience to follow, he had burlesqued it and treated it as a joke.[3] He introduced a kind of ballet when four servants came on with step-ladders to light the electric candles; some of the costuming was too fantastic; Witwoud carried a muff though the weather was warm enough to sit in the park; and there was too much play with lace handkerchiefs and snuff-boxes.

3. *Hammersmith Hoy* (London, 1930), p. 244.

Some critics were churlish enough to condemn Elsa Lanchester's dance, inspired by Hogarth's 'Shrimp Girl'. The *décor* by Doris Zinkeisen was in poster style, inferior to the similar work of Lovat Fraser for *The Beggar's Opera*.

There were faults in the casting. Harold Anstruther was too modern as Fainall, and Margaret Yarde was too modern and farcical as Lady Wishfort. Harold Scott as the bogus Sir Rowland exaggerated so absurdly that he could not have deceived even Lady Wishfort. These flaws made Hubert Griffith in the *Observer* speak of *The Way of the World* 'as a farce that had its dull patches'. But although the play was 'perhaps just a teeny-weeny bit popularised', because, as James Agate suggested, Playfair 'was afraid to trust us with the pure distillation of the Comic Spirit', it was amply redeemed by the three performances I have mentioned and by Norman V. Norman as Petulant, Playfair himself as Witwoud, and by Scott Russell as an endearing and tuneful Sir Wilfull.

Agate thought that Robert Loraine's Mirabell was a trifle on the sober side and that he had too much heart. I think myself that this criticism is due to a misunderstanding of the part. Loraine was better than Godfrey Tearle and Sir John Gielgud, who have both played the part to the Evans Millamant, and his seriousness contrasted nicely with her gaiety, with the foppishness of Witwoud, and with the caddishness of Fainall. 'The part was beautifully spoken, and the actor used only the suavest and most gentle notes in his voice. He listened exquisitely.'[4] Dorothy Green, as Agate said again, 'made great music of her lines' as Mrs. Marwood; and she lived up to her name in the wormwood bitterness of her voice.

As for Edith Evans, who emerged as our greatest actress in a single night, the critics had no reservations. Playfair, in his book of reminiscences, *Hammersmith Hoy*, declares that the character ran away with the author:[5]

4. Winifred Loraine, *Robert Loraine* (London, 1938), p. 302, said that Mirabell 'may be classed as the most ungrateful and difficult part ever written. Mirabell has to balance Millamant, with scarcely a line from the author to help him do it.' This is absurd; but Mrs. Loraine was influenced by an accident on the first night when the curtain fell by mistake before Mirabell's soliloquy near the end of Act II.

5. Ibid., p. 244.

What started as a comedy of manners is suddenly rapt from our sight in one of the most blinding visions of character that have ever been dramatized. And it was that which gave Miss Evans her real chance. The Millamant of that last final surrender to Mirabell is something far more than the Millamant who comes 'full sail, with her fan spread, and her streamers out, and a shoal of fools for tenders': it is a woman wittier, more fascinating and more tender, probably, than has ever been seen off the stage, or elsewhere on it. Here is no 'character rendered ridiculous by an affected wit': here is a character rendered sublime by the poignancy and the sincerity of its wit. ... It is a most extraordinary tribute to Edith Evans that she was able to take on her shoulders the weight of such an enormous conception, and play it almost as if the conception were purely her own rather than the author's.

That it was rather the author's conception is supported, I believe, by the description of how Anne Bracegirdle, for whom the part was written, played it. As Colley Cibber said,[6] the discretion of her life

contributed not a little, to make her the *Cara*, the darling of the theatre. For it will be no extravagant thing to say, scarce an audience saw her that were less half of them her lovers. ... She had no greater claim to beauty than what the most desirable *brunette* might pretend to.

She had, in fact, a slight deformity:

But her youth and lively aspect threw such a glow of health and chearfulness, that, on the stage, few spectators that were not past it, could behold her without desire. ... When she acted Millamant, all the faults, follies, and affectation of that agreeable tyrant, were venially melted down into so many charms and attractions of a conscious beauty.

Hubert Griffith remarked that Edith Evans was a comedienne by training and an emotional actress by instinct:[7]

the formality of eighteenth-century comedy is too rigid a mould into which to pour a personality that needs the freedom of great emotional tragedy to be seen in its full splendour. I admit she did it marvellously. One hung upon the lips of her Millamant and delighted in her. But one noticed something else. At the lightest of Millamant's remarks, from the first scene of courtship onwards, one felt strangely moved, an

6. A. N. Nagler, *A Source Book in Theatrical History* (New York, 1959), pp. 228–9.
7. *Observer.*

inward disturbance of spirit that neither wit nor gaiety nor the art born of perfect technique can produce. It comes only in the presence of power and beauty. And I am perfectly sure it was Miss Edith Evans who was providing in her own personality the power and beauty that Mr. Congreve in his lines was not. She kept Millamant an eighteenth-century flirt, and because she is of the line of great tragic actresses, transformed her also into a poem.

To which we may retort that, except in *Rosmersholm*, Edith Evans was never a great tragic actress; that the power and beauty were in Congreve's lines; that Millamant is not really a flirt (like Célimène) but a woman in love who fears disillusionment.

The brilliance of the performance was best described by James Agate.[8] Edith Evans's countenance

is replete, as was said of Congreve's style, 'with sense and satire, conveyed in the most pointed and polished terms'. This acting is 'a shower of brilliant conceits, a new triumph of wit, a *new conquest over dullness*' . . . Her Millamant is impertinent without being pert, graceless without being ill-graced. . . . Never can that astonishing 'Ah! idle creature, get up when you will' have taken on greater delicacy, nor 'I may by degrees *dwindle* into a wife' a more delicious mockery . . . all this is breathed out as though it were early Ronsard or du Bellay. . . . There is a pout of the lips, a jutting forward of the chin to greet the conceit, and a smile of happy deliverance when it is uttered, which defy the chronicler. This face, at such moments, is like a city in illumination, and when it is withdrawn leaves a glow behind.

Arnold Bennett had been one of Playfair's financial backers, but he announced publicly that the production 'was bound to be a complete frost, the plot being silly and the dialogue far too subtle for the public'. To his astonishment the play was 'a tremendous success', the booking far exceeding that for *The Beggar's Opera*, and (as he said) 'the gallery nightly "eats it" '. He thought that Edith Evans gave the 'finest comedy performance' he had ever seen. He went behind afterwards to tell her so and she replied, 'How exciting!' But perhaps the best indication of Bennett's conversion as a result of the performance is to be found in his letter to André Gide a fortnight later: 'It is a wonderful play.'

When the production was revived in 1927, *The Times* critic remarked that beneath Millamant's gaiety there was a depth of

8. *Sunday Times*; A. Bennett, *Journal* (London, 1933) and *Letters* (London, 1966), 12 and 25 February 1924.

sentiment and a fastidiousness of feeling. Edith Evans's performance had not been dimmed:

She shines and glitters and bedazzles, varying her laughter and the
ripple of her voice with superb artistry, while provokingly hiding her
cheeks behind her fan, as if to conceal her own delight from those who
delight in it.

None of these critics, however, pointed to the fact that this Millamant was fully alive to her own absurdities. When, for example,
she declared that she never used prose letters for doing up her
hair, she was not stating a fact but spinning a delightful fantasy.

By all accounts there was a better Fainall in this revival (Henry
Hewitt) and a worse Lady Wishfort. The tiny part of Betty in the
opening scene was played by Peggy Ashcroft. Some critics
preferred Godfrey Tearle to Robert Loraine: he was 'courtly,
polished, poetic, sincere, splendidly clear-cut'.[9] Ion Swinley, who
played the part for some performances—I think in this revival—
was not so polished in manner, but he brought out the music of the
Congrevean prose more successfully.

The Playfair production, enjoyable as it was, made the mistake
of guying the plot and ignoring the Horatian epigraph. Not only
is there an economic basis for the plot, but none of the characters
belongs to the real aristocracy. Witwoud, though a fop, had once
been an attorney's clerk; Sir Wilfull is a boorish country squire;
Fainall has to marry for money, and even takes money from his
mistress; and Mirabell cannot afford to marry without Millamant's
dowry. An ideal production would make all this clear.

The fame of Edith Evans's Millamant deterred rivals for a good
many years. I did not see the Ashley Dukes production at the
Mercury Theatre in 1942, with Sonia Dresdel as Millamant and an
otherwise undistinguished cast. Six years later, in October 1948,
Edith Evans, now Dame Edith, appeared again in *The Way of the
World*, this time as Lady Wishfort. All the critics agreed that the
production as a whole was a failure, partially redeemed by the
performances of Dame Edith, and of Robert Eddison as Witwoud.
The rest of the cast reduced Congreve's subtle rhythms to 'a sort
of English Films version of eighteenth-century diction'. As
Harold Hobson said:[1]

9. *Times.*   1. *Sunday Times.*

You cannot jump from the shorts and lustiness of suburban tennis into the frills and flounces of Restoration comedy.

Harry Andrews as Mirabell took his speeches

like a dose of cascara, to be swallowed manfully and, above all in the shortest possible time.

He seemed to disbelieve in the value of Congreve's language.[2] Faith Brook, as Millamant, had to contend with the Edith Evans of 1924, as well as with the Edith Evans of 1948. Millamant, said Mr. Darlington, is a personage; 'Miss Brook makes her a nice young person'.[3] She was 'too naïvely self-conscious in her playfulness' and without the necessary social assurance. She lacked 'the comic force, the full sweep of haughty raillery, the glorious mischief'.[4] Somebody should tell her, said Mr. Hobson, 'that there are certain words in Congreve that ought to be stroked and fondled like a lap-dog'. Miss Brook's 'freshness and charming vivacity are wasted since they have the effect of turning Millamant into a girl who seems naïvely surprised at the witty things her author has given her to say'.[5]

Dame Edith's Lady Wishfort was 'a gloriously over-ripe piece of petulance, grossness and pathos'. When she signified 'her intention to *loll* on the sofa at her first meeting with Sir Roland, Dame Edith put into that word a comic sensuality that made it leap out of the dictionary as if it were the active incarnation of humorous lechery'. 'Commanding as she does the combined styles of Lady Bracknell and Sir Thomas Beecham she can make any line pregnant with meaning.' For example, 'when it is suggested that the plot against her did no harm, she gave an overwhelming shout of "No damage?" comparable to the indignation with which as Lady Bracknell the actress hailed "A handbag?" '.[6] As T. C. Worsley said,[7]

When Dame Edith Evans speaks, the words cascade and check, pause and then gush, straight from a living person who has always, you are convinced, spoken just so. How she confounds Dr. Johnson, who pronounced of Congreve's plays: 'His characters are commonly fictitious

2. *Manchester Guardian.*   3. *Daily Telegraph.*
4. *Times, Observer.*   5. *Tatler.*
6. *Tatler, Sunday Times, Evening Standard, Manchester Guardian.*
7. *New Statesman and Nation.*

and artificial, with very little of nature, and not much of life'. This Lady Wishfort has so much of both that, laughable, ridiculous and ridiculed as she may be, she is yet not a mere figure of fun. She touches our pity as well as our laughter.

II

Sir John Gielgud's production followed five years later on 19 February 1953. It was at the Lyric Theatre, Hammersmith, and it was suggested by one critic that the unlaid ghost of the legendary performance of 1924 interfered with the success of the production. There was an unexpected air of heaviness about it, the lack of any consistent style, and there were several loose ends and blurred performances.[8] But T. C. Worsley, who came to see it after it had been running for a week, recorded that 'the hesitancies and imperfections of the first night are now ironed out and the production is smooth, uncreased and shining'.[9] But Mr. Worsley, who had not seen the Evans Millamant, was almost alone in regarding Pamela Brown's as masterly:

What superb attack and bravura, what precision and mastery of diction, what absolute perfection of phrasing both in speech and gesture, so that each small passage is rounded off and complete with no untidy ends, what jets and spurts of unforced gaiety springing from a vitality unquenchable yet controlled in the prevailing idiom of superficial indifference!

The *Daily Express* absurdly saluted Pamela Brown 'for giving the theatre's wickedest lady something very like a heart'; and the *Daily Mirror* thought it was praising Pamela Brown when it declared she continued to dazzle 'with the rolling eye of a very attractive ventriloquist's dummy'. Many of the reviews were much less favourable. Miss Brown gave the impression 'that she was not in love with the idea of Millamant'. She was 'an ice-maiden, learned no doubt in classics and philosophy'. Her words 'leaked from her, half apologetically, in dribs and drabs'. She was 'never for a moment Congreve's heroine'. She had 'the air of repeating brilliantly the *bons mots* heard at a party the previous evening'

8. *Manchester Guardian, Punch, New Statesman and Nation.*
9. *New Statesman and Nation.*

and she had the habit of 'interrupting her speeches with expulsions of breath that resemble the escape of air from a punctured tyre'.[1] Philip Hope-Wallace, with an unusual imperceptiveness, suggested that[2]

Miss Brown is simply too intelligent for Millamant; there is and should be a natural silliness in the woman which was lost in so 'knowing' an interpretation, one which continually and wittily seized the regard of the audience in a silent embrace of complicity.

Something of the same misunderstanding of the part colours the review in the *Tatler*. Miss Brown, we are told,

conceived a sort of distaste for the witty, idle, shallow creature who is nothing more than a superior lady of fashion ... Millamant is, of course, a type of the superior ladies who do not think. . . . It pleases her to talk exquisitely, but, for all her wonderful play with irony and paradox and wit, she remains an inveterate trifler, perfectly happy to pose elegantly in the social mirror. Miss Brown cannot bring herself to enter into the delicious make-believe of such an essentially empty mind, and this imperfectly concealed antipathy is ruinous to the comedy.

One may ask both critics if it is possible to be witty, paradoxical, and ironical without intelligence, and whether Millamant's love of the poets bespeaks an empty mind.

Gielgud, too, was something of a disappointment. Perhaps because of his anxieties as producer he stumbled over his lines on the first night, and even afterwards he mangled the rhythm of some of his speeches. The most popular performance, however deplorable, came from Margaret Rutherford as Lady Wishfort. It was, to my mind, disastrous. 'Comic business is not enough here', said T. C. Worsley. She 'was not born for Restoration comedy', commented the *Sketch*. She was 'firmly imprisoned in the W.R.N.S. wardroom'. She reminded another critic of St. Trinian's.[3] Only Harold Hobson thought her as good as Edith Evans in the part. The best performances in this production came from Paul Scofield as Witwoud and Pauline Jameson as Mrs. Fainall.

The John Clements production of the play at the Saville Theatre in December 1956—I saw it on tour—was generally

1. *Times, New Statesman and Nation, Evening Standard, Sunday Times.*
2. *Manchester Guardian.*
3. *New Statesman and Nation, Tatler.*

regarded as a disappointment. The Zinkeisen sets were arty and effete. The whole performance was dull, plodding, lacking in style.[4] John Clements made a tolerable Mirabell; Margaretta Scott was good as Marwood; Margaret Rutherford, looking like 'an abandoned stone quarry' or 'a huffing and puffing head-mistress', was at least funny; and the Witwoud and Petulant (Reginald Beckwith and Geoffrey Dunn) were generally praised.[5] But Kay Hammond's Millamant was a major disaster. She spoilt the witty dialogue 'by drawing it out as though intent on piling affectation on affectation'. Her speech sounded 'like cream being squeezed over chocolate'. She delivered 'each word as if it were on the end of a long wad of chewing gum she was reluctant to give up'. She was not so much acting the part, as holding the character 'up for inspection'. She gave not merely 'the fine lady posing wittily in the social manner but also the actress imitating the fine lady posing wittily in the social manner' [? mirror]. 'She ceases to be Lady Wishfort's problem-niece and becomes Miss Hammond echoing herself'. 'In her sulks she is positively morose.'[6] One should, perhaps, add that as Kay Hammond had been seriously ill, she was less good than everyone had expected, and this may explain the tone of some of the remarks I have quoted.

I will say little about the current production of *The Way of the World* at the National Theatre. *The Times* critic pointed out that it 'goes a long way to disproving the old idea that nobody can follow the plot. . . . Audiences will have no difficulty in following the stratagems of sexual and economic acquisitiveness on which the action turns.' The text was 'delivered with exceptional clarity and bite', though another critic thought it was rather tame in its effect.[7] Michael Langham, the producer, was a little too anxious to dot the i's and cross the t's. At one point, at the end of Act III, Fainall and Marwood locked the doors and started to undress—a risky proceeding in Lady Wishfort's house. But one may sympa-thize with the producer's wish 'to reveal the natural man under the fine clothes'. This was apparent, too, in Hazel Hughes's Lady Wishfort. Although some critics compared her to a pantomime dame or a figure from a Whitehall farce, she subtly modulated 'her

4. *Observer, Times.*   5. *Evening Standard, Times.*
  6. *Times, Daily Mirror, Evening Standard, Manchester Guardian, Times, Punch, Observer.*
  7. *Times, Sunday Times.*

performance from the grotesque and cruel into the civilized and pathetic'. As *The Times* critic remarked, 'There is a real savagery in seeing her reeling under the blows of sexual humiliation and turning on her servants in revengeful fury'.[8]

Robert Lang's Mirabell and John Moffatt's Fainall were generally admired; but Geraldine McEwan's Millamant divided the critics. To Philip Hope-Wallace, she seemed miscast, quacking through her lines in imitation of Danny La Rue. To another critic, whose style hardly suggests much literary sensibility, Miss McEwan was[9]

a languid, gurgling female casting her witty affectations in all directions with a giggling disinterest (*sic*) in their impact. Hooded-eyed and open-mouthed, she seems at times fey rather than adorable.

But to the *Daily Telegraph* she was *radiant* and *The Times* rightly suggested that she wore 'her vocal and bodily affectations like a suit of armour' and left you in no doubt that these were 'a necessary safeguard against the sexual disasters rife among the other characters'. She spoke her marriage provisos 'with an attractive wistfulness'.[1]

III

There have been few productions of *The Double-Dealer*. It was done at the Edinburgh Festival by the Old Vic company in August 1959 and, in the following month, in London. The *Daily Mirror* critic said he defied 'anyone to follow the intrigues, the asides, the plots and counter-plots' of the play; but both *The Times* and the *Manchester Guardian* praised the speed and clarity of Michael Benthall's production. As Philip Hope-Wallace said, 'the plot comes out bold and clear', and even though

The play is like a motionless car in which the characters make conversation until the author at intervals cranks the starting handle madly;

and even though, as *The Times* remarked, 'the play is written in a series of entertaining zigzags ... the narrative has become as simple to comprehend as the alphabet'.

8. *Daily Telegraph, Evening Standard, Sunday Times.*
9. *Manchester Guardian, Evening Standard.*
1. *Sunday Times.*

The main complaint levelled at the production was that there was 'an assortment of individual acting styles in the kind of play that is more dependent than almost any other on perfect unity of style'. The intonation varied 'as though no one had given much thought to the overall sound of the speaking'. There was ugliness of speech and movement. For example both Maggie Smith (as Lady Plyant) and Moyra Fraser (as Lady Froth) played 'in broad revue style with *naice* Kensington accents'. Maggie Smith, indeed, at one point interjected 'the screams of an unregenerate Eliza Doolittle' and lacked 'a sense of period style'.[2]

All the critics praised Miles Malleson as Sir Paul Plyant. He was described as 'a joy almost touching in his embodiment of stupidity, complacency and good nature'. He managed

to look facially like a classic sculptor's idea of an animated sheep, and to speak in tones of a furiously confidential turkey cock. Never has there been so much rich gobbling and cawing: never has chin dropped like Malleson's or eyes popped so constantly.

Most critics approved of Ursula Jeans as Lady Touchwood, oddly enough because her 'emotional volcano' did not disrupt the play, her evil being seen under a comic light. Donald Houston was effective as Maskwell, Judi Dench and John Justin were sympathetic, if sententious, as the true lovers; and Alec McCowen (as Brisk) and Joss Ackland (as Lord Froth) were very funny indeed.[3]

The critics as a whole seem to have been astonished at their own enjoyment. They thought it would have, at best, a mild collector's interest. They found it exhilarating. One critic confessed that he had

enjoyed it as much as any comedy of the period: it may lack the style of the major Congreve or the breadth of some of the other dramatists; but it has a crazy joy in life that I find infinitely and unexpectedly attractive.

Another critic said that the play[4]

has too many brilliantly entertaining scenes to deserve a neglect that has lasted for nearly half a century. .... The characters in this comedy have the inestimable advantage of speaking a dialogue which in its easy volubility and exquisite precision is unlike the dialogue of any other Restoration playwright.

2. *Tatler, Manchester Guardian, Times.*
3. *Times, Illustrated London News, Times.*
4. *Illustrated London News, Tatler.*

The only other revival of *The Double-Dealer* of which I have any information is that at the Liverpool Playhouse in 1956. They chose the play at my suggestion and (as they lost several thousand pounds on the production) they are never again likely to take my advice. But the failure of the production was not, I think, Congreve's fault. Lady Touchwood's incestuous passion was treated as a joke, and her scenes with the Iago-like Maskwell were treated as burlesqued melodrama. As a result, the scenes of high comedy were destroyed by their juxtaposition to the scenes of melodrama. The only proper way to play Lady Touchwood is with deadly seriousness.

The only public production of *The Old Batchelour* was in 1931 at the Lyric Theatre, Hammersmith, when Sir Nigel Playfair presented it with a splendid cast. It was in his best manner, said one critic; it was produced with 'infinite care and taste'. But the text was cut and rearranged.[5]

Handling the text with a surgeon's skill and discretion, he has excised *longueurs*, purged it of some period blemishes and stitched up the wounds again so neatly that the scars are scarcely noticeable.

The Fondlewive scenes were run together. One critic said 'it would be absurd to regard such a plot as sacrosanct' and Ivor Brown, who regarded Congreve as obscene, remarked in his carping review that[6]

The extent to which Congreve has to be trimmed and titivated to become tolerable to a modern audience is proof of his incompetence as a dramatist.

Even Mr. Brown admitted that the Fondlewife episode was delightful, and 'handled with a brilliance beyond praise' by Edith Evans as Laetitia, O. B. Clarence as Fondlewife, and Eric Portman as Bellmour. 'You wonder whether even Garrick could have had Mr. Clarences sere and gentle pathos.' He played what one critic said was an easy part with the 'most delicate skill'. As for Edith Evans, 'a leaping fountain of humour, of amorousness, of vivacity and duplicity', she played 'with a roguery, an abandon, a zest, a fertility of expression, and a happy suiting of Millamant's great air to the more approachable class next below'. Although

5. *Punch.*   6. *Times, Week End Review.*

Laetitia is one of the secondary characters, she was drawn by Edith Evans 'with a whimsical, shameless grace'.[7]

To see Miss Evans, torn between hope and fear, speed her old *Nykin* on his way and presently fail to cover the retreat of her gallant is to enjoy one of the tardier fruits of the Fall ripened by comic genius.

The other member of the cast who was universally praised was Miles Malleson as Sir Joseph Wittol. We are told that he was

In aspect a transmogrified shrimp; in manner sublimely absurd; his timing and deportment lovely; the laughter that greets his looks is kept bubbling by his art.

'Was there ever', asks another critic

so full, so rich, so varied, so blessed an inanity? This actor's Wittol proves that he must be the next great Aguecheek, and incidentally the character shows that Congreve had no silly scruples about borrowing, and like a good borrower could do it with a grace.

Malleson was 'infinitely funny', 'a delicious mannikin' ... 'the darling innocent in a world whose innocence we are foolish to protest'. Even Mr. Brown admitted that Miles Malleson was 'almost successful' in his 'efforts to wring some fun from the part'.[8]

IV

There have been three notable revivals of *Love for Love*, in 1934, 1943 and 1965. The first of these was given by the Old Vic company at Sadler's Wells, and was produced by Tyrone Guthrie. This was the famous season when Charles Laughton played Henry VIII, Angelo, and Lopahin, and Tattle was one of his best parts. Mr. Darlington in the *Daily Telegraph*, despite his generally low opinion of Congreve as a dramatist, had to admit that there was 'a delightful sense of style about the whole production, which fits admirably with the brilliance of the author's English and the sureness of his characterisation'. James Agate spoke of 'The grandeur of the evening as both enterprise and entertainment'. Ivor Brown called it a 'tremendous comedy—both stylish and robust';[9] and

7. *Sunday Times, Sketch, Sunday Times, Times, Punch.*
8. *Punch, Sunday Times, Observer, Week End Review.*
9. *Sunday Times, Observer.*

The Times critic (probably Charles Morgan) remarked that in performance all traces of Congreve's tendency to mingle reality with fantasy 'surprisingly disappeared'.

We have only to see a few scenes played to realise that, as readers, dazzled perhaps by the unending flicker of wit across the printed page, we have been led into a too easy acceptance of Lamb's theory that all these characters were intended to inhabit a world of fantasy.

He points out the difference between the 'realistic' and the 'fantastic' studies of character 'is the perfectly natural distinction between persons belonging to town life and personages belonging to country life'.

As the dialogue flashes along drama is constantly being struck out of some scene or incident. A whispered confidence or a bout of raillery, and two or more portraits are drawn and placed in dramatic relation to each other and to life.

Charles Laughton, we are told, had

composed the picture of this vain, blabbing, affected creature with the care, the insight, and the humour that have carried him so far . . . in his profession.

He was 'a delicious figure of fun and under-breeding, a mixture of wiggery and waggery, at once coy and servile, male yet mincing'. He was brilliant as an instructor in the art of love. Ivor Brown complained that Laughton has credited 'the toad with a certain proletarian oafishness'—a description that does not accord with my own memories of the performance—but Mr. Brown went on to say that 'the richness of his comedy was absolute'.[1]

Mr. Laughton's acting is, as always, a form of total immersion; he is Tattle to the writhing shoulders, the twisted mouth, the garrulous finger-tips.

Equally delicious was Elsa Lanchester's performance as Miss Prue. She was described as 'a deliciously effective character', and 'a glorious fantasia on a bucolic theme'. But *The Times*, while admitting she was great fun, thought she ought to have been a trifle more demure; and James Agate said that her hoydenism seemed to him urban rather than rustic. 'Such a chit has climbed more steps of areas than trunks of trees.'[2] I don't agree.

1. *Daily Telegraph, Sunday Times, Observer.*
2. *Morning Post, Daily Telegraph, Sunday Times.*

Three of the Livesey family were in the cast. Sam as Sir Sampson Legend had 'a certain pig-headed splendour'. He appeared as a 'benevolent ogre' who loomed 'large and round and over-red, like the sun seen through fog'. Roger Livesey, as Ben, was a 'jolly personable salt' who hardly deserved 'to be likened to a porpoise' by Miss Prue. One critic compared him to a drawing by Morland. Barrie Livesey as Valentine was less successful. He was in too much of a hurry and he made little of the feigned madness. Two critics blamed Congreve for the fact that Valentine was never very entertaining. It is 'the play's worst part, being no more than a peg for the actor's own airs and graces'.[3] This, in view of Gielgud's later performance, is clearly absurd.

Angelica was played by Ursula Jeans, variously described as charming, enchanting, and 'floating gaily through Mrs. Bracegirdle's part'. Athene Seyler, an old hand at comedy of manners, was splendid as Mrs. Frail. She kept 'a Restoration tongue in her cheek' and her performance and that of Flora Robson as Mrs. Foresight 'one could hardly ask to see bettered'. This, I think, is true; though Flora Robson's triumph was unexpected in view of her preference for more serious roles. Morland Graham as Foresight was 'a shining focus of fun' in a brilliantly entertaining evening. Inevitably two critics punned on Foresight's name. The performance was 'a saga of senility almost dazzlingly ludicrous'. Morland Graham 'tops the pedigree of this Foresight Saga with a wonderful picture of the superstitious coney'.[4] It may be added that the small part of Jeremy was played by James Mason.

Gielgud's wartime production was even better. He had played Valentine years before at the Oxford Playhouse and although they had only a week's rehearsals they had to give a number of extra performances. Sir John tells us that the play was given in a very full version, but that as the 'audience consisted largely of dons and the highbrow intelligentsia of North Oxford the text was easily followed and understood'. He decided in 1943 that with a less academic audience it was necessary to cut the text more drastically. He had the problem of playing in very large theatres and, as he thought, 'of trying to make the wordy, classic text seem alive

3. *Times, Sunday Times, Times, Sunday Times, Times, Observer, Sunday Times.*
4. *Daily Telegraph, Times, Morning Post, Times, Daily Telegraph, Times, Sunday Times, Observer.*

and truthful to audiences unfamiliar with this type of dialogue'.[5]

Gielgud produced, as well as taking his old part of Valentine. He assembled a star cast, but some of the casting was a little odd. Yvonne Arnaud, with her carefully cultivated accent, was a strange choice for Mrs. Frail, the only excuse for turning the character into a French-woman being that Miss Arnaud had played Mrs. Pepys in *And so to Bed* with notable success. James Agate asked how Leon Quartermaine as Scandal could convey vitriol with a voice of honey; Leslie Banks's Tattle was not as funny as Laughton's had been; and the Angelica of Rosalie Crutchley, though she had 'an agreeable suggestion of devil', had little of the requisite style. Marian Spencer, as Mrs. Foresight, had not merely style but, we are told, 'a certain cadaverous charm'. Everyone liked Cecil Trouncer as Sir Sampson, 'glowing with choleric splendour', Angela Baddeley as Miss Prue, and George Woodbridge as Ben. But the two best performances were those of Miles Malleson and of Gielgud himself. Malleson's Foresight was a continual joy:

his fears and agonies are so authentic and his little, peering, anxious face becomes a haggard question-mark of pallid and twitching perturbation.

Agate thought the part of Valentine was not a good one; and Ivor Brown said it was a dull part in the First Act. It did not seem dull to me. I agreed with *The Times* critic who said that Gielgud played the part 'with a witty grace, a perfect comand of the Congrevean prose rhythm and the nicest sense of Shakespearian parody in the mad scene'. The production owed a lot to Rex Whistler's settings and the performance captivated 'the mind in the right way, lapping it, so to speak, in laughter and delight'.[6]

The National Theatre production in 1965 was by Peter Wood. He believed that Congreve was satirizing 'the fortune-hunting materialism of the new upper classes'. He therefore stressed the play's social relevance. As a result the props had 'that battered, worn, Berliner-Ensemble look'. Valentine's lodgings were like a pig-sty, and he himself was 'pasty-faced from long confinement, blue-jowled', and wearing a 'frowsy wig'. He had reached 'the seedy last stages of bachelordom'.[7] Some critics approved of the

5. *Stage Directions* (London, 1963), p. 65.
6. *Sunday Times, Times, Observer, Times, Observer, Times.*
7. *Sunday Telegraph, Spectator.*

realism of the production, but others complained that the fun had been dampened, that the pace was too slow, that the play was 'frost-nipped'. Milton Shulman said the wigs were so unkempt that one could only assume 'that the nation at the time was undergoing a national strike by either hair-dressers or comb manufacturers'. Angelica suffered particularly. Geraldine McEwan's spirited performance was spoilt by 'an ugly frizzed wig and a pallid sickroom make-up'. Even an admirer, who spoke of her 'delicious, beady little Angelica', complained of her 'distraught and distracting hair'—what another critic described as 'a Harpo-Marx hair-do'. Joyce Redman's sense of style was universally praised— perhaps an indication that style was elsewhere lacking—and so was Lynn Redgrave's Miss Prue, 'in her most irrestistibly lumpish vein', 'charmingly hoydenish', 'the last and most perfect of her studies in lumpishness'.[8] (No critic had a word to say of the fourth woman, Mrs. Foresight, so we must suppose that Madge Ryan made little impression.)

Miles Malleson again played Foresight, and he was 'a continuous doddering joy', 'whose mass of chins become the outward and visible sign of the vulnerable, wobbly inner man', reminding one critic 'of an anxious and wobbly whale about to blow'. But another critic, comparing this performance with the earlier one, thought Malleson was subdued. Colin Blakeley's Ben was criticized for his Irish accent, and it suffered too from the producer's conception:

Suddenly a lurching figure appears in the mouth of the lane by the park, short, stout, top-heavy, weighed down by a lumpy kitbag and an incongruous, feather-light birdcage. At first glance he seems a dwarf, but this is because his trousers were built for a giant, snipped off raggedly below the crotch, but still hanging ludicrously loose and wide around his knees.

He was dressed, said another critic, 'in the scourings of a quayside rag-and-bone man'. Why, asked another, was he dressed like a pirate-beggar?[9]

8. *Daily Telegraph, Evening Standard, Sunday Telegraph, Sunday Times, Evening Standard, Times, Guardian* (formerly *Manchester Guardian*), *Spectator.*

9. *Spectator, Illustrated London News, Queen, Guardian* (formerly *Manchester Guardian*), *Spectator, Sunday Times, Guardian* (formerly *Manchester Guardian*).

Robert Lang's Scandal, 'stalking through the play like an embodiment of lonely scorn', delivered 'his marginal cynicisms as if they [caused] him some private disgust'. One critic, who regarded Scandal as 'a naive romantic who is appalled by the loucheness of the world about him', thought that Mr. Lang failed to find any meaning in the part; but Hilary Spurling disagreed:[1]

Perhaps Mr. Lang's finest moment is when the plot begins to dawn: 'Tattle and Frail leagued for eternity'. Light seems to irradiate Scandal's bleak, bony face as he savours the prospect, delighted, incredulous, like a child given the star off the Christmas tree: 'It is magnificent'. A shadow crosses his brow, humour is replaced by a maniacal fixity of purpose, we know that he would die in the attempt, even as he says: '*It must not fail*'. An Iago stands revealed.

I find this circumstantial description baffling. Congreve's Scandal merely says:

I have discover'd something of *Tattle*, that is of a piece with Mrs. *Frail*. He Courts *Angelica*, if we cou'd contrive to couple 'em together —Heark'ee.

It is difficult to understand how any actor could convey the thoughts provided for him by Hilary Spurling, unless the producer inserted some additional dialogue.

Sir Laurence Olivier's Tattle was naturally the star performance He reminded J. C. Trewin of

an agile, scandalous cat, now thrusting out a paw, now exploring the roof, now purring secretively, now (as if his tail had been trodden on) wailing in inarticulate despair—'I never liked anybody less in my life'.

This line, when he finds himself married to Mrs. Frail, impressed *The Times* critic too, who adds that Olivier at this point burst into tears. The part was played as 'a chalk-lipped fop with enormously padded calves'. Olivier was 'superbly funny in that dry-mouthed and mincing manner he has perfected in parts like Justice Shallow'. He was 'a little unbalanced, with the long-lipped slack-mouth, nosy look of Hylda Baker under a Bette Davis head of curls'. 'He primps, pouts and piruoettes his way through one slapstick intrigue after another.'[2]

1. *Sunday Times, Queen, Spectator.*
2. *Illustrated London News, Queen, Sunday Telegraph, Evening Standard.*

The production had been taken to Moscow before it opened in London, and according to the *Evening News* the most successful moment of the performance in the Kremlin Theatre was when Tattle escaped from Miss Prue's bedroom window:

This involved Olivier sliding down a roof and in dishevelled wig and clothes running along a narrow wall balancing himself like a drunken tightrope walker. Coming to a wide gap, this uncertain tomcat paused, closed his eyes in silent prayer and jumped across. This would be funny in any language. It brought deserved applause last night and is going to be cherished by collectors of Oliviana.

Here, obviously, was a legitimate piece of business.

It will, I hope, have become apparent that Congreve is still a living dramatist; that his plays offer wonderful parts to good actors and actresses, especially to those who allow the wonderfully differentiated speech to possess them; that the plays are not artificial in any straightforward sense of the word; that the characters are not at all heartless; that the plots are not unintelligible to audiences if the plays are properly directed and not reduced to farce or fantasy. It may be observed that the verbal felicity of Congreve has enabled dramatic critics to excel themselves. Finally, I may add that every actor, whether amateur or professional, to whom I have spoken on the subject, agrees that after acting in Congreve they find all other dramatic prose inferior and more difficult to deliver effectively.

The Way of the World

	1924	1927	1948
Fainall	Harold Anstruther	Henry Hewitt	Peter Copley
Mirabell	Robert Loraine	Godfrey Tearle	Harry Andrews
Witwoud	Nigel Playfair	Guy Boulton	Robert Eddison
Petulant	Norman V. Norman	Norman V. Norman	Mark Dignam
Sir Wilfull	Scott Russell	Scott Russell	Nigel Green
Waitwell	Harold Scott	Harold Scott	Meadows White
Lady Wishfort	Margaret Yarde	Ruth Maitland	Edith Evans
Millamant	Edith Evans	Edith Evans	Faith Brook
Marwood	Dorothy Green	Dorothy Green	Pauline Jameson
Mrs. Fainall	Ruth Taylor	Ruth Taylor	Mary Martlew
Foible	Hilda Sims	Renée de Vaux	June Brown
Mincing	Kathleen Hilliard	Kathleen Burgis	Penelope Munday
Peggy	Elsa Lanchester	Penelope Spencer	Josephine Stuart
Betty	Miss Dixon	Peggy Ashcroft	Margaret Chisholm
Producer	Nigel Playfair	Nigel Playfair	John Burrell

The Way of the World (cont.)

	1953	1956	1969
Fainall	Eric Porter	Douglas Wilmer	John Moffatt
Mirabell	John Gielgud	John Clements	Robert Lang
Witwoud	Paul Scofield	Reginald Beckwith	Edward Hardwicke
Petulant	Richard Wordsworth	Geoffrey Dunn	David Ryall
Sir Wilfull	Brewster Mason	Raymond Francis	Michael Turner
Waitwell	Peter Sallis	Harry H. Corbett	Edward Petherbridge
Lady Wishfort	Margaret Rutherford	Margaret Rutherford	Hazel Hughes
Millamant	Pamela Brown	Kay Hammond	Geraldine McEwan
Marwood	Eileen Herlie	Margaretta Scott	Jane Wenham
Mrs. Fainall	Pauline Jameson	Valerie Hanson	Sheila Reid
Foible	Jessie Evans	Anne Leon	Helen Burns
Mincing	Mairhi Russell	Rosalind Knight	Jane Lapotaire
Peggy	Charlotte Mitchell	Sheila Grant	Suzanne Vasey
Betty	Gillian Webb	Megan Latimer	Gabrielle Laye
Producer	John Gielgud	John Clements	Michael Langham

Love for Love

	1934	1943	1965
Valentine	Barrie Livesey	John Gielgud	John Stride
Jeremy	James Mason	Max Adrian	Tom Kempinski
Scandal	Dennis Arundell	Leon Quartermaine	Robert Lang
Buckram	Marius Goring	D. J. Williams	Peter Cellier
Tattle	Charles Laughton	Leslie Banks	Laurence Olivier
Frail	Athene Seyler	Yvonne Arnaud	Joyce Redman
Foresight	Morland Graham	Miles Malleson	Miles Malleson
Mrs. Foresight	Flora Robson	Marian Spencer	Madge Ryan
Angelica	Ursula Jeans	Rosalie Crutchley	Geraldine McEwan
Sir Samson	Sam Livesey	Cecil Trouncer	Anthony Nicholls
Ben	Roger Livesey	George Woodbridge	Colin Blakeley
Prue	Elsa Lanchester	Angela Baddeley	Lynn Redgrave
Producer	Tyrone Guthrie	John Gielgud	Peter Wood

The Double-Dealer

	1959
Lord Touchwood	Charles West
Mellefont	John Justin
Careless	John Woodvine
Brisk	Alec McCowen
Sir Paul Plyant	Miles Malleson
Lord Froth	Joss Ackland
Lady Touchwood	Ursula Jeans
Maskwell	Donald Houston
Cynthia	Judi Dench
Lady Froth	Moyra Fraser
Lady Plyant	Maggie Smith
Saygrace	Norman Scace
Producer	Michael Benthall

The Old Batchelour

	1931
Heartwell	James Dale
Bellmour	Eric Portman
Vainlove	Henry Hewitt
Belinda	Diana Wynyard
Laetitia	Edith Evans
Wittol	Miles Malleson
Bluffe	Harvey Braban
Setter	Hay Petrie
Fondlewife	O. B. Clarence
Araminta	Grace Wilson
Silvia	Marda Vanne
Producer	Nigel Playfair

12

The Plays of
Henri René Lenormand[1]

The literary historian of the future, when tabulating the trends and influences of our age, will doubtless observe that the influence of Freud and Adler on the novel was more considerable and more permanent than their influence on the drama. Many modern dramatists show a nodding acquaintance with a mother-fixation or an inferiority complex; but it cannot be said that their basic outlook has been greatly altered by their knowledge of psychological theory. The Auden-Isherwood plays are one notable exception; and it may be admitted that Harry's neurosis in *The Family Reunion* owes something to psychoanalysis, even though Eliot, by writing of sin and expiation, lifts the subject to a higher plane. *Mourning becomes Electra* is another example of the application of modern theories of psychology to an ancient dramatic theme.

In much continental drama, however, until the beginning of the 1930s, the psychoanalytic treatment of sex had been the favourite theme. Most of these plays have not worn well; but the best plays of Henri René Lenormand, in all of which modern psychological theory is used as a basis for tragedy, are likely to survive.

Lenormand was born in 1882, but his best work was not written till after the First World War. In spite of the attempts of John Palmer, Peter Godfrey, Ashley Dukes, and Miss Orna to familiarize the English public with his work, he is still comparatively unknown in this country. *In Theatre Street*, a work of minor importance, is the only one of his plays which has had a run in London. There have been private and amateur performances of two or three other plays; but the neglect of this great dramatist is a lamentable reflection on the state of the English stage between the two wars.

1. From *Proceedings of the Leeds Philosophical and Literary Society* (1949).

In the present essay I must confine my attention to the contents of the first nine volumes of Lenormand's plays. Some of the sixteen plays are of minor interest. *La Dent rouge and Une Vie secrète* were written before 1918, though not published until after Lenormand's first successes. He had to contend with initial neglect, which gave him an insight into the psychology of failure. *Asie* and *La Folle du ciel*, written in the 1930s, seem to show a decline in dramatic power. I shall, therefore, discuss only the ten plays produced between 1919 and 1931. For two of these (*Le Mangeur de rêves* and *L'Homme et ses fantômes*) I shall make use of Miss Orna's translation.

Nearly all these plays are studies in neurosis. *Les Ratés* is a study in the psychology of failure; *Man and his Phantoms* is a psychoanalytical interpretation of Don Juan; *In the Shadow of Evil* is a study of a man who loves cruelty and injustice; *The Coward* is about an artist who feigns illness so as to avoid military service; *Love the Magician* deals with the morbid effects of suppressed desire; *Mixture* displays the conflict in a woman's soul between maternal love and criminality; and, most psychological of all, *The Eater of Dreams* is the revelation of the psychology of a psychologist.

Time is a Dream (1919) is about the death-wish. Nico van Eyden, the hero, is obsessed with problems of death and time. He believes that man, though free in space, is imprisoned in time, and that his end is determined. He complains of the 'ferocious and useless stupidity of the laws of life'. From the East he has brought the idea that past, present, and future coexist, and his fiancée, Romée, who has had a waking dream in which she sees him drowned, fears that it may be prophetic. When he was a small boy, Nico had tried to commit suicide by hanging; and at the end of the play he makes the dream come true by drowning himself.

With such a theme, everything depends on the atmosphere and the characterization. Lenormand succeeds in conveying the influence of the Dutch countryside on Nico, but the introduction of the Javanese servant never quite justifies itself. Nico's neurosis is finely revealed, and it is given individuality by a curious mingling of theories of eastern mysticism, the heart-searching fears of a Hamlet, and the yearning of Shelley to shatter the illusion of life and solve the great mystery by dying. But Nico's neurosis is intended to be an acute form of a very common one, and there is a suggestion that there is no such thing as perfect mental health. When a character remarks that Nico is ill, Romée replies: 'Yes. But who isn't? Doubt can be an illness . . . Faith is probably one. Some people are ill with certainty.'

Matthew Arnold objected to the treatment of situations

in which the suffering finds no vent in action; in which a continuous state of mental distress is prolonged, unrelieved by incident, hope, or resistance; in which there is everything to be endured, nothing to be done.

In *Time is a Dream*, Romée offers some resistance to Nico's suicide; but Arnold's words can be applied accurately enough to the play. It provokes the gloom, but does not arouse the exhilaration, of the best tragedy.

To some critics, *Failures* (1920), suffers from the same defect; and certainly its plot is somewhat forbidding. The nameless hero is an unsuccessful dramatist. His wife, who is equally unsuccessful as an actress, takes a job with a third-rate touring company. Her meagre salary is not enough to keep them both, and she is gradually driven to prostitute herself. Finally, in a drunken rage, he shoots her; and, on the arrival of the police, he commits suicide. All the other characters are likewise failures, from the manager of the touring company, who once had lofty ambitions and a theatre of his own, to the players, who had once expected to become stars at the Comédie Française and are now reduced to performing in third-rate plays to stupid provincial audiences. A composer, who at the beginning of the play regarded himself as a great genius, is driven to play the piano in a cheap provincial café, though he still believes that his derivative tunes are masterpieces.

Such a theme might well have become morbid, but Lenormand redeems it by the subtlety of his characterization, and still more by the profundity of his analysis of the psychology of failure. When the full horror of their poverty and degradation begins to dawn on the dramatist and his wife, they realize that they have been driven to it by some impulse in themselves:

SHE: But we foresaw it.
HE: Yes. That's the most absurd thing about it. We knew that if I accompanied you we should, before two months were out, be at the end of our resources—and yet you insisted.
SHE: I couldn't endure this job if I were alone.

HE: That's what you imagine. But there's another thing you don't mention, which perhaps you don't consider.

SHE: What's that?

HE: Not only did you foresee our present situation, but you awaited it, and almost looked forward to it . . . All living creatures rush towards joy, but some obscure instinct drives you away from it. . . . It would seem that you were afraid of it, and that a secret power inclined you towards sadness. . . . You aspire to suffer. . . . You hope secretly for misfortune.

The hero comes to think that love in itself will not make one's passion living and fertile:

Perhaps one must defile what one loves. . . . Perhaps greatness, beauty and love are obtained at that price. . . . One has only to look at life to see that health and purity of soul are become as empty as corpses . . . and that all power, all fulfilment, all plenitude come from evil.

For a week or two his love is increased by his wife's degradation, and she has found that

a door opens in the depths of sorrow, and a light shines through, a tenderness never known before. . . . One is peaceful . . . one doesn't get worried any more. . . . There is no more trouble. . . . One has arrived. . . . How strange it is!

But this peace which springs from evil and suffering does not last, and is, perhaps, merely an illusion. The hero is more and more shattered by his wife's prostitution, and he takes to drink.

After the murder he quotes 'One always ends by killing the thing one loves', and he adds:

Yes. . . . Or else it is she who kills us. The one or the other is bound to happen. It's only a matter of time. I was drunk . . . and yet I have done a wise deed. We shall no longer suffer, my dear. We shall not grow old like the others . . . in weariness and destitution . . . till we are sixty . . . till the hospital. I have given death to you. . . . I don't know what it is . . . but it can't be more terrible than life.

The Simoon, performed in the same year, is not so closely knit and it has a number of short scenes which violate the unity of action and slacken the tension. The melodramatic elements in the plot are not converted into tragedy, and our attention is not sufficiently concentrated on the figure of Laurency, who falls in love with his own daughter because of her resemblance to her mother as she had been during the first weeks of their marriage. The jealous half-caste mistress who fosters his incestuous passion, and who stabs his daughter with a poisoned dagger is an impressive figure; and the Simoon itself coincides with the tragedy, so as to make the climax very effective on the stage. But on the whole it must be said that Lenormand does not quite succeed in blending the exotic setting with modern psychology.

Lenormand again chose an African setting for the final scenes of *The Eater of Dreams* (1922) and for the whole of *In the Shadow of Evil* (1924)—his two masterpieces. Luke de Bronte, the protagonist of the former play, is a psychologist who devotes his life to the cure of neurotics by revealing the secrets of their childhood. He is 'like Bakou, the Japanese demon, whose special function is to devour evil dreams. . . . And even as they are devoured so the sleeper is delivered of them. He changes fear to joy.' In the course of the play we are introduced to one of Luke's former patients, an Englishwoman named Fearon. Before treatment she had been highly respectable. Luke convinced her that she was a natural criminal, and he persuaded her to live accordingly; so that when we meet her she is a successful criminal, without morals and without scruples—but happy. It is from Fearon that we get hints of Luke's hidden motives. We learn that he usually chooses pretty women for his patients, and that he is actuated more by curiosity than by the desire to heal. Fearon tells him that he loves 'the seduction and corruption of a pure conscience'. We are not, of course, intended to take these accusations at their face value, but they prepare us for the peculiar ambiguity of Luke's relations with Jeannine, which is the main theme of the play.

Jeannine Felse is separated from her middle-aged husband. She has spent some time in an asylum and has attempted to commit suicide. She is haunted by feelings of guilt with regard to her dead mother. Luke discovers from her that her mother was killed by bandits in North Africa. Jeannine was a child at the time of the tragedy, but when she dreams of it she always awakens with a morbid feeling of guilt. Luke shows that she had been in love with her father and jealous of her mother, and this afterwards made her marry a man twice her own age. Luke tells her:

From your earliest childhood your emotional life was warped, perverted. So much so that now you cannot love without wishing to die! That, in brief, is the secret of your illness.

Jeannine at first recoils in horror from this diagnosis; but when she realizes it is true, her feeling of guilt is lifted. She and Luke become lovers, and they go on a trip to North Africa, because Jeannine wishes to revisit the scenes of her childhood. At this point there is an interesting twist in the plot. Jeannine, when she arrives in Africa, finds that her feelings of guilt and remorse return to her in a more terrible form: instead of dreaming that her mother is dead, she dreams that she herself is killing her. She is convinced that her conscience is diseased because it suffers for an unpunished crime. At the same time she comes to suspect that Luke loves only 'the provocative enigma lurking in the innermost folds of the mind'; and Luke has to admit that his passion for knowledge prevents him from giving himself unreservedly, though he claims that this passion springs from love, the love of the innocence underlying crime.

Fearon, who is also in Africa—on a gun-running expedition—meets the brigand who had been present at the supposed murder of Jeannine's mother. As Fearon is still in love with Luke, she gets the brigand to tell her rival the truth: Jeannine, when a child of six, had signalled to the brigands, who were thereby enabled to kidnap her mother. Jeannine, recognizing this as the truth, rushes out into the darkness; and as she goes, Fearon gives her a revolver, ostensibly to protect her, but really so that she should kill herself. Fearon admits to Luke that she drove her rival to suicide, but she accuses him of being an accomplice:

LUKE: Don't say *us*! You alone are guilty.

FEARON: Stop that! Who's been raking over her past for months? Who's been digging up her childish loves and hates? Who re-opened the abscess? I'm ashamed of your stupidity, you vain little busybody!

LUKE: You know quite well I wanted to save her!

FEARON: No hypocrisy! Something within you wanted her death. It was you who brought her here. It was you who revived her memories.

LUKE: I loved her! I loved her!

FEARON: Yes. . . . And you hated her! You loved and hated me, too. You love and hate all the women you meet. You are as diseased as your victims. Like them, you are loaded with unanswered riddles and unconsumed dreams. Learn at last something about yourself, you specialist in burdened consciences.

She tells Luke that she is going to marry him, because they are chained to the same corpse. The forces unchained by the psychologist always turn against the man who liberated them. 'You made a thief and criminal of me. The evil spirits you let loose will throttle you.' She tells him that she will teach him to be a thief like herself. At the end of the play is heard the laughter of the hyena, come for the body of Jeannine. Fearon tells Luke that the hyena, like him, scents her meat from afar. 'And she dismembers bodies far better than you dissect souls. Her meal leaves no traces.'

It would be a mistake to regard this play as an attack on psychoanalysis; for psychoanalysts neither recommend their patients to become criminals, nor do they normally have love-affairs with their patients. Nor can it be said of them, as Fearon says of Luke, that they are not out for truth but for sensation, when they slowly prod the shameful secrets confided in them. Even the death of Jeannine is not due to psychoanalysis. She is a very exceptional case, in that the truth is more painful than the imaginary feeling of guilt which hides it, and the truth comes to her as a brutal shock. Nevertheless, the play uses psychological theories for dramatic purposes, and uses them with brilliant effect. For though orthodox psychoanalysts would not advise their patients to follow their criminal impulses, it may be said that the effect of Freud's ideas on those who pick up a smattering of knowledge about them is probably to weaken their sense of moral responsibility. The popular view of psychoanalysis is simply that repression is bad, though, in fact, Freud uses the term 'repression' in a technical sense quite different from the popular one. So that Fearon represents in an extreme form the impact of a distortion of psychoanalysis on society. Jeannine represents another danger of psychology—the danger of believing that we can pigeonhole everyone, of assuming that the mystery of human personality can be reduced to scientific terms; and Luke himself exemplifies the third danger of psychology—that the psychologist may himself be neurotic and that his scientific task may deprive him of the joy of natural and spontaneous human relationships. The relationship between doctor and patient vitiates the relationship between lover and lover.

The Eater of Dreams is a particularly revealing play because of the close connection between psychologist and artist. Fearon tells Luke:

You consider yourself a scientist, a sort of apostle? You're an artist. And I've never seen anything more akin to a female crook than an artist.

The dramatist, as a dissector of the human heart, is akin to the psychoanalyst; Shakespeare had something of Iago in his disposition, and Lenormand himself has much in common with the psychologist. A reviewer in *The Times Literary Supplement* pointed out that Lenormand struggles to approach every human phenomenon 'in a spirit detached from the spirit of right and wrong', but 'from this detachment he is perpetually falling away, swept into unwilling judgments by a conscience within him which, though the man of science forbid it, captures the artist'. This verdict must be qualified in two ways. Firstly, it should be pointed out that the great poetic dramatists have always approached human phenomena in a spirit detached from *preconception* of right and wrong. Keats, in his famous analysis of the poetical character, declares that the poet 'has as much delight in depicting an Iago as an Imogen'. He, like Lenormand, is not concerned with praise or blame, but with understanding. Secondly, the detachment from preconceptions of right and wrong does not mean that Lenormand is swept into unwilling judgements. It means merely that the judgement takes place at a deeper level of consciousness. Neither Freud nor Jung refrains from moral judgements. The powers of the unconscious take the place of Fate in Lenormand's tragedies; but the compulsion of the unconscious, though it may explain, does not exonerate. This fact is brought out in nearly all Lenormand's plays, most clearly, perhaps, in *In the Shadow of Evil*, which has the greatest compression and intensity of them all.

Before we turn to that play, it will be convenient to consider two plays which are related in theme to *The Eater of Dreams*. *Mixture* (1927)—the original title is in English—reintroduces Fearon, the crook who finds happiness in her criminality; but the main theme of the play is the divided personality of Monique. She is a 'mixture', as Fearon acutely notices, at once a devoted mother and a natural criminal. She has, like several of Lenormand's characters, *la nostalgie de la boue*. We first see her at the moment of desertion by her lover, who tells her:

You will always accuse men of being the instruments of your ruin. They will only be the accomplices. There is in you, as in all your family, a secret taste for change and disorder.

Monique is driven to earn her living, first as a chorus-girl in the provinces, and then as the partner of a half-caste dancer. She leaves him when he demands that her little girl shall take part in the act. She wants her daughter to be the respectable girl she has failed to be herself, and, rather than let her become a performer, she would prostitute herself. At the end of the first act, Monique murders a particularly unsavoury client—a homosexual who wishes to arouse the jealousy of another man, and then refuses to pay her—and steals the money from his pocket-book. She flees to London and, in association with Fearon, makes her living as a thief. In one scene she leaves her daughter, Poucette, with a receiver of stolen property; and the girl, frightened that he will murder her or corrupt her, picks up a revolver left in the room by her mother. Meanwhile, Monique is told by Fearon that she is not merely a devoted mother. (The italicized words are in English in the original, and it will be seen that Lenormand is not always happy in his use of colloquial English.)

There is something in you which wills the contrary of what it ought. ... You are double, like everyone nowadays. *By Jove*, in my youth a thief was a thief, and a clergyman a clergyman. Now one has bits of the other in him. There is the skin of a bishop round the insides of a murderer, and the thoughts of puritans in the brains of coiners. ... *All mixed up, my dear.* ... I know a judge who likes to have his pants stolen and a fire-brigade captain who trembles with joy when the fire gets out of control. Oh, if it were wickedness, treachery or hypocrisy, *all right! But it's worse!* It's like a cocktail, the mixture, the yellow liqueur which runs into the green ... and the orange bitter in which everything is mixed. Pigs! They don't even know they're mixed! They think they are all gin or all syrup. ... What about you? What's gnawing you and splitting you asunder? Oh, a mother's heart's not simple either. *What's the matter with you?*

We realize later in the play that Monique is thinking of her daughter being left with the receiver. Fearon explains that it is her double travailing—the other mother 'who curses the child for having spoilt her figure'. Monique faints, and when she recovers Fearon tells her that she looked like a woman she had seen two hours after she had strangled her baby.

In the third act, some years later, Monique has climbed again into respectability. She works in a beauty parlour—for men—and Poucette, now a girl of nineteen, is a dancing hostess in the

same hotel. Monique tries to marry her daughter to an aged client;
but Poucette, who is in love with a young man, refuses. There is
a violent quarrel, and Poucette answers her mother's account of
her life of self-sacrifice by saying:

You have sacrificed yourself for me, it's true. You have suffered,
endured, dared, renounced for love of me—it's true. But there is
another mother in you who wants me to suffer, wants me to endure,
renounce and risk in my turn. You have undergone for me the most
horrible humiliations, but you have not accepted them. . . . You have
always waited for your revenge. . . . And your revenge is to see me
humiliated and soiled in my turn! Me, whom you love more than your
own life! That's what would be for you the justice of which you're
always talking: to see me flounder in the same muddy roads where you
floundered for fifteen years! That's what you want, my good, my cruel
Mummy!

Monique repudiates the suggestion with horror, but Poucette
suddenly realizes why years before, her mother had left the
revolver where she would find it: she wanted her to kill the
receiver, so that she also would become a murderess. Monique
recognizes this as the truth, and she consents to Poucette's
marriage to the man she loves.

In the last scene Monique again meets Fearon, who has also
turned respectable. They talk over past times, and Monique
admits:

I have always had a mysterious need of vice, of danger, of fear, and
perhaps of crime. But as I was too feeble to lead this monstrous life
without a noble pretext, maternal love furnished me with it. . . . I have
committed my crimes in the shadow of a little girl. I didn't sacrifice
myself. I followed my bent. There is something in me of terrible
vileness, some foul secret which drags me into the mire.

Fearon says, contemptuously, 'Everyone has a cloven foot . . .
and also little wings on the back'. They are both still tempted
when they see a valuable pearl necklace, and they lament together
that they have nothing to look forward to except the dull life of
respectability.

The theme is a development of one which had been stated in
The Eater of Dreams. The character of Monique, with its mingling
of conflicting passions, is more subtle than that of Fearon in the
earlier play. Another theme touched on in *The Eater of Dreams*,

the psychology of the artistic temperament, is developed in *The Three Rooms* (1931). The hero of the play, Pierre, is a dramatist whose wife, Florence, agrees to his infidelities on condition that he never conceals anything from her, and on the understanding that if he falls genuinely in love, she will divorce him. She pretends not to be jealous, and she is confident that he will continue to love her. Pierre tends to be attracted by neurotic women, partly because they are more interesting to him as a dramatist, as they had been to Luke as a psychologist. Rose, his neighbour in a Swiss hotel, is on the verge of a breakdown, because she is still in love with a man who has deserted her. She and Pierre commit adultery, and Pierre duly tells Florence. Rose, feeling guilty towards Florence, suddenly leaves the hotel and does not answer Pierre's letters. A year later they meet again, and Pierre begins to suspect what Rose had known from the start, that they are in love with each other. At first Pierre conceals this fact from his wife, but when he finds that his failure to keep to their bargain is destroying his integrity as a writer, he finally tells her. Florence commits suicide, and Rose intends to break with Pierre for ever; but when he threatens to kill himself, she consents to marry him. The last scene takes place some years later at the same Swiss hotel as in the first act. Rose is now in Florence's place. Pierre makes friends with a girl in the neighbouring room as he had done with Rose. The audience realizes that Rose now has to put up with Pierre's infidelities as Florence had done before.

The play is partly an examination of the artist's temperament, ever in quest of new sensations; but much more it is an examination of the unwritten contract between Pierre and his wife. Is it possible to treat sexual infidelities as of minor account and no cause of jealousy to a reasonable person? Is it possible to dissociate sex and love? Is it wise in such a marriage to adopt the principle of absolute frankness? There is no complete answer to these questions, but after Florence's death, Pierre tells Rose that the two women were 'two halves of a being, a body and soul unjustly separated'.

I exhausted myself in re-uniting you in my heart. And not for a single hour have I known wholeness. I was torn, paralysed by my double tenderness. There are moments when I have hated you for being two. I have wished that one of you would disappear. And now that she is gone, I am still more cruelly divided and chained than before.

In the last scene Pierre tells the girl, who is about to fill the place taken by Rose in the first act, that complete frankness is undesirable in marriage:

Well, I, who have suffered my whole life long from that principle, feel that I have never been able to attain it. A conjuror makes it vanish with a stroke of his wand when I'm on the point of reaching it. Avoid the superstition of truth. ... The tragedy which I have recounted to you to-day would have been averted by a few lies and a little silence. It was by pursuing this chimera of truth that I unchained everything. And the most frightful thing is that this so-called truth, the revelation of which killed my wife, was probably not really the truth. In proclaiming to her my love for another, I wasn't lying—no, but I yielded to an obscure attraction for the tragic. I gave myself up to the tragedy of the dividing of hearts. And death, who must have been waiting in the wings, forthwith took me at my word. In reality, I don't believe that the sharing of love need be a tragedy. Our love was a good working-arrangement. I had ended by seeing in Florence a second mother. But I did not love her less on the eve of her death than ten years before. I merely loved her in a different way. ... It is my wretched writer's imagination which has corrupted everything. Who knows if in cherishing two beings at the same time, I may not have committed a crime against love?

Pierre is rightly given a considerable measure of self-knowledge, but he does not know that, in spite of his new reticence, Rose is aware of his infidelities.

In this play, the truth proves as disastrous as it had been to Jeannine in *The Eater of Dreams*; and, by an additional irony, Pierre is doubtful whether it was the truth after all. Lenormand's own irony is exercised at the expense of the psychological theories which provide him with the framework of his plays.

As with Ibsen's later plays, most of the action of *In the Shadow of Evil* (1924) takes place before the rise of the curtain. The play itself, which obeys all the unities, gives us the last act of a drama which stretches over fifteen years. Rougé, the hero, had been in his youth a trader in French Equatorial Africa. He had been stationed in a lonely settlement up-country, 400 kilometres from Grand-Bassam. The Resident at Grand-Bassam, Préfailles, played a number of cruel practical jokes on him: when he asked for quinine, he was sent sugar; when he asked for a bed, he was sent a child's cot. Rougé's whole character was warped by this experience. He had been a young idealist. Now he determined to inflict on others the injustice and cruelty from which he had himself suffered; and to provide himself with opportunities he joined the colonial service.

The play opens fifteen years later. Rougé has risen to be the Resident at Kadiéso, and he deliberately rewards the wicked and punishes the innocent, thereby outraging his subordinate's sense of justice. He orders a chieftain, Maélik, to be flogged, though he knows him to be innocent of the crime of which he is accused, just at the time when his old tormentor, Préfailles, arrives at Kadiéso. At the request of Le Cormier, Rougé's subordinate, Préfailles raises the question of the flogging with Rougé, who retorts that the ultimate guilt rests on Préfailles's shoulders. Ironically enough. Préfailles had undergone a sudden conversion to good, at the same time as Rougé had been converted to evil; so that he is horrified at the revelation of the results of his own cruelty. He begs Rougé to break the chain of evil:

Promise me that you will strive to make this fountain of injustice run dry, this fountain I have made to spring up within you.

Rougé replies that even if he were to promise, he could not answer for those to whom he had been cruel:

I tell you that once the fountain of injustice is liberated among men, no one can know how far it will flow—above all, no one can make it dry up.

At the end of the play his fears are confirmed. Maélik has his revenge, not on the man who has wronged him, but on the innocent Madame Le Cormier, who goes to bandage his wounds. Rougé's terrible hypothesis is confirmed. He tells Préfailles: 'It is we who have killed her. She loved. . . . She had pity, even on me! Justice is done.'

The play has the inevitability of a theorem in Euclid. It is a brilliant technical achievement to compress into a few hours the gradual spread of evil, and to let us see at the same moment the whole chain: Préfailles—Rougé—Maélik—Madame Le Cormier. It is a superb commentary on the moral process which Auden summed up in the lines, written on the outbreak of war:

> Those to whom evil is done
> Do evil in return.

Lenormand does not show us the effect of the murder of Madame
Le Cormier on her husband. Logically, he, too, is involved in the
chain of evil; but the dramatist does not take the extreme determinist position. Préfailles had broken away from his evil heritage,
and Le Cormier need not, and probably will not, revenge himself
on the innocent. It is Rougé, in his own justification, who puts
forward the determinist thesis. It is he, with his perverted will,
who argues that though justice is a human invention, injustice is
vital and inextinguishable. It is he, not the dramatist, who argues
that

to do good is to draw disaster on one's own head. . . . The converse is
also true. Hate and cruelty preserve us! To do harm keeps oneself from
harm! If we are still alive after twenty years of Africa, twenty years of
massacre, plague and treachery, it is because we have both lived *in the
shadow of evil.*

Préfailles replies:

I don't know whether Justice is only an idea of man, but I do know that
your pretended law is one of man's—mean and cruel, like him! You
think you've plucked out the secret of the universe . . . and the solitude
you question whispers to you abject superstitions, negro beliefs!

If it is true that the victims of injustice themselves become unjust,
it is also true that those who receive love and justice become
righteous and loving. That is the unexpressed corollary to the
play's theorem.

In the Shadow of Evil is only indirectly influenced by theories of
psychology; but *Man and his Phantoms* (1924) written about the
same time, is a psychoanalytical interpretation of the character of a
Don Juan. The rake who spends his life in seducing an endless
series of women is told by Luke, who reappears in this play, that:

A man who has had and rejected dozens of women in his life has
suppressed woman, because he has suppressed love. . . . He takes
without giving. He thinks he gives chase, and he runs away. . . . He
thinks he wants joy; all he wants is solitude. To sleep with every
woman is equivalent to sleeping with none. . . . Don Juan's body is
that of a man; his soul, that of a woman. In woman, he seeks for the
phantom of man. That is why each of his victories proves a secret
defeat. That is why he flees women, raging at finding them enriched
with a treasure he can never possess. He hates them with a pauper's
hate, and inflicts suffering on them. He revenges on them his own
incapacity for happiness.

That this is a true explanation can be seen from the man's confession to Patrick in the first scene of the play: 'When a man makes love, he is groping vainly for his own skeleton.' From one point of view the play would have been more effective if Lenormand had reserved this disclosure for a later scene; especially as one of the phantoms in the last scene makes the same revelation—and this time the Man recoils in horror. But the dramatist has one card up his sleeve. When the Mother's Phantom puts the others to flight and the Man dies in her arms, we are left to assume that behind his inversion, and the cause of it, is an inverted Oedipus complex, in which the child protects himself from his father's hate by identifying himself with his mother. It may be noted that the hero of this play, like Luke and Pierre, is mainly attracted by neurotic women.

Several critics regard *Man and his Phantoms* as Lenormand's masterpiece. It is certainly magnificent, but there is occasionally a shifting of convention which is disconcerting. The Old Woman in the first scene, who warns the Man of approaching nemesis; Alberta's story of the ghost who haunts her faithless lover; the madness of Laura, another of the Man's victims; and the concourse of ghosts in the last scene are unrealistic devices which remind us of the Elizabethan dramatists: but the play as a whole is realistic, and Lenormand prepares the way for the ghosts by a spiritualist séance and also by Luke's warning that the apparitions are imaginary:

You, who disguised your pursuit of solitude in debauchery, people it with apparitions, now that it is granted you. You, who denied love and suffering, affirm the existence of pure illusions, of images created by you. . . . You asked me the other evening with what you could replace women. But with other women! The accusing or forgiving phantoms which rise up in your unconscious mind.

I suppose this rationalist interpretation is necessary today for the suspension of disbelief, though to spectators conversant with poetic drama the explanations weaken the grandeur of the last scene. Elsewhere Lenormand seems to admit a supernatural agency: he offers no rational explanation of a mysterious fire, from which the Man is saved only by flight.

It is remarkable that in plays which are rooted in modern theories of psychology, Lenormand should feel the need of the supernatural. The phantoms which hound the Man to his death are similar in effect to the Eumenides. The sense of doom and the vast forces of evil unloosed by Rougé are suggested by the appearance of the witch-doctor; and in *Love the Magician,* the prophecies of the Breton witch prepare us for the death of Béatrice at the end of the play.

Love the Magician (1926) is a study of the effects of sexual repression on Béatrice, an Irish girl who is the secretary of Albert Carolles. The play opens soon after the drowning of his wife off the coast of Brittany. Her body has not been recovered, and it is suspected that she committed suicide. One evening Béatrice falls into a trance, and the dead wife seems to speak through her. Albert half believes, but he wants a rational proof that he is in touch with his wife. The voice of the dead woman tells him that she did commit suicide, and that she had been unfaithful to him. He searches amongst his wife's papers for proofs of her infidelity, but without success. In the final scene, Albert tells Béatrice that he no longer believes that his wife has spoken through her: 'It has surged up from the depths of your soul, unconsciously, for my torment and yours.' Béatrice asks what motive she could have had, and Albert replies:

At first to console me. . . . Yes, to save me from despair. . . . But after a while, you could not bear the happiness which her presence gave me. . . . It was through jealousy that you stopped her from coming. . . . And when you allowed her to reappear, it was to accuse her. You pretended that she no longer loved you: you were afraid of her vengeance . . . and it is you who are avenged on her. You try and make me suspicious of her memory. You charge her with faults . . . like a rival.

Albert realizes, as Lenormand himself does, that 'one can be both innocent and guilty of one's crimes'; but Béatrice indignantly demands proof that she is a monster. He replies, in words that give the play its title:

I don't believe in monsters. . . . As soon as he ceases to know himself, the purest man amongst us becomes a monster—but a monster led by love, by such a thirst for happiness, that he creates worlds to withstand death, that he defies the dead themselves, or calls them to his aid to assure him of his joy. Yes, love in us uses every weapon. It can restore corpses to life by magic, and send them back to the grave, laden with faults.

We are left with the impression that the supposed messages from the dead woman are the unconscious fabrications of the love-sick secretary. But at the very end of the play Albert confesses to Béatrice that he has fallen in love with her; and, at the very moment of his confession, Béatrice feels that she is being strangled by invisible hands. To the superstitious servant, Béatrice needs exorcism; and the Witch tells Albert: 'It's not choking, M. Carolles . . . It's your dead wife strangling her.' Béatrice's death at least exonerates her from deliberate deception as a medium; but we can assume that she dies not as the result of supernatural agency, but rather from an acute sense of guilt because she had supplanted the dead woman. It is one of the best examples in Lenormand's work of his blending of the natural and the super-natural, so that the incident can be taken by the audience in either sense.

The Coward (1925) is about an artist who escapes into Switzer-land during the last war, and poses as a consumptive to avoid being called up. A French spy blackmails him with the threat of exposure unless he consents to join the secret service. He is given the job of stealing documents from a hotel acquaintance, Professor Hirtz. He bungles the job, and is tricked into giving Hirtz the names of his French colleagues. As a result he is suspected of treachery, and at the end of his play he is taken off to be murdered. The play is a long one, and it is less concentrated and less inevit-able than Lenormand's best work. Jacques's fate is perfectly possible. The punishment may even fit the crime. But we do not feel that the tragedy springs directly from character. On the other hand, Jacques is depicted with considerable subtlety. He is not merely, not even mainly, a coward. Though it may be rationaliza-tion, his view on the respective claims of art and patriotism com-mands respect: and, by a typical stroke of irony, he begins to develop the symptoms of the disease he is counterfeiting.

The effect of psychology on the work of Lenormand is to eliminate the villain. He, like Albert Carolles, does not believe in monsters; and, like Fearon, he believes that we are all mixtures, with angel's wings as well as cloven hoofs. The revelation of the forces of the Unconscious has the effect of adding a new dimension to tragedy—though all great dramatists, often by means of the soliloquy, have made use of unconscious desires and motives. It might be argued that just as Jonson utilized the theory of

Humours as a basis for comedy; so Lenormand uses the theories of psychoanalysis for tragedy; and just as Jonson's characters seem rather systematized compared with Shakespeare's, so Lenormand's are sometimes too obviously based on recognized psychological types. But this is not true of his best work. In that he combines the ruthless analysis of a scientist with the charitable understanding of a healer. Nothing to him is common or unclean. He adopts Lear's attitude:

> None does offend, none, I say, none; I'll able 'em.
> Take that of me, my friend, who have the power
> To seal the accuser's lips.

This combination of ruthlessness and humanity is a genuine source of the pity and terror of tragedy; and Lenormand, in his best work, is one of the finest dramatists of our time.

13

The Pursuit of Relevance[1]

The demand for relevance in literature, and especially in drama, takes a variety of forms. It is apparent in the way in which undergraduates pick modern optional courses, in their plea that Orwell and Miller should replace Yeats and Conrad in the syllabus, in the popularity of 'sociology of literature' courses, in Brecht's rewriting of *Coriolanus* to make it more relevant to the political situation in the present century, in Günter Grass's *The Plebeians Rehearse the Uprising*, in the tendency of theatre directors to present the classics in modern dress, and in their admiration for Jan Kott's theories.

In some ways this desire for relevance is healthy. It springs from a distrust of a literature divorced from life. After all, it is generally accepted that the novel should offer a relevant criticism of life; that *Vanity Fair*, for example, although set in the past, was not irrelevant to the Victorian present, nor to ours; that *Felix Holt*, another historical novel, was as relevant as *Silas Marner*; and that Dickens in all his novels, and especially in the later, greater ones, had a powerful message for his age—he wanted to reform the world by showing us what was wrong with it. On the other hand, the plays of Victorian poets—Tennyson's *Becket*, Browning's *King Victor and King Charles*, Swinburne's plays on Mary, Queen of Scots, Bridges's *Palicio*, even Hardy's *Famous Tragedy of the Queen of Cornwall*—had little to say to their own age, and nothing to say to us. Elizabethan dramatists rarely made this kind of mistake. Not merely did Jonson, we are told, give an allegorical account of the Gunpowder Plot in *Catiline*, and Shakespeare introduce allusions to the same plot in *Macbeth*—to remind the audience that king-killing could happen in 1605 as it had done in Scotland 'in the dark backward and abysm of time'—but even Lyly's delicate and artificial structures were as topical as

1. From *Essays and Studies*, ed. John Lawlor (1973).

the Goon Show. It was not simply that by the deliberate use of anachronism Elizabethan dramatists called attention to parallels between ancient and modern. Historians, no less than dramatists, were all anxiously didactic, satisfying the voracious appetites of their readers for facts about the past, at the same time as they were exhibiting the workings of Providence (as Ralegh did in his great Preface), or pointing out the horrors of civil war and the blessings of the Tudor settlement; or even, as Machiavelli did in his *Discourses on Livy*, using particular events to illustrate general historical or political principles. It can easily be seen that in the English Histories, besides writing exciting and popular entertainment, Shakespeare was using the past to influence the present. It is assumed that *A Midsummer Night's Dream* contains allusions to the bad weather of 1594; it has been plausibly maintained that *King Lear* exhibited the dangers of a divided kingdom at the time when James I was advocating the union of England and Scotland; and it has often been suggested that *Coriolanus* took the form it did because of the Midlands insurrection.

In two of his Roman plays Shakespeare makes his characters allude to the future dramatization of the events in which they are concerned. Cleopatra is terrified lest some squeaking actor should boy her greatness in the posture of a whore; and Cassius, carried away by the solemnity of a historical occasion, exclaims:

> How many ages hence
> Shall this our lofty scene be acted over
> In states unborn and accents yet unknown!

Brecht-minded commentators have assumed that in both cases Shakespeare was deliberately shattering the illusion and reminding his audience that they were listening to a play. This, surely, was the precise opposite of what he was doing. The reaction of his original audience—although it is dangerous to generalize about its members—would be to think:

Yes, that is exactly what is happening; the murder of Julius Caesar *is* being enacted in accents unknown to the Romans, in what was then a barbarous island, as Cassius foretold, and therefore the play is true. A boy actor is playing Cleopatra now, even as she speaks these words, although happily he has not got a squeaky voice, and this paradoxically establishes the truth of the character who prophesied it.

Even though the temporary effect may be to remind the audience they are watching a play, the ultimate effect will be to reimpose the theatrical illusion more securely than before. It may be added that all the main characters in *Julius Caesar* seem to be conscious of the fact that future ages will be the audience of their lofty scene: they are acting for posterity. Coriolanus postulates an even loftier audience; the culmination of his many theatrical images is when he thinks of himself as having an audience of gods:

> Behold, the heavens do ope,
> The gods look down, and this unnatural scene
> They laugh at.

It is important to realize, however, that neither the cunning use of anachronism, nor even the use of historical material to express orthodox views on order, were the most important means employed by Shakespeare for the achieving of relevance. If that had been so, directors would have been justified, now that anachronisms are explained in footnotes and Tudor views on politics are as quaint as the honour of Marvell's mistress, in seeking some other way of making the plays relevant to a modern audience.

A play which is merely a careful historical reconstruction, or even a competent dramatization of a historical event, of no special relevance to the thought of the day, is doomed to failure. In this connection it may be worth while to compare three plays about Becket. Tennyson's play, saved from disaster by Irving's acting, is unlikely to find an audience again, though it was revived at Canterbury in living memory. Whereas *In Memoriam*, concerned as it was with the doubts and difficulties of Victorians, spoke directly to their hearts, and King Arthur, in the *Idylls of the King*, could be regarded as the embodiment of popular ideals, *Becket* seems to be completely removed from the interests of a nineteenth-century reader. T. S. Eliot did not make this mistake. *Murder in the Cathedral* was written for performance in Canterbury Cathedral before a nominally religious audience, one that could be relied upon to have a kind of domestic interest in the martyrdom of the local saint. The subject of the play, moreover, involved two themes in which Eliot was deeply interested—the relationship between Church and State and the nature of sainthood. One has only to think of *The Idea of a Christian*

Society and *The Cocktail Party* to see how these themes continued
to engage his interest. Unfortunately Eliot, who had had little
dramatic experience, seems to have lost his nerve. He was afraid
that his audience would fail to see the relevance of his play to the
world of 1935; so he made the four murderers address the audience
in speeches which parodied the clichés of modern oratory. Either
Eliot, or his producer, made one of the knights wear plus-fours
and practise golf strokes. The audience was told that if they
approved of the subordination of the Church to the State, they
shared the guilt of Becket's murderers. Whatever one may think
of this, the speeches are funny in themselves and they jolt the
audience out of its complacent reverence; but they are nevertheless a worse blemish than the feeble farce which mars the sublimity
of *Saint Joan*. Anouilh's *Becket*, though inferior to Eliot's play in
poetic quality and high seriousness, nevertheless appeals more to a
modern secular audience, not by drawing parallels between
Becket's day and ours, but by showing that the relationship
between Becket and the King can be interpreted in modern
psychological terms, and related therefore to the experience of
members of the audience. There is sexual rivalry in the play and
incidental comments on the treatment of subject-races and of
women.

Quite apart, then, from any special interest a play may have
when it is first performed, it may well appeal to later ages for
different reasons. The scenes in *Venice Preserved* which were
designed to satirize Shaftesbury's sexual tastes have been successful on the modern stage; but often, when the topical interest fades,
the play becomes a bore. Middleton's *Game at Chess*, phenomen-
ally successful in its day, and brilliantly ingenious as it is, did not
survive for many months; and Addison's *Cato*, that extreme
example of neo-classical flummery, was applauded only for party
reasons. On the other hand, *Julius Caesar* remains viable on stage
and screen because Shakespeare convinces us that this is how men
in such circumstances do behave. Brutus, for example, who fears
that a crown will turn Caesar into a tyrant, being blissfully
unaware that he is one already, appears as a timeless portrait of a
political idealist. In *Coriolanus* we can recognize in the Tribunes
some characteristics of demagogues of all ages, no less than the
ignoring of moral scruples characteristic of 'the right-hand file'.
The scene in *Macbeth* between Malcolm and Macduff used to be

criticized as being tedious and improbable; but a performance just before the Second World War, after the influx of refugees from Germany, made the scene startlingly realistic. The fear of betrayal and the report on the state of the nation no longer sounded exaggerated:

> Alas, poor country,
> Almost afraid to know itself! It cannot
> Be call'd our mother, but our grave; where nothing,
> But who knows nothing, is once seen to smile;
> Where sighs, and groans, and shrieks, that rent the air,
> Are made, not mark'd; where violent sorrow seems
> A modern ecstasy; the dead man's knell
> Is there scarce ask'd for who; and good men's lives
> Expire before the flowers in their caps,
> Dying or ere they sicken.

Directors, to their credit, have recognized the essential truth in all these cases, and they have sought to make assurance double sure, so that the audience too will recognize it. Their favourite method is by the use of modern dress. If Caesar's guards are dressed as SS men, and the conspirators, as in Roy Fuller's splendid poem, are 'comrades', then the drachma will drop. Even the dullest members of the audience will thrill to the play's relevance and return home in the self-congratulatory glow of people who have taken part in an anti-Nazi demonstration. In *Coriolanus* Brutus and Sicinius may be dressed as Bevin or Bevan, or Scanlon and Feather; Menenius may figure as Baldwin or Macmillan; and Coriolanus can appear as Montgomery or Mussolini, according to political taste.

In the recent National Theatre production of *The Merchant of Venice*, the modern dress of Shylock immediately reminded the audience of the Nazi persecution of the Jews. This was clearly the director's intention, and Shylock emerged as the baffled hero of the play. It need hardly be said that this interpretation runs counter to the text. Shylock's real role is that of villain, as we can see from his first aside:

> How like a fawning publican he looks!
> I hate him for he is a Christian;
> But more for that in low simplicity
> He lends out money gratis, and brings down
> The rate of usance here with us in Venice.

> He hates our sacred nation; and he rails ...
> On me, my bargains, and my well-won thrift,
> Which he calls interest.

This hatred may spring partly from Antonio's contemptuous rudeness, but it is fanned by religious and especially economic motives. There is nothing in Shakespeare's character to suggest the generous, cultured Jew portrayed by Laurence Olivier: he is a miser, and he hates music—two indications of what the poet thought of him. Of course, there are moments in the play when we are allowed to pity him; but even the scene where he hears of the sale of the ring given him by his dead wife shows that he is more perturbed by the loss of his ducats than of his daughter. If the sympathies of the audience are enlisted for Shylock—because of our modern feelings of guilt—the fourth act will be tragic and the last act will be imbued with bitterness. One can imagine an admirable play in which a noble and cultured Jew is hounded to death by a pack of Philistines, in which Bassanio pursues Portia's fortune rather than her person, in which Jessica is a treacherous thief with Lorenzo her accomplice, and in which the Duke's court is as obviously corrupt as the one where Volpone is tried—but Shakespeare's script cannot be used to mean anything like this. I have more sympathy with the point of view expressed in a recent pamphlet, wrong-headed as it is, that *The Merchant of Venice* should not be staged so long as people remember Belsen and Dachau. One might reply that so long as people remember the concentration camps, the play is unlikely to do any harm.

In defence of adaptations, it has been urged that Shakespeare himself took other men's plays and rewrote them to suit his own purposes, and that therefore Marowitz and others should have the right to adapt Shakespeare's old-fashioned scripts, and so create a new *Hamlet* and a new *Othello*. Directors, retaining the words of the original, should even more clearly have the right to slant the plays to make them relevant to our own time. It may, perhaps, be doubted whether it makes *A Midsummer Night's Dream* more relevant if Hippolyta, that sensible Amazon, is supposed to be cured of her bestial tastes by experiencing as Titania a passion for a donkey. In any case, most people would agree that Shakespeare improved on the old *Hamlet* play and on *Promos and Cassandra*, and few people share Tolstoy's opinion that *King Lear* was better than the play Shakespeare made of it. On the other hand it is by no means certain that the various adaptations of Shakespeare, from Dryden's *Troilus and Cressida* and Tate's *King Lear* to Shaw's *Cymbeline* and Barton's *Wars of the Roses* are improvements on the originals. Shaw, at least, recommends Shakespeare's *Cymbeline* in preference to his own.

A favourite method of bringing home to an audience the relevance of Shakespeare's plays is to associate them with some contemporary fashion. There was a period at Stratford-upon-Avon when nearly every production was adorned or cumbered with a waggon borrowed from *Mother Courage*. This was the outward and visible sign that the history plays were to be treated as epic theatre, complete with *Verfremdungseffekt*. Then we had a diet of Shakespeare the existentialist, with iron in the soul and nausea in the guts. Next we were assured by Jan Kott that *King Lear* was Shakespeare's *End Game*, and that Shakespeare was a proleptic contributor to the Theatre of the Absurd. Finally, under the influence of Artaud and later of Weiss, we were asked to accept him as an honorary member of the Theatre of Cruelty. Did he not write *Titus Andronicus*? And is not the extrusion of Gloucester's vile jelly more significant that Lear's address to the poor, naked wretches? Kozintsev wisely thought otherwise.

None of these Shakespeares is totally without foundation. There are absurdities and cruelties in *King Lear* and *Titus Andronicus*; but the attempt to present *Macbeth* or *King Lear* in such limited terms immeasurably impoverishes them. If the keyline of *King Lear* is thought to be—

> As flies to wanton boys are we to the gods:
> They kill us for their sport—

Gloucester's later prayer to the 'ever-gentle gods' will seem ironic. The loyalty of Kent, the loving-kindness of Cordelia, the heroism and endurance of Edgar must all appear less significant than the blunt realism of the man who hangs Cordelia. 'If it be man's work, I'll do't.' Gloucester must be thrust out of the castle-gates to smell his way to Dover, but Cornwall's servants must not be allowed the lines in which Shakespeare showed the human-kindness of the humble and made them comment authoritatively and authorially on the wickedness of Regan and Cornwall, as this would undercut the play's cruelty.

Existentialism is not without attractions and it may be said—
it has indeed been said by me—that in the world of Elsinore and
in the situation in which Hamlet is placed, he has to create his
own morality. But whereas Sartre believes that this is the universal
state of man, there being no god and no divine sanctions, Hamlet
knows that he has to work out his own salvation in fear and
trembling. Only in *King Lear* is there any doubt of the existence
and nature of the gods; but even if we accept this view of the play,
this would not mean that we had the slightest difficulty in dis-
tinguishing good from evil. There may be some ambiguity about
Shakespeare's metaphysics, but none about his morality.

There are, then, at least four objections to the attempt to
impose a modern and arbitrary relevance on an old play. Such an
attempt distorts the meaning; insults the intelligence of the
audience; substitutes a partial and temporary interpretation for a
more universal one; and, as we shall see, it limits the options.
These objections overlap. It is not possible to distort the meaning
without insulting the audience and if we impose a partial interpretation we obviously limit the options.

Some examples have been given above of directorial distor-
tions. Those responsible presumably fear that audiences would be
bored by a straightforward presentation because they themselves
have seen the play many times before. Taking Shakespeare's own
excuse for his infidelity—

> Like as to make our appetites more keen,
> With eager compounds we our palates urge—

directors offer audiences not Shakespeare's play, but something
new and allegedly more relevant. Not that they imagine, as
Dryden and Tate apparently did, that they can improve on
Shakespeare, excepting in minor details, but they believe that their
versions will appeal to an audience more than the originals would
do. If one were to judge by the reactions of certain dramatic
critics, saved from boredom at their twentieth production of *The
Merchant of Venice*, or of some other play that has often been
clapper-clawed by the palms of the vulgar, one might suppose
that directors were right in their calculations. A tape-recording of
audience reactions would tell a very different story. They came to
see Shakespeare and, to their disappointment, were given something else, and something inferior.

It is reported in *The Elizabethan Theatre* (edited by David Galloway, 1969) that a questionnaire was issued to members of the audience at the Royal Shakespeare Memorial Theatre, in order to discover facts about their social and educational background. Terence Hawkes, in his analysis of the replies, showed that nearly all the respondents were middle-class, two-thirds of them were under thirty, over 60 per cent were teachers or students, and over 70 per cent were graduates, undergraduates, or hoping to enter a university in due course. The significance of these figures is twofold: most of the audience were young enough not to have seen many productions of the plays and their intellectual level was remarkably high. This means that directors at Stratford and at the National Theatre have no need to temper the icy wind of pure Shakespeare to an audience of semi-literate Philistines. They may be as literate as the director himself and quite unlikely to feel that Shakespeare's plays were remote stories of

> old, unhappy, far-off things,
> And battles long ago,

with small relevance to the twentieth-century mind. Such an educated audience is apt to resent both the distortion involved in the modish productions we have been describing and what is surely the arrogant assumption that they would not notice the relevance of *Coriolanus* or of *Troilus and Cressida* unless it is made so blatantly clear that only a moron could miss it. They feel as Queen Victoria's correspondents must have done when they received her epistolary underlinings.

If Coriolanus is depicted as a fascist dictator and the Tribunes as Labour politicians, the audience is thereby prevented from seeing the play steadily and seeing it whole. Between 1609 and 1970 the political changes were so enormous that we can no longer look at the play with Jacobean eyes. In 1609 democracy was condemned by all political theorists, and as an actual form of government it was unthinkable in England until much later. A modern-dress production divides the audience on party lines; the association of Coriolanus with a corrupt and defeated régime either undercuts the tragedy or perverts the spectators; and the saving graces of the hero—his courage, his unwillingness to play the hypocrite, his love for Virgilia—tend to be passed over. By inventing a spurious relevance the director hides the genuine and more universal relevance of the play.

When we are reading great literature of the past—*The Canterbury Tales* or *Paradise Lost*—or witnessing Elizabethan plays, we should not be thinking all the time of their relevance. We should rather by the exercise of imagination be partaking in the life of distant ages, and so extending our horizons and enlarging our sympathies. We ought as often to be aware of strangeness and difference as of resemblance and familiarity. Often, no doubt, there will be moments of recognition when, as Wordsworth said,

in spite of difference of soil and climate, of language and manners, of laws and customs, in spite of things silently gone out of mind and things violently destroyed,

the literature of the past illuminates the present, so that we think not 'How unlike!' but 'How like . . .!' Such relevances, as Keats said of poetry, should 'appear almost a remembrance'. This provides a subtler pleasure than the kind of relevance which is obtained by obliterating temporal distinctions.

W. H. Auden, in his elegy on W. B. Yeats, remarked that

> The words of a dead man
> Are modified in the guts of the living.

We can never read a Jane Austen novel or a satire by Alexander Pope in the way their first readers did. We have different backgrounds, different educations, different literary experiences somewhat different moral principles, and different sensibilities. With plays the obstacles to understanding are even greater: we can never hope—even in an exact replica of the Globe Theatre—to experience a play in the same way as the original audience did. The text, familiar to us, was not to them; our style of acting is different; our dramatic conventions have changed; our ideologies and superstitions are not the same as theirs; even our hygiene, our medicine, our dentistry, our diet, and our expectation of life are all different. However much, therefore, the director is anxious to bridge the gulf of the years, he will never wholly succeed; but he should try, at least, not to make the gulf wider.

It has been suggested above that the frantic pursuit of relevance limits the options. In other words, it forces one particular interpretation on an audience, when there are a number of others equally valid, and some less forced. Of course it may be argued that even before rehearsals begin any director must choose some options and reject others. We cannot have a neutral production, and if we could it would be both confusing and dull. This point has been put forcibly by John Barton in an interview printed in *Shakespeare Survey 25*:

I think it's certainly impossible, and I question whether it's desirable. It's impossible because, as I've said, you have to be specific with actors. Actors have got to know what effect they're trying to make with a given line, what they mean and what they feel. When one reads the play in the study one can say again and again of a given line, 'I'm not sure what Shakespeare intends here; it could be this or it could be that'. But however unsure one may be, one can't leave things uncertain for the actor; he has to be specific.

This does not quite answer the point; for, although Mr. Barton later admits that directors cannot completely control an audience's response, he sums up his position by saying:

I think the only point at which the play can be said to be absolutely open-ended is when it exists as a mere text waiting to be performed or studied.

To this one may ask: 'What if the fact that you are not certain of Shakespeare's meaning is a sign not of some failure of expression, or of comprehension, but, as Maurice Morgann suggested, of deliberate ambiguity?' 'We have no right', he declared, 'to call upon Shakespeare for explanations upon points which he means to obscure.' The director can be entirely specific in his instructions to each of his actors, without necessarily jeopardizing the freedom of interpretation of the play as a whole. He can say to his Hamlet that 'Get thee to a nunnery' means what it says, or alternatively 'Get thee to a brothel'. He can say 'Hamlet still loves Ophelia' or 'He no longer loves her'. The words can be said sadly. or bitterly, or savagely. But, in any case, the mystery of Hamlet's character is still a matter for debate: a perfectly unambiguous Hamlet would falsify the poet's meaning.

The point we are making can be clarified by two or three examples. Stanley E. Hyman, in a book on Iago mentioned above, shows that a number of different interpretations can be squarely based on the text of the play. Critics have traced his ancestry to the devils of Moralities and Interludes; to Othello he is a demi-devil;

Iago himself refers to hellish theology—'divinity of hell'—and compares himself to devils. Yet he may equally well be regarded as a stage villain, as a follower of Machiavelli, as an unscrupulous artist as Bradley, Swinburne, Hazlitt, and others suggested and as a latent homosexual. Oddly enough Mr. Hyman does not mention the two most obvious interpretations of the character's motives: that he is professionally jealous of Cassio's promotion, and that he was jealous of Emilia. Even the motivation provided by Cinthio —that his love for Desdemona has been thwarted—finds some slight support in the text, as when he confesses: 'Now I do love her too.' The temptation facing a director is for him to choose one only of these interpretations, and for him to instruct his actor accordingly. Fresh from a study of Dr. Leavis's essay, he may decide to treat Iago merely as a stage villain; after reading S. L. Bethell or G. R. Elliott, he will be driven to make him a devil, and he will be deterred from making him Satan only by the knowledge that the Prince of Darkness was a gentleman; after a diet of Freud and in the post-Wolfenden climate he will make Iago a homosexual; and, indeed, at the present day, he is likely to motivate his actions by the colour of Othello's skin. It is surely apparent that a complete commitment to any one of these interpretations would wreck the play. If Iago is simply a devil, then the tragedy is reduced to a Morality; if he is simply a stage villain, the play becomes a melodrama; if he is simply a racialist, it becomes political propaganda; and if he is a homosexual, it becomes a psychological drama. Any of these directional choices would be an impoverishment of the play Shakespeare wrote, although the critics must share the blame.

If we were to analyse the reactions of a member of an audience to the delicate balance maintained in an uncommitted production —one in which the director tried to keep the options open—we should find that his attitude to Iago changed from scene to scene. He would assume at the beginning that Iago's hatred of Othello was caused by Cassio's promotion, though he would realize that Iago was a hypocrite and a Machiavel. The words with which he rouses Brabantio might suggest to the spectator colour prejudice. In his soliloquy at the end of Act I, he reveals his fear of cuckoldry, and after framing his plot he invokes hell and night. In Act II he again reveals his jealousy, confesses his 'love' for Desdemona, and compares himself to devils. This ambiguity about his character will continue throughout the play until his very last words; and it is surely the duty of a director to preserve this ambiguity and not attempt to impose a clarity alien to Shakespearian dramaturgy. It is in pursuit of relevance that a director is most likely to sacrifice complexity; and there are apparently some dramatic critics who would prefer to witness a play on homosexuality or colour prejudice, and so be relieved of the tedium of unadulterated Shakespeare.

What has been said about Iago applies, to a lesser extent, to Othello, and to most of Shakespeare's major characters. Hamlet can be played in a variety of ways; but in whatever way it is played the audience should be given glimpses of the rejected ways. So with *Troilus and Cressida*. It has been interpreted as tragedy, comedy, tragical satire, and comical satire; and whichever interpretation a director decides to adopt it is essential that the audience should be made aware of the discrepancies in the text which have led to such divergent opinions. There is the same problem with regard to *Measure for Measure*. Is the Duke a self-satisfied, blundering busybody, or a symbolic representation of God? Is Isabella a saint or a self-centred prig? Is the play a Christian parable on the necessity of forgiveness, or a satirical comment on the government of the universe? If the Director decides to make the Duke a symbol of 'power divine', we should not be prevented from laughing, with Lucio, at him; and if Isabella is presented as a saint, we ought nevertheless to recoil from her when she lashes out at the condemned Claudio. Or again, if *Troilus and Cressida* is presented as a comical satire, woe betide that director who will deny Troilus his moment of tragedy! In the great scene in Act v, where Troilus watches Cressida's swift infidelity, the point of view is continually changing; but the choric comments of Ulysses and Thersites—neither of them sympathetic characters—ought not to do more than act as counterpoint to the agony of the hero.

Not one of Shakespeare's major characters can be summed up in a few sentences: they carry a penumbra of uncertainty. The sense we have of their truth to life is very largely due to the conflicting evidence we have of them—what is said of them, what they say themselves, the tension between theatrical convention and psychological realism. As Morgann pointed out, the greatest dramatists introduce an apparent incongruity of character, and

Shakespeare was able to give life to his characters, partly because he lived in them, and partly because 'his mimic creation agrees in general so perfectly with that of nature'. This being so, an attempt to bring the plays up to date, and to make them relevant to the fashions of the day, upsets their metabolism. We do not need such desperate remedies; for even without them the plays continue to offer something fresh to each new generation. His profundity has been revealed little by little, and we may be sure that its depth is 'deeper than did ever plummet sound'.[2]

2. A sequel to this essay appeared in *The Triple Bond*, ed. Joseph G. Price (1975).

I 4

Poetry as a Criticism of Life[1]

I

The title of my paper refers, of course, to Matthew Arnold's often-expressed view,

that poetry is at bottom a criticism of life; that the greatness of a poet lies in his powerful and beautiful application of ideas to life.

Poetry, Arnold declared, interprets life in two ways:

by expressing with magical felicity the physiognomy and movement of the outward world [and] by expressing with inspired conviction the ideas and laws of the inward world of man's moral and spiritual nature.

The moral profundity which Arnold demanded of poetry and, oddly enough, did not find in Chaucer or Pope, was indispensable to him partly because he wanted to use poetry as a substitute for religion. Many years later Thomas Hardy expressed a similar and what he admitted was a forlorn hope, for an alliance between religion and complete rationality 'by means of the interfusing effect of poetry'.

We may sympathize with Arnold's description of great poetry, while doubting whether his method of quoting short passages as touchstones is a reliable one. We may pass over the fact that, quoting from memory, Arnold did not always quote accurately. But the quotations from Homer, Dante, Shakespeare, Milton, and Keats, however admirable, are taken out of context; and one has the unworthy suspicion that Arnold did not always remember what the context was. The lines from *Paradise Lost*, for example,

> And courage never to submit or yield,
> And what is else not to be overcome—

1. The Dill Lecture, delivered at Queen's University, Belfast, 7 May 1975.

display moral profundity only if we remember that they are put into the mouth of Satan after his fall. (And Arnold did not believe, with Blake, that Milton was of the devil's party without knowing it!) Hamlet's lines—which seem like a copybook maxim—

> There's a divinity that shapes our ends
> Rough hew them how we will—

are spoken to justify his killing of Rosencrantz and Guildenstern.

I must spend a little time on this question of context, as it would be wrong to imagine that Arnold was looking in literature for moral sayings, *sententiae*, such as are marked with marginal inverted commas in Elizabethan quartos. The importance of context is particularly significant in dramatic poetry; and one of the besetting temptations of biographers and critics is to quote speeches from plays as the considered opinion of the poet. Bernard Shaw, in most ways the best of all dramatic critics, declared in one of his attacks on bardolatry that Shakespeare emerged from his reflective period (i.e., his tragic period) 'a vulgar pessimist, oppressed with a logical demonstration that life is not worth living'. Notice that Shaw made no attempt to consider the total meaning of the plays in which Hamlet, Lear, and Timon play their parts; instead he relied on lines divorced from their contexts: Hamlet's longing for death, Gloucester's anguished protest,

> As flies to wanton boys are we to the gods:
> They kill us for their sport;

and the words spoken by Macbeth in his castle of Dunsinane, when news is brought to him that the 'fiend-like queen', for whom he had killed Duncan, was dead:

> She should have died hereafter:
> There would have been a time for such a word.
> Tomorrow and tomorrow and tomorrow
> Creeps, in this petty pace, from day to day
> To the last syllable of recorded time,
> And all our yesterdays have lighted fools
> The way to dusty death. Out, out, brief candle!
> Life's but a walking shadow, a poor player
> That struts and frets his hour upon the stage
> And then is heard no more: it is a tale
> Told by an idiot, full of sound and fury,
> Signifying nothing.

Shaw's remarks on acting and production are invariably sound; his criticism of plays other than Shakespeare's is often penetrating; his comments on the delivery of Shakespeare's lines excellent; his style is continuously witty and trenchant; but in the remark I have quoted about Shakespeare's pessimism he made the elementary mistake of assuming that Shakespeare's characters necessarily express the poet's own views. He would have been the first to protest if critics had made the same mistake about his own plays— if they had regarded any one character as his spokesman. And, in fact, critics to this day delight in telling us that Jack Tanner, Andrew Undershaft, or Captain Shotover are Shaw's mouth-pieces. The more perceptive critics, however, have realized that the meaning of *Major Barbara* is not embodied in the speeches of Undershaft (powerful as they are) but in the dialectically opposed views of Barbara, Cusins, and Undershaft: the Christian salva-tionist, the Fabian Socialist who translates Euripides, and the Nietzschean manufacturer of armaments. Such a mistake is relatively pardonable in Shaw's case since he claimed at the begin-ning of his career that he was using the stage for propaganda pur-poses, even though he was not doing it so crudely as his critics liked to think. With Shakespeare the mistake is particularly absurd since he had the power—more perhaps than any other dramatist—of completely losing his identity in that of his characters, so that, to take an extreme example, the anonymous Captain who agrees to murder Cordelia becomes for us in less than twenty words fully alive and fully individualized:

> I cannot draw a cart or eat wild oats:
> If it be man's work I'll do it.

Shakespeare, one may say, allows his characters to speak for them-selves.

It may perhaps be argued that some of his major characters do nevertheless express his personal views. When Hamlet debates whether to escape from the miseries of this life by stabbing him-self with a bare bodkin, can we not say that here at least the poet was speaking through his character—especially as the Prince himself did not suffer from the miseries he enumerates, and es-pecially as Shakespeare writes on the same miseries in his sixty-sixth sonnet?

> Tired with all these for restful death I cry:
> As to behold Desert a beggar born,
> And needy nothing trimmed in jollity,
> And purest faith unhappily forsworn,
> And gilded honour shamefully misplaced,
> And maiden virtue rudely strumpetted,
> And right perfection wrongfully disgraced,
> And strength by limping sway disabled,
> And Art made tongue-tied by authority,
> And Folly, doctor-like, controlling skill,
> And simple truth miscalled simplicity,
> And captive good attending captain ill—
>   Tired with all these, from these would I be gone.

Hamlet, of course, was a great generalizer; and in the 'To be or not to be' soliloquy he was speaking of Everyman more than of himself. Anyone who enumerates the evils of life is drawing on a long tradition, through the Middle Ages to pagan times, and it is not surprising that Hamlet's and Shakespeare's lists overlap. Similarly when Timon bewails the long sickness of living, or when the mad Lear declares that the great image of authority is that a dog's obeyed in office, these passages are perfectly appropriate to the characters at particular moments in the plays. Neither Timon nor Lear could have spoken in such terms in Act I, and Shakespeare is again hidden behind his masks.

If we turn back to Gloucester's bitter words about the gods, accusing them of sadistic cruelty—much as Thomas Hardy upbraided the President of the Immortals at the end of *Tess of the D'Urbervilles*—we find that the words were spoken soon after his eyes had been gouged out by Cornwall, and after he had learnt that Edgar was innocent, and that both he and Edgar had been betrayed by Edmund. Physical and mental agony combined made him long for death. Nevertheless, only a few scenes later, only a few minutes later in stage-time, Gloucester prays to the same gods, whom he describes, apparently without irony, as ever-gentle. Why should we assume that the first quotation expresses the views of the poet while the second does not? Why, indeed, should we suppose that any of Gloucester's opinions were Shakespeare's own, since the poet provides us with at least four characters who are frequently used to comment on the action, and to guide the responses of the audience? I am thinking of Kent in the first scene of the play, condemning Lear's foolishness, of the Fool before he fades from the play, of Albany in Act IV, and of Edgar throughout the last three acts. Consider, for example, some of Edgar's remarks on Lear:

> He childed, as I fathered

or

> O matter and impertinency mixed,
> Reason in madness!

or his advice to his father:

> Men must endure
> Their going hence, even as their coming hither;
> Ripeness is all.

As for Macbeth's speech on his wife's death, the context is again all-important. It is spoken as the forces of liberation besiege the castle of Dunsinane. Macbeth is unable to mourn for his wife, not merely because of the desperate military situation, but because he has lost the capacity to feel. He has supped full with horrors. He can no longer be moved, either by fear or by sympathy. Life, therefore, seems to him to be completely meaningless. I have quoted elsewhere some remarks on this speech by Lascelles Abercrombie, who declared that at this moment in the play the hero's world 'turns into a blank of imbecile futility', yet he 'seizes on the appalling moment and masters even this'. The worst of evils, in tragedy as in life, is the conviction that life has no meaning; but 'Macbeth's personality towers into its loftiest grandeur' by seizing on this conviction and relishing it to the utmost. Abercrombie was not quite so wrong as Shaw had been; but he seems nevertheless to confuse two things: the poetic power of Shakespeare which enchants us, and the words as the expression of Macbeth's character and situation. We cannot deduce that Macbeth has risen above his sense of nothingness by his expression of it, any more than we should pretend that all Shakespeare's tragic heroes were poets because they have great poetry to speak. Macbeth, by his own deeds, has destroyed for himself the meaning of life. It could indeed be argued that by showing that Macbeth's nihilism is a direct result of the murders he has committed,

Shakespeare vindicates the meaningfulness of life, in a way that an obstinately cheerful criminal would not.

Even if we were to ignore both the character of the speaker and his immediate situation, we should have to recognize that the resonance of the lines comes partly from the echoes from the Bible:

The light shall be dark in his dwelling and his candle shall be put out with him.

For we are but of yesterday and are ignorant; for our days upon earth are but a shadow.

We bring our years to an end, as a tale that is told.

Shakespeare was thinking of Man as a poor actor in a meaningless melodrama—thus giving a sinister twist to the commonplace that all the world's a stage, one that goes back to the pagan Petronius and forward to the Christian Calderón.

Macbeth is set in a Christian era and Shakespeare made full use of this fact by stressing the saintliness of Duncan and Edward the Confessor, and the reality of hell and damnation. *King Lear*, however, unlike the play on which it is based, is set in a pre-Christian era, unless we assume (as Kozintsev did in his great film) that Britain had lapsed into paganism. Everyone remembers, and all critics have noted, that the answer to Albany's prayer for the preservation of Lear and Cordelia is the cry of the King, 'Howl! Howl! Howl!' and his entrance, bearing the body of one who, we are told, redeemed nature from the general curse. Many critics have regarded this as the poet's sardonic comment on the efficacy of prayer; and William Elton in his extremely learned book on the play has argued that Shakespeare, while ostensibly showing the powerlessness of the pagan gods was hinting for the benefit of the more sophisticated members of the audience that the world was not providentially governed. Other critics have gone further. Professor Jan Kott, in his regrettably influential book, *Shakespeare Our Contemporary*, rechristened *King Lear* as *End Game*; and Peter Brook, whose production of *Titus Andronicus* had rightly been eulogized by Kott, returned the compliment by introducing Kott's ideas into his production of *King Lear*, which he tried to present as Shakespeare's contribution to the Theatre of the Absurd and the Theatre of Cruelty. This involved some major surgery on the text of the play. One example must suffice. As Shakespeare wrote it, the scene of the blinding of Gloucester ended with Regan assisting the wounded Cornwall, after he had ordered the servants to throw the corpse of their fellow on the dunghill, and to thrust Gloucester out of gates to let him smell his way to Dover. The two surviving servants are left on stage and they comment on the scene we have just witnessed.

> 2. I'll never care what wickedness I do
> If this man come to good.
> 3.   If she live long
> And in the end meet the old course of death,
> Women will all turn monsters.
> 2. Let's follow the old Earl, and get the Bedlam
> To lead him where he would; his roguish madness
> Allows itself to anything.
> 3. Go thou; I'll fetch some flax and whites of eggs
> To apply to his bleeding face. Now, heaven help him!

This concludes the scene and the third act of the play. Peter Brook cut these lines and ended the scene with Regan shrinking away from her wounded husband. The moral condemnation of Regan and Cornwall, the prophecy that they will not die a natural death, the concern for Gloucester's suffering, the servants' attempt to alleviate it, their refusal to carry out Cornwall's brutal commands, and the prayer with which the scene ends—all these things are demanded by the horrified audience, and they prevent us from regarding the actions of the evil characters as *normal*. In Brook's production it was the good characters who seemed abnormal.

It may be legitimate to rewrite the classics to make them more 'relevant', more contemporary, to a modern audience, as Brecht rewrote *Coriolanus*, for example. But perhaps classics should be defined as works that are perenially relevant, and therefore in no need of face-lifting. Brook's *Lear*, indeed, was less relevant than Shakespeare's because it reflected a narrower, and ultimately a falser, view of human nature and of the human condition. Not that the reinterpretation of Shakespeare's masterpieces to make them conform to modern prejudices is confined to Polish dramatic critics and brilliant theatre directors. One of the sanest books on *King Lear*, by S. L. Goldberg, published last year, is a valiant attempt by the author to speak what he feels, not what he ought to say, to use Edgar's words at the close of the play. But Professor Goldberg, I believe, is led astray more than once because he believes that Edgar's moral aphorisms were as irritatingly smug to Shakespeare as they are to his modern critic.

II

You may be thinking that I have adopted the method of Polonius who told his servant 'By indirections [to] find directions out'. But this indirect method was a convenient one for showing that the meaning of a play or poem is not to be arrived at by a consideration of short passages taken out of context; nor can it be reached by imposing on the work a modern interpretation at odds with its original meaning. Arnold rightly pointed out that scholars were liable to overvalue minor literature by considering it historically; and this is a fault which flourishes in some university departments in the frantic search for new topics for doctoral theses. But he would not have denied that to detach literature from its historical roots could only lead us astray. In other words, just as lines must be considered in their context, so must the whole work be considered in the context of its age.

The differences between the first Elizabethan age and the second are obviously vast. Shakespeare and his contemporaries expressed in their writings a view of the world which by and large they shared with their audiences and their readers. Not everyone, of course, would accept the Elizabethan World Picture as painted by the late Dr. Tillyard. Some of the greater writers would doubtless temper the ideology of the age with personal ironies and reservations; and the thought of all the great writers was dynamic rather than static. Perhaps, as Theodore Spencer once argued, the impact of the ideas of Montaigne, Machiavelli, and Copernicus on Shakespeare had profound effects on his views; although I doubt whether he was at all worried by Copernicus, and I imagine that he hailed Montaigne as a kindred spirit. Yet it is certainly true that in his Jacobean period, Shakespeare ceased to expound the blessings of a god-given political order which reflected a cosmic order. When he last expressed this idea it was through the mouths of the old fox, Ulysses, and the timeserver, Rosencrantz (or was it Guildenstern?). Nevertheless Shakespeare, along with his contemporaries, relied on a generally accepted ideology. They wrote for a nominally Christian society, for people who went to church as often as to the theatre; and in spite of violent and mortal differences between the sects, we can see that the extremists were closer to each other, 'united in the strife that divided them' (in Eliot's phrase) than they are to most people of the present day.

The pervasiveness of received ideas can be seen most clearly perhaps by a brief consideration of two writers who were branded as atheists by their contemporaries: Christopher Marlowe and Sir Walter Ralegh. Marlowe's table-talk, as we know from the evidence of Kyd and others, was often blasphemous and deliberately designed to shock; he had copied out passages denying the divinity of Christ; and he was rumoured to have delivered an atheist lecture before Ralegh. If not atheistical, he was at least heretical. In *Tamburlaine*, *The Jew of Malta*, and *The Massacre at Paris* he had satirized Machiavellian Christians; but if one reads *Doctor Faustus*, the play of his which deals most directly with religious matters, one cannot but be struck by the orthodoxy of his treatment. Faustus, unwilling to admit that he is a sinner needing repentance and redemption, falls through the sin of pride; he sells his soul to the devil for the sake of knowledge and power; and at the end of the play he is taken screaming to hell. It used to be argued that Faustus represented Renaissance man in conflict with the restrictive dogmatism and superstition of the medieval church; and that his meeting with the shade of Helen of Troy was an allegory of the rediscovery of the literature of the ancient world. But it is now generally accepted that to have sexual intercourse with a devil (which is what the shade of Helen really was) was to commit a sin for which there was no forgiveness. The act, therefore, seals the damnation of the hero.

In one of the most impressive speeches of the play, Mephistopheles speaks of the reality of hell:

> Why, this is hell, nor am I out of it!
> Thinkst thou that I who saw the face of god
> And tasted the eternal joys of heaven
> Am not tormented with ten thousand hells
> At being deprived of everlasting bliss?

It is the villains in Marlowe's plays

> Who count religion but a childish toy
> And hold there is no sin but ignorance.

My point is not that Marlowe, despite his reputation and the iconoclastic nature of his conversation, believed and trembled; but that, writing for a popular audience in 1592, and trained in theology as he had been, he was bound to treat the subject in the way he did.

As for Ralegh, whose private conversation was equally shocking to the conventionally pious, his *History of the World* was written to prove that the world was providentially governed, that the judgements of God are for ever unchangeable; and that God,

a power ineffable and virtue infinite,
a light by abundant clarity invisible,
an essence eternal and spiritual,
of absolute pureness and simplicity
was and is pleased to make Himself known by the work of the world.

What I am suggesting is that in Shakespeare's day there was a fair measure of agreement among writers and their public. The heretics took care to conceal their heresies, so that even in the middle of the seventeenth century the reader of *Paradise Lost* could be excused for failing to notice that Milton subscribed to a dozen or more heresies. He had been dead for more than a century before anyone dared to publish his *De Doctrina*.

Shakespeare, of course, is notoriously elusive. He hides behind the masks of his characters, behind the demands of the subject and the imperatives of his art, and (even in the *Sonnets*) behind the persona of the Poet. Books have been written to prove that he clung to the old faith, that he was a rigid follower of St. Augustine, that he was profoundly sceptical, and that he was a conformist. One play, *Measure for Measure*, has been used in support of all these conflicting views: Duke Vincentio has been regarded as an allegorical presentation of the deity, as a sardonic comment on the workings of providence, and as a partial portrait of James I. We are on safer ground if we confine ourselves to facts: that Shakespeare read two versions of the Bible—the Bishops and the Genevan—and that he was acquainted with the prayer-book version of the Psalms; that he had read some of Erasmus and Montaigne; that he knew the Homilies and at least the early part of Hooker's *Laws of Ecclesiastical Polity*.

There are similar disagreements about Shakespeare's political views. Generally he is regarded as a supporter of the Tudor settlement; but some critics think of him as a supporter of feudalism, one who regarded the beginnings of capitalism with disgust and horror; and to others he belonged to the left of centre of advanced bourgeois opinion. In other words, he was slippery as an eel. Whatever his private views, the ideas expressed in his plays—and even in the sonnets—were those of his age: not just mirroring them, but refracted through the prism of his mind; expressing received ideas only after they had been proved upon his pulses. Austin Warren, in one of his early books, spoke of 'the poet's passionate desire to perceive order for himself (not to accept it as a stereotype, given, handed down)'. And this is something we should never forget in considering the views of any great poet.[2]

III

If one turns now to the poets of the Romantic Revival, one finds that their attitude to the public was quite different from that of Shakespeare and his contemporaries. They no longer attempted to express generally received ideas: they questioned them. As a result, their public, except Byron's, was absurdly small. Wordsworth became popular only long after his truly creative period; Shelley paid for the publication of his poems; it was possible to buy the first editions of two of Keats's volumes years after his death; and Blake appears to have sold not a single copy of *Jerusalem*, his last important work. Blake, indeed, was the archetypal romantic poet, reacting against neo-classical attitudes in art and literature, a fervent supporter (like Wordsworth and Coleridge) of the early phases of the French Revolution, a supporter of the American colonists, a bitter opponent of the industrial revolution, a severe critic of the religion and philosophy of the Establishment. He found in the England of his day,

A pretence of Art to destroy Art; a pretence of Liberty
To destroy Liberty; a pretence of Religion to destroy Religion.

2. Perhaps it is necessary to say that I don't agree with Orwell, who thought Shakespeare was too timid to give expression to his subversive views, except through the mouths of madmen.

He had good reason to complain of the aspersion of madness cast on the inspired by the poetasters of the day. And, indeed, it has often been pointed out that the eighteenth century drove half its poets to mental breakdowns: Collins, Smart, Cowper, and (later) Clare went mad; Thomson, Gray, and Green suffered from melancholia; and even Dr. Johnson was a prey to obscure terrors and spoke of the hunger of the imagination which preys upon life. Blake's extraordinary mythology was invented by him because of his fear of being enslaved by the commonplace, the cliché, the received idea.

If Blake was eccentric, Keats was perhaps the sanest of the Romantic poets, and he had no inhibitions about using classical mythology—but he used it for his own purposes. I am old-fashioned enough to cling to the belief that *Endymion* is a kind of allegory; and most critics agree that the two versions of *Hyperion* are partly an attempt to find a positive meaning in suffering (of which Keats had plenty of experience in his short life) and partly to define the conditions of poetic greatness. You will recall that in the first *Hyperion* one of the old gods describes the top of sovereignty as a stoic acceptance of whatever disasters occur; but Apollo, who represents the new gods, is a sensitive, suffering human being, who is deified only in the concluding lines of the poem by gazing into the eyes of Mnemosyne, reading therein the tragic sufferings of humanity, and taking them on himself. In Keats's terminology, Apollo is a man of achievement rather than a man of power, a Shakespeare rather than a Napoleon. But it is probable that when Keats abandoned this version of the poem early in 1819, he did not fully comprehend his own symbolism; so that when he wrote his account of the Vale of Soul-making to his brother and sister-in-law, he was really writing an interpretation of his own poem. This section of a journal letter was written on 21 April, just before the composition of the first of the great Odes:

The common cognomen of this world among the misguided and superstitious is 'a vale of tears' from which we are to be redeemed by a certain arbitrary interposition of God and taken to Heaven—what a little circumscribed straightened notion! Call the world if you please 'The Vale of Soul-making'.

After describing how intelligencies are made into souls, he asks:

Do you not see how necessary a world of pains and troubles is to school an intelligence and make it a soul? A place where the heart must feel and suffer in a thousand diverse ways!

In the revised version of *Hyperion* Keats made his meaning plainer. Instead of Apollo and Mnemosyne, he writes of the dreamer (his own persona) and the prophetess Moneta, who instructs him that true poets are

> those to whom the miseries of the world
> Are misery, and will not let them rest.

Obviously Keats believed that poetry should be a criticism of life, and so did Blake, Shelley, and Wordsworth. To Shelley poets were (in his grandiloquent phrases) the hierophants of an unapprehended inspiration, the unacknowledged legislators of the world. Keats thought his ideas superior to those of Christianity; Wordsworth declared that poetry was the breath and finer spirit of knowledge; and Blake reiterated that his prophetic books were necessary to salvation. Whereas Shakespeare and his contemporaries were the spokesmen of their age, the Romantic poets were all on the opposition front bench. The subsequent history of ideas makes it easy for us to see these poets as the real spokesmen of their age, but to themselves, and to their contemporaries, they were voices crying in the wilderness. They had, one may say, rediscovered the prophetic function of poetry.

In the Victorian period, it was the prose-writers rather than the poets who engaged in a serious criticism of life. Morris described himself as the idle singer of an empty day, but this was before he became a busy propagandist for a new society. Arnold's attempt to divorce religion from the supernatural belonged to the period when his poetical powers had withered away. Of course some of the verse of Tennyson, Arnold, and Browning can be regarded as a criticism of life in the Arnoldian sense, but it is less significant in this respect than the prose of Newman or Ruskin, or even the novels of George Eliot and Dickens.

Arnold's inadequate definition of religion as morality touched with emotion and his demand that poetry should constitute a criticism of life brought poetry and religion into an uneasy juxtaposition, if not into a misalliance. But Arnold himself was aware of the dangers, as we can see from his sardonic account of an imaginary Social Science Congress at which some didactic verses of Wordsworth were quoted:

One can call up the whole scene. A great room in one of our dismal provincial towns; dusty air and jaded afternoon daylight; benches full of men with bald heads, and woman in spectacles; an orator lifting up his face from a manuscript written within and without to declaim these lines of Wordsworth; and in the soul of any poor child of nature who may have wandered in thither, an unutterable sense of lamentation, and mourning, and woe!

At the end of the nineteenth century poets reacted against the use of poetry for uplifting purposes, and against the spirit of the age which produced such titles as *The Moral System of Shakespeare*, and against the didactic bent of the Browning Society. They proclaimed that the poet's one aim should be the creation of beauty, that he should not be concerned with the inculcation of morality, or even with ideas. The strange device of 'Art for Art's sake' adorned their banner. It was useful and necessary at the time; it was a recognition, as Eliot put it, 'of the error of the poet's trying to do other people's work'. Yeats was a close associate of the poets of the 1890s—he *was* a poet of the 1890s—but altogether tougher than the others. He shared their distrust of poetry which (in Keats's phrase about Wordsworth) had a palpable design on the reader. But like all dramatists he wanted to do more than 'leave great verse unto a little clan'; and his concern with a specifically Irish literary movement counteracted his early aestheticism.

IV

Soon after the First World War in his magnificent and terrifying poem, 'The Second Coming', Yeats observed that

> The best lack all conviction, while the worst
> Are full of passionate intensity.

At about the same time T. S. Eliot, recovering from a nervous breakdown, was demonstrating the truth of these words in the poem originally entitled *He do the Police in different Voices*, but afterwards rechristened and condensed as *The Waste Land*. It is a poem which seemed to lack all conviction. Looking back from the standpoint of *Four Quartets*, we can see that I. A. Richards was wrong to declare that *The Waste Land* 'effects a complete severance between poetry and all beliefs'; but when the poem first appeared it seemed (and not merely to stupid reviewers) to be about the breakdown of civilization and the meaninglessness of life. The quotations from Buddha, St. Augustine, and the Upanishads, even the allusion to the journey to Emmaus, are not statements of conviction, but fragments that the poet has shored against his ruins, useful literary symbols, like the impotent Fisher King, or the references to Dante, Webster, Marvell, Goldsmith, Spenser, and Shakespeare.

It is, I believe, more than a coincidence that at the same time that Eliot was writing *The Waste Land*, E. M. Forster was writing *A Passage to India* and James Joyce was finishing *Ulysses*. When Mrs. Moore in Forster's novel hears the echo in the Marabar Caves, the curious 'boum' seemed to signify:

Pathos, piety, courage—they exist, but are identical, and so is filth. Everything exists, nothing has value.

In his earlier novel, *Howards End*, Helen Schlegel, at a concert, listening to Beethoven's Fifth Symphony, had an image of goblins walking over the universe, 'who merely observed in passing that there was no such thing as splendour or heroism in the world . . . Panic and emptiness. Beethoven scatters the goblins, but they could return.' Art restores meaning to life, but Mrs. Moore never recovers from the sense of utter meaninglessness.

Joyce had two ways of combating the sense of futility. His idea of secular epiphanies, what he called the sudden 'revelation of the whatness of a thing', to be found 'in casual, unostentatious, even unpleasant moments' were for an artist what Hardy called 'moments of vision'. They gave at least the illusion of significance. In *Ulysses* Joyce went further. He made a single day in the life of very ordinary characters 'forms more real than living man, Nurslings of immortality'; and to demonstrate his rage for order, for the creation of order out of chaos, every episode is given a Homeric parallel.

The case of Yeats is equally interesting. You may recall Eliot's gibe about Blake's philosophy, that 'we admire the man who has put it together out of the odds and ends about the house'. This is unfair to Blake, but would not be unfair to Yeats. There were literary sources for his ideas—Blake, Shelley, and Swift; philo-sophical influences—Plotinus, Vico, Berkeley; magic and spiritualism, Eastern mysticism; Celtic and Greek mythology; and the influence of his sense of ancestry, which was not without some mythological exaggeration. All this was the raw material of his poetry, and we may suspect that this was its prime function. When he asked the spirits who ostensibly dictated *The Vision* whether he should devote the rest of his life to expounding their system, they conveniently replied: 'No, we have come to give you metaphors for poetry.' In his last period—the period of *The Tower, The Winding Stair,* and *Last Poems*—Yeats gathered the rich harvest of his eclecticism. The pieces fell into place; the perfected work, achieved only after the scrapping of draft after draft, seemed in the end to mirror reality.

V

I have attempted to trace three different ways in which poets have written what may be called a criticism of life. I have suggested that the poets of the Renaissance, including Shakespeare and Mil-ton, expressed the common wisdom of the age, refracted pris-matically through their individual minds. The Romantic poets, on the other hand, were generally critical of the ideas and attitudes of the Establishment; but they all, to a greater or lesser degree, wished to influence the minds of their readers, as well as to give them delight. Wordsworth might speak of 'this unintelligible world', but he did not regard it as meaningless or absurd. Shelley declared in the preface to *Prometheus Unbound* that didactic poetry was his abhorrence, not because he did not believe in the moral effect of what he wrote, but because he believed that good poetry increased the imaginative power of its readers, and hence their ability to put themselves in the place of other people: this, he believed, was the true basis of moral conduct. The modern writers I have been discussing, lacking all conviction, nevertheless sought in the exercise of their art to find a meaning in life, or to impose a meaning on it.

It is interesting to compare Yeats's 'Sailing to Byzantium' with Keats's 'Ode on a Grecian Urn', since both the Urn and Byzan-tium symbolize art in opposition to life. Keats contrasts the figures on the urn with ordinary human beings. The lovers cannot embrace, but they remain eternally in love, and forever beautiful, 'All breathing human passion far above'. But in the last stanza we are not left with the bleak opposition of art and life. The cold pastoral instructs the observer in 1819, and in the future (where it will remain amid other woe than ours):

> Beauty is truth, truth beauty—that is all
> Ye know on earth and all ye need to know.

We have to take this in relation to Keats's similar aphorisms in his letters: 'What the imagination seizes as beauty must be truth' and 'The imagination may be compared to Adam's dream: he awoke and found it truth'. If I may be forgiven for telescoping the argument, Keats is implying in the ode that human life, considered *sub specie aeternitatis*, could be as meaningful and significant as a work of art.

Yeats's poem, on the contrary, contrasts himself, the ageing poet, with the young, at the height of their sensuous, active life:

> This is no country for old men—the young
> In one another's arms, birds in the trees,
> Those dying generations, at their song,
> The salmon falls, the mackerel-crowded seas,
> Fish, flesh and fowl, commend all summer long
> Whatever is begotten, born and dies.
> Caught in that sensual music, all neglect
> Monuments of unageing intellect.

The flux of existence cannot be brought under the dominion of art. The dying poet seeks for consolation in the immortality of his poetry, as Keats in his 'Ode to a Nightingale' contrasted the mortality of man with the immortality of the bird's song,

> the self-same song that found a path
> Through the sad heart of Ruth when sick for home
> She stood in tears amid the alien corn—

a song that clearly symbolizes poetry itself. But in Yeats's poem there is some ambivalence about his posthumous existence: the mechanical toy song-bird keeping a drowsy emperor awake or entertaining the lords and ladies of his court is hardly an exalted symbol of Poetry—even if it sings of the future as well as of the present and the past.

I have referred to Joyce, Eliot, and Yeats as modern writers; but although I read the works I have been discussing when they first appeared, that was half a century ago. During the intervening period, there have been further changes of attitude, to which I can allude only briefly. You will recall that the poets of the 1930s mostly wrote political verse. A poet of that period would have had to be very insensitive to have remained unmoved by the results of the world slump, by the successive failures of the League of Nations, and of its constituent members, to halt aggression in Manchuria, Abyssinia, Spain, and Czechoslovakia, and by the horrors of the concentration camps. Nor is it altogether surprising that many of the poets used Marxist terminology, since History seemed bent on demonstrating the truth of Marx's theories. Nevertheless the overtly political poems are now embarrassing to read. They are naive, one-sided, propagandist, expressing a party point of view, accepted intellectually but not by the whole man. Even worse, they are imbued with the immature notions current in single-sexed private schools. The Revolution often appears more like a schoolboy rag than a dangerous commitment. This is not what Arnold meant by criticism of life. It is therefore understandable that Auden should have scrapped many of the poems he wrote before 1940, and that he should have altered some poems that were too good to repudiate altogether. Some of the alterations, however, can hardly be justified on literary grounds. For example, in the poem on the outbreak of war, Auden repented of the sentence 'We must love one another or die' because we die whether we love one another or not. One might as well scrap the 'Ode to a Nightingale' because the bird that Keats heard was not the one that sang to Ruth. It was natural too that Auden should come to react against the whole idea of political poetry, partly because it was absurdly ineffective, and partly because the poetry itself suffered from its dual motivation. But although Auden turned his back on politics, disclaimed any didactic function, and advanced more modest claims for poetry than any good poet since the Renaissance, he could not eradicate the habit of teaching and preaching. His finest volume, *The Sea and the Mirror*, comprising a religious treatment of psychology and a psychological treatment of religion, attempts (in the words he used earlier about the finest poetry) to teach people to unlearn hatred and to learn love.

I have no time to discuss later poetry—whether by Larkin or Heaney—but I want to say something about the theatre of the Absurd, which will link up with the beginning of my lecture and the effect of this kind of drama on criticism of Shakespeare. The drama of Samuel Beckett starts from the same assumptions as those of the existentialists: that there is no god, and therefore no divine sanction for morality; but whereas the existentialists believe that social morality is created by an infinitude of choices by individuals (who therefore have to make their choices with an anguished sense of responsibility) the absurdists are left in moral chaos, believing that life is without a meaning. Beckett's best play, *Waiting for Godot*, dramatizes the human situation in a godless universe, for we realize long before the end of the play that Godot will never come, because as a character in Balzac's play, *Le Faiseur* puts it, 'Godeau is a myth, a fable! Godeau's a phantom, as well you know!' Beckett, of course, must depict life as he sees it. His plays are, in a sense, a criticism of life; and we may say he succeeds in doing, what Abercrombie wrongly praised Macbeth for doing, namely of facing and expressing life's utter futility. It would be absurd to regard the Theatre of the Absurd as in any sense consolatory; but it could be argued that Beckett, by bringing home to us the reality of the human condition, enables us to construct our lives on more solid foundations than on the hopes and delusions of the past. I think one can detect in Beckett's work not merely a conviction that life is absurd, but also an agonized cry of protest that this is so.

There is, perhaps, some ambivalence in absurd literature: for if life is completely futile, literature is futile too. Yet Beckett continues to write, and obviously not for the money; and if the act of writing, or the consciousness of writing well, or the influence his work may be thought to have, gives the author some small satisfaction, one is driven to assume that life retains for him a modicum of meaning.

VI

We may, then, accept Beckett's plays as a criticism of life, whether we agree with the criticism or not. But it is not difficult to imagine what Arnold's comments would have been. Indeed, we may be certain that he would have applied to *Waiting for Godot* or *End*

Game the reasons he gave in 1853 for suppressing his own poem, *Empedocles on Etna*. He argued that

A poetical work . . . is not yet justified when it has been shown to be an accurate, and therefore interesting representation . . .

What then are the situations, from the representation of which, though accurate, no poetical enjoyment can be derived? They are those in which the suffering finds no vent in action; in which a continuous state of mental distress is prolonged, unrelieved by incident, hope, or resistance; in which there is everything to be endured, nothing to be done. In such situations there is inevitably something morbid, in the description of them something monotonous.

This is not at all fair to Arnold's own poem, which is not in the least morbid; but it is, I think, an accurate criticism of much of Beckett's work. The quotation from Arnold's preface may provide a return passage to the beginning of our discussion—the way in which critics and directors of Shakespeare's plays seek to make them more 'relevant' to modern audiences and readers by linking them to contemporary fashions. What is wrong—apart from the fact that a great dramatic poem does not require such cosmetic surgery to make it relevant—is that the process is horribly reductive. *End Game*, with all its merits, is not an adequate substitute for *King Lear*, any more than Kott is an adequate substitute for Coleridge or Bradley. Shakespeare did not believe that life was absurd: the tragic and the absurd are opposites.

I have tried to show that during the last four centuries there have been radical changes in the criticism of life offered by poets: expressing to a greater or lesser degree the ideology of the age; rebelling against the ideology of the age; and seeking in what Henry James called 'the luminous paradise of art' the significance they can no longer find in life itself. One is tempted to misapply Yeats's little poem entitled 'Three Movements':

> Shakespearean fish swam the sea, far away from land;
> Romantic fish swam in nets coming to the hand;
> What are all those fish that lie gasping on the strand?

But this would be unfair. For if they are gasping, it is not because of some deficiency of talent but because of the intellectual climate into which they have been born. It may be that with the fusion of the two cultures, and with the solution of the problem of reconciling freedom and justice, we shall have a second renaissance, and the poets will fulfil once again—or, it would be truer to say, fulfil at last—the splendid manifesto of Wordsworth:

In spite of difference of soil and climate, of language and manners, of laws and customs; in spite of things silently gone out of mind, and things violently destroyed; the Poet binds together by passion and knowledge the vast empire of human society, as it is spread over the whole earth, and over all time.

Index

Abercrombie, Lascelles, 7
Adler, A., 123
Andrewes, Lancelot, 35
Anouilh, Jean, 201
Appian, 2
Archer, William, 94, 136
Arnold, Matthew, 10, 212, 224, 231
Auden, W. H., 207, 229

Baker, G. P., 147
Barton, John, 208
Beaumont, Francis, 84
Beckett, Samuel, 217, 230
Beerbohm, Max, 109
Bennett, Arnold, 163
Bethell, S. L., 11, 27, 85
Blake, William, 222
Bodin, J., 18
Bond, Warwick, 56
Bonjour, A., 85
Bonnard, Georges, 11
Bowers, F., 10
Bradley, A. C., 1, 4, 15, 124
Brecht, B., 198, 204
Bridges, Robert, 92
Bright, Timothy, 120
Brook, Peter, 89, 217
Brooks, Cleanth, 34
Bryant, J. A., 85
Bulthaupt, H., 76

Calderón, 149
Campbell, Thomas, 77
Charlton, H. B., 4
Christie, Agatha, 93

Cicero, 3
Clemen, Wolfgang, 9
Coghill, Nevill, 88
Coleridge, S. T., 2, 21, 56, 77, 93
Collins, Churton, 144
Congreve, William, 129, 159; casts, 159 ff.

Danby, J. F., 17
Daniel, Samuel, 2, 106
Dickinson, Emily, 124
Digges, D., 18, 59
Donne, John, 35
Drummond, William, 92
Dryden, John, 20, 92

Eliot, T. S., 7, 11, 36, 67, 77, 94, 105, 112, 113, 200, 225
Elliott, G. R., 11, 19
Ellis-Fermor, Una, 128
Empson, William, 33, 66, 94
Euripides, 78

Famous Victories of Henry V, 39
Faucit, Helen, Lady Martin, 78
Flatter, R., 125
Flaubert, Gustave, 125, 135
Fletcher, John, 38
Forman, Simon, 81
Forset, E., 18
Forster, E. M., 226
Freud, S., 110
Fry, Christopher, 36
Fulbecke, W., 18

Gardner, Dame Helen, 11
Gielgud, Sir John, 79
Goethe, 14, 71
Godwin, William, 56
Goldberg, S. L., 218
Golding, Arthur, 26
Granville-Barker, Harley, 80
Grass, Günter, 198
Greene, Robert, 76, 80, 90, 138

Hardy, Thomas, 212, 215
Harsnett, Samuel, 119
Holinshed, Raphael, 31
Hunt, Leigh, 20
Hyman, S., 105, 131, 208

Ibsen, Henrik, 130
Irving, Washington, 94

James, D. G., 9
Jones, E., 110
Johnson, Samuel, 20, 77, 92
Jonson, Ben, 20, 68, 92

Keats, John, 14, 34, 57, 88,
   128, 223, 227
Kipling, Rudyard, 125
Kitteredge, G. L., 12
Knight, G. Wilson, 9, 66, 94
Knights, L. C., 6, 62
Kott, Jan, 217
Kozintsev, G., 124
Kyd, Thomas, 6

Lamb, Charles, 20
Leavis, F. R., 11
Lennox, Charlotte, 76
Lenormand, H. R., 180 ff.
Lewis, C. S., 56, 112

Lodge, Thomas, 139
Lowell, Robert, 126
Lyly, John, 148

Macready, Charles, 78
Madariaga, S. de, 6
Marlowe, Christopher, 4, 38,
   220
Marx, Karl, 57, 67, 71
Maxwell, J. C., 19
Mirror for Magistrates, A, 5
Molière, 126, 130, 151
Moore, Henry, 37
Morgann, Maurice, 95, 109,
   134, 137, 208
Morley, Henry, 17
Morozov, Mikhail, 13
Moulton, R. G., 87
Mozart, 137

Newman, John Henry, 15

Olivier, Laurence (Lord
   Olivier), 127, 203
Otway, Thomas, 201
Ovid, 26

Pasternak, Boris, 125
Peele, George, 38, 54
Pembroke, Mary, Countess of,
   2, 99
Playfair, Sir Nigel, 160
Pope, Alexander, 92

Rabkin, Norman, 133
Racine, Jean, 130, 149
Ralegh, Sir Walter, 220

Rilke, Rainer Maria, 126
Robertson, J. M., 147
Rymer, Thomas, 103

Schelling, F. E., 147
Seneca, 3, 15–16, 26–27
Sewell, Arthur, 9
Shakespeare:
 All's Well, 106, 146
 Antony and Cleopatra, 17, 129
 Comedy of Errors, 97
 Coriolanus, 18, 201
 Hamlet, 6, 56, 110, 132
 2 Henry IV, 59, 129
 Henry V, 51
 Henry VI, 96
 John, 59, 68
 Julius Caesar, 17, 199
 Lear, 13, 32, 63, 90, 116, 179, 204, 213, 217
 Macbeth, 2, 15, 22 ff., 93, 114, 201, 213, 217
 Measure, 33, 52, 93, 106, 128, 210, 221
 Merchant of Venice, 115, 202
 Midsummer Night's Dream, 100
 Much Ado, 102
 Othello, 11, 103, 131, 208
 Pericles, 86
 Richard II, 4, 100
 Richard III, 4
 Romeo and Juliet, 5, 24, 101
 Tempest, 75
 Timon, 65
 Titus, 3
 Troilus and Cressida, 210
 Two Gentlemen, 96
Sharpe, Ella Freeman, 117

Shaw, George Bernard, 56, 93, 124, 128, 136, 213
Shelley, Percy Bysshe, 224
Siddons, Sarah, 77
Sidney, Sir Philip, 3, 8, 9, 27
Smirnov, 56
Spassky, 56
Spencer, Theodore, 58
Spurgeon, Caroline, 9, 66
Stewart, J. I. M., 122
Stoll, E. E., 11, 94
Strachey, Lytton, 77
Strindberg, August, 133
Swinburne, Algernon Charles, 42

Tennyson, Alfred (Lord), 105, 200
Tillyard, E. M. W., 57
Tolstoy, Leo, 56
Trilling, Lionel, 117
Troublesome Raigne of King John, 39
Turgeniev, Ivan, 125

Webster, John, 153
Wertham, F., 112
Whiter, Walter, 34
Wilbur, Richard, 126
Wilde, Oscar, 94
Wilson, J. Dover, 11, 121
Wordsworth, William, 232

Yeats, W. B., 225, 231

Zola, Emile, 125